MANIFESTO OF A TENURED RADICAL

CULTURAL FRONT

GENERAL EDITOR: MICHAEL BÉRUBÉ

MANIFESTO OF A TENURED RADICAL

CARY NELSON

MANIFESTO
OF A TENURED RADICAL

CARY NELSON

NEW YORK UNIVERSITY PRESS
NEW YORK AND LONDON

NEW YORK UNIVERSITY PRESS
New York and London

Copyright © 1997 by New York University

Library of Congress Cataloging-in-Publication Data
Nelson, Cary.
Manifesto of a tenured radical / Cary Nelson.
p.   cm. — (Cultural front)
Includes bibliographical references and index.
ISBN 0-8147-5794-4 (clothbound : alk. paper).—ISBN
0-8147-5797-9 (paperbound : alk. paper)
1. Education, Higher —Aims and objectives—United States.
2. English philology—Study and teaching (Higher)—United States.
3. Humanities—Study and teaching (Higher)—United States.
4. Critical pedagogy—United States.   5. Canon (Literature)
6. College teachers—Tenure—United States.   7. Education, Higher
—Political aspects—United States.   I. Title.   II. Series.
LA227.4.N45   1997
378.73—dc21   96-51305
                          CIP

New York University Press books are printed on acid-free paper,
and their binding materials are chosen for strength and durability.

Manufactured in the United States of America

10 9 8 7 6 5 4 3 2 1

CONTENTS

MANIFESTO OF A TENURED RADICAL

INTRODUCTION

Walk the halls of almost any large university anthropology, English, or history department and you will meet faculty and graduate students who feel personally empowered by decades of innovative disciplinary and multi-disciplinary work. Yet those same hallways may be peopled by adjunct and part-time faculty who cobble together what is at best an uncertain, nearly impoverished existence on the margins of their disciplines. And those intellectually ambitious graduate students, as they near completing their degrees and start contemplating the disastrous job market, will begin to wonder if they have any future in the field they have come to love. A graduate student who had just completed defending his dissertation in the fall of 1996 turned to me and said, "Now I can see the tunnel at the end of the light." The tenured faculty rarely think of such matters. Focused on their careers, they assume we all earn our fates. The scholarship of the last half century has not, unfortunately, encouraged many of these people to ask searching questions about academic culture. Meanwhile, if we have any doubts about the difficulties we face in healing ourselves, we might recall that bond-rating services consider it a sign of financial health and good management if universities make heavy use of adjuncts: it shows they have a *flexible* (disposable) work force. This is a book about these contradictions.

It is also a book that sometimes offers radical solutions to the problems confronting higher education as it approaches the next millennium. My title, *Manifesto of a Tenured Radical*, is, however, both serious and ironic. The book is very much a manifesto for a series of progressive cultural commitments within academia. As the country has moved to the political Right, such commitments have gradually been radicalized, and the notion of the tenured radical, first popularized by Roger Kimball, has now established itself within popular common sense.[1] As far as the Right is concerned then, I am a tenured radical, a status I must view somewhat whimsically, but which I am nonetheless willing to claim as a provocation. Notably, no one seems to get equally upset about *un*tenured radicals, since it is the aura of permanence, invulnerability, and cultural warrant around tenure that makes tenured radicals an affront. Of course no contemporary "tenured radical" with a sense of history would put him- or herself in the same company as beleaguered university radicals in the 1950s or those radicals outside academia who risk everything in the causes they serve. My field of operations is not the mountains of Mexico but the groves of academe. But I believe in the importance of higher education as a field of work; *Manifesto of a Tenured Radical* draws on some decades of left-wing pedagogy and research to make a series of statements about what higher education must do to heal itself.

Manifesto thus examines the dynamic interrelationship between the intellectual and political present and future of the academy. Of course higher education's controversial commitments to research, its fractured sense of community, its economic peril, its limited capacity to reflect on its disciplinary divisions, and its troubled political and cultural image are already in conflict. What this book seeks to do is to describe these realities clearly and convince readers to take their interrelationships seriously.

I use my own discipline of English simultaneously as a representative case and as an exaggerated instance of forces at work widely in the humanities and throughout higher education. More narrowly, I also use my own period specialization in modern American poetry repeatedly to show how a faculty member's teaching and historical research can have wider social implications and can be positioned in relation to contemporary debates. More perhaps than any other discipline, literary studies has reformed and opened its intellectual life in such a way as to fulfill a commitment to democratic values. Yet because English departments often hire large numbers of graduate students or part-time faculty to teach lower-division courses, the discipline also harbors some of the most exploitive labor practices in the academy. In English, therefore, democracy is fulfilled in scholarship and betrayed in the workplace. As in other disciplines, some of those who have helped lead the field's intellectual revolution are among those most indifferent to the fate of their more vulnerable colleagues. When we turn our attention to the workplace, part of the vanguard becomes a rearguard. The discipline as a whole is in almost complete denial about these contradictions. Yet they must be addressed. I have tried not only to say why that is the case but also how the process of reform might begin.

English has also been at the forefront of the culture wars of the last decade. That has puzzled some commentators, but on reflection the prominent position of English seems unsurprising. First, its size makes its scholarship more visible. Its widespread responsibility for freshman rhetoric or composition requirements means that large numbers of students are exposed to English courses. The discipline has also played a large role in formulating the theory revolution of the last twenty-five years and demonstrating its relevance to textual interpretation. And finally, more than any other disciplinary caretaker of high cultural objects, literary studies is articulated to our sense of national identity. Far more members of the general public feel they have access to (and a modest stake in interpreting) novels than symphonies, paintings, or classic works of philosophy. National literatures are often sites of struggle over cultural and political representation, and the disciplinary organization of literature into national groupings frequently serves myths of national exceptionalism and conflict over national identity.

So the debates over symbolic investments in the changes in English studies have been singularly intense. And if some of those outside the university have been willing to use developments in literary studies to delegitimate and defund public education, many inside higher education have simply ignored the material conditions in which they work.

Part of what is startling about faculty passivity and indifference is its blindness to anything except short-term self-interest. Longer-term self-interest—even self-interest focused on, say, a five-year plan—would suggest that some collective action to secure individual options is now critical. Thus many scholars scramble to publish their own books and essays, without troubling to notice that the whole system of university press publishing is dying. If they did notice, they would be ill-prepared to take collective action. Meanwhile, the cost of printing scholarly books keeps increasing while the number of copies sold has declined steadily for nearly two decades, in part because library budgets are falling farther and farther behind acquisition costs. A scholarly book that could easily sell 2,000 copies in 1970 now regularly sells but 500, and some sell even fewer copies than that. All over the country English professors are doing research for books they will not be able to publish. Nevertheless, the enterprise of writing traditional literary criticism continues despite the fact that opportunities to publish it will soon be nearly nonexistent.[2]

Whether this problem really matters is another issue. Publishing books that virtually no one will read is perhaps not a national priority, but books that could make a difference will likely be threatened as well. This is not, in any case, one of the issues I take up here, but there are other crises that clearly do matter, and, like the one in scholarly publishing, they can only be addressed by collective action. One such crisis is the declining percentage of tenured or tenure-track faculty among college and university teachers. These are the people with the greatest protection for their free speech and, moreover, the people with the greatest potential for commitment to the institutions in which they teach.[3] Despite media and legislative assaults on tenure, its real crisis is one of gradual diminution, as retiring faculty are increasingly replaced with part-timers, adjuncts, or graduate assistants. The precise pattern varies, with many private institutions relying heavily on adjunct or part-time faculty and many public universities employing graduate assistants, but the trend away from permanent, full-time faculty appointments is nationwide.

Tenure will thus gradually disappear—not with a bang but a whimper. There may never be an event or a critical decision that provokes a national confrontation over the issue, though the 1996 effort by the University of Minnesota Regents to eliminate almost all tenure guarantees will certainly test faculty resolve. The Regents' rules would make it easy to fire tenured faculty or cut their salaries not only for programmatic but also for political reasons. Meanwhile, some junior colleges now argue over whether every department needs to include at least one full-time, tenure-track faculty member. The alternative is a faculty of part-timers who are given their marching orders by bureaucrats with no disciplinary expertise and no intellectual commitments beyond cost accounting. When tenure is gone, then anyone who questions corporate authority can be summarily fired. Do any faculty members think such a system would serve students well? Hardly. Yet disciplines like English continue to flood the market with unemployable Ph.D.s and make such "innovations" easier and easier to institute. We are repeatedly told that the job crisis, the focus of the third part of *Manifesto,* is about to end.

For some years I have been puzzled by the good cheer of our high-profile faculty in the face of the long-term collapse of the job market. The reality is that the academic job crisis began in 1970 and 1971. We have had intermittent periods of relative improvement since then, but even the best years have left many long-term candidates unemployed. In other words, over a quarter of a century we have never been able to eliminate the backlog of Ph.D.s without full-time tenure-track employment. There are now people who have spent their whole professional lives—twenty or more years—on the margins of the academy, making do with part-time work, cobbling together courses at multiple institutions, going on unemployment, covering their own health insurance when they can. It is astonishing that the more privileged members of the profession can declare "we're all in this together," when some of us are clearly so much more equal than others. But most astonishing of all is the decades-long claim that the job crisis is temporary. At the 1994 annual meeting of the Modern Language Association, the main disciplinary organization in English, I ran into glad-handers who declared "we're back" and "the crisis is over" in response to a miserable 2 percent increase in the number of jobs listed that fall. For them the glass was apparently 2 percent full, not 98 percent empty. But the greatest puzzle to me has remained the political and economic blindness of some of our most distinguished scholars. In the spring of 1996 the MLA president again declared the job crisis temporary. These delusions are not unique to English, of course, but it is in English that the numbers are particularly staggering. It is likely that no more than 25 percent of the English Ph.D.s produced in the 1990s will end up becoming tenured faculty members.

This interplay between English and the rest of academia runs through the entire book. *Manifesto* opens with a critical review of the way a succession of influential interpretive theories have accommodated themselves to disciplinarity. English is the model, but the pattern is repeated throughout the humanities and social sciences. The same is true of the role anthologies can play in imaging social life, the subject of chapter 2, and the possibilities opened up by a relativistic historiography, the focus of chapter 3. Chapter 4, a polemical account of the Americanization of cultural studies, speaks directly to all the fields where cultural studies has made inroads.

The book's second section, "The Academy and the Culture Debates," also moves outward from English to the academy as a whole. Its opening chapter uses modern American poetry to mount a plea for a historically grounded progressive pedagogy, while the last chapter poses the challenge of left research and teaching at a more abstract and general level. In between, *Manifesto* addresses the debates over the canon and hate speech regulation. In the latter case, I try to make it clear that a progressive politics need not support restraints on speech.

If *Manifesto* is unapologetically on the Left then, it is not programmatically or conventionally so. In a number of areas—from its commitment to maintaining substantial portions of the traditional canon in the curriculum to its rejection of hate speech ordinances—the book negotiates a principled passage through issues the press usually treats as politically given and dichotomous. In its support for teaching assistant unions, for example, *Manifesto* breaks with more traditional campus liberals who find graduate student unions unacceptable. Indeed, I criticize those who do progressive research but resist applying its lessons to employment practices on their own campus. Far more than the media has encouraged the public to believe, this kind of mix of positions is common among progressive faculty. Perhaps *Manifesto* can make a small contribution to dispelling public myths about unanimity of opinion on campus.

Finally, as I suggested above, the last section of the book uses English departments and the Modern Language Association as key examples because they display the problems of other disciplines writ large. "Lessons from the Job Wars" also opens and closes with anecdotes and comments about the efforts to unionize graduate teaching assistants in New Haven. The reactions of Yale faculty and administrators to such efforts highlight the difficulties we face in trying to make campus communities more equitable places to live.

Here and there the contradictions become rather stark. At Yale, after years of organizing, cafeteria workers won the right to be assigned other duties in the summer rather than be laid off and have to go on welfare. That also gave them year-round benefits and some security for their families. But the Yale Corporation remained restless about its concessions. Other schools were more ruthless; why should Yale waste money and decrease its profits? So in 1995 a Yale spokesperson declared the university to be looking for a "humane" way to reduce salaries and benefits. Step one: break the local union. Some faculty cared deeply; others were indifferent to the nature of the community they worked in or the values of the institution to which they were devoting their labor. After all, their lives proceeded on a higher plane.

Institutions that mistreat whole classes of employees, we need to realize, have little claim to public respect, let alone an exalted self-image. With higher education under assault and under scrutiny, it is no longer so easy to maintain public acceptance of the academy's self-idealization, especially when higher education's labor practices too closely resemble those long associated with California agriculture. "Health care for me but not for you" does not seem a particularly saintly faculty slogan. Nor does "living wages for tenured faculty only."

Part of the problem is the increasing spread of the ideology of careerism through the postwar academy. A faculty member who entered the profession in the 1960s remarked to me that the first thing he did when he arrived at his first job was join the American Association of University Professors, a group devoted to defining and promulgating general professional principles, not to individual career advancement. Membership in the AAUP has declined by over half in two decades.

One is tempted to conclude that some faculty members see the profession as a whole primarily as an audience for their scholarship, an applause track in the background of their lives celebrating their personal accomplishments. When they wonder whether the job market will improve, they look for an answer to the only evidence that signifies: their publications. A good job market would be just one more confirmation of their own value. Given what they themselves have produced, how can the country but reward them yet again? Careerism encourages us to take everything personally; there is no other measure that counts.

For some time there was no large-scale institutional problem either with faculty doggedly supporting their own rights and privileges while seeing no need to grant anything comparable to anyone else on campus, or with faculty focusing exclusively on their own careers and ignoring the common good. In the 1990s it is another matter. There is a name for this ideology—capitalism—and it is not so compatible with expectations of public largesse, let alone with passivity.

Meanwhile, the basic categories of university life are in doubt. A shakeout of research universities is under way; many of them will not merit the designation a decade from now. As it is, less than 10 percent of our institutions of higher education devote a significant portion of their resources to research. Yet despite their centrality to the effort to keep higher education current everywhere else, including the majority of institutions whose faculty have neither time nor money to do research, these schools lack public support for their mission. Tenure is increasingly and falsely viewed as a "problem," a source of excessive costs, indifferent performance, and an undemocratic prestige of intellect. To a considerable degree, views like these are installed as unquestioned common sense in the media and public opinion. At the same time, the political Right wants only cultural indoctrination, respect for authority, and either unfettered greed or technical expertise from college graduates. Even those few academics who glimpse these threats mostly express helplessness before them. "What can we do?" they ask. *Manifesto for a Tenured Radical* tries to begin answering that question.

Is there, then, any reason for hope in the picture I paint? First of all, the intellectual life in many disciplines—including English—is at a higher level than it has been in more than half a century. As always, there is no shortage of mediocre work, but the sheer quantity and inventiveness of the best work is remarkable. This scholarship has theoretical resources we have not yet used to examine either ourselves or the social formations in which we as academics are embedded. It is critical to do so collectively.

Secondly, here and there are sources of inspiration. In September of 1995 I had dinner with a group of graduate student union activists and their faculty supporters in New Haven; in May of 1996 I had a similar meal with student union leaders in San Diego. Both groups were rainbow coalitions of multiple races, ethnicities, and economic backgrounds. They were working together, sharing their varied pasts and their more parallel presents. The Yale and University of California administrations were gearing themselves up to threaten or fire these people. The administrators were unable to realize they are an inspiration, not only for New Haven and San Diego but also for America. Here was our multicultural present and future in miniature, and it worked. They were engaged in an alliance politics that extended from the classroom to the maintenance shop and the cafeteria. Yale or California may break these unions for now, but each one of these students has been turned into an agent of change. It is happening all across the country.

Higher education almost certainly faces if not a kind of meltdown, at least a future that is likely to be economically mean and brutish. It cannot be altogether resisted, but it can be partly blocked, and we can create communities that are in some important ways better than those we will lose. The difference between this partial success and failure will be the difference between a form of higher education that is and is not worth working in a decade from now.

For faculty members, higher education is a career that entails relearning your discipline as it changes over time. Many faculty members in fact remake themselves repeatedly in the course of their careers. If higher education becomes like high school, or like community college teaching, so thoroughly crammed with scheduled responsibilities that it offers little time for independent intellectual pursuit, then it will lose the difference that makes it what it is. In the false name of a repressive efficiency, corporate-style administration would make higher education pay people as little as possible and extract the maximum labor from them. It will be done in the service of several narratives, including, ironically, the need to compete in the global environment. Of course American higher education already attracts students from all over the world. But if current trends continue—such as the wholesale shift from tenure-track faculty to underpaid part-timers and adjuncts—quality will decline and we will no longer compete so effectively.

Meanwhile, higher education remains the only proven means of social mobility, the only antidote to poverty, and the only large-scale corrective for the ravages of capitalism. It is in short the only workable solution to some of America's worst social problems. Yet many conservative politicians would drastically reduce its size and reduce student access to it at the same time. All these forces must be resisted, but faculty members cannot do so without collectively

8

INTRODUCTION

looking outward at the world for the first time in decades. The process can only succeed if we understand our disciplines in terms of their larger social meaning and prove ourselves worthy, as communities, of the respect and support we ask of the public. Using the discipline of English and my own historical specialization, modern poetry, as examples, *Manifesto* offers some prescriptions for how we might begin. My aim is to help make the book's predictive warnings untrue.

Manifesto has benefited from thoughtful and suggestive comments from several readers, including Michael Bérubé, Karen Ford, Robert Parker, Matthew Hurt, Carine Melkom-Mardorossian, John Carlos Rowe, Paula A. Treichler, Richard Wheeler, and Eric Zinner. Earlier versions of portions of a number of the chapters, now revised and updated, appeared in *Academe, American Literature, The Chronicle of Higher Education, College Literature, Illinois Law Review, Journal of the Midwest Modern Language Association, Profession, Social Text,* and *Works and Days,* and in the collections *Teaching Contemporary Theory to Undergraduates* (ed. Dianne F. Sadoff and William E. Cain) and *Changing Classroom Practices: Resources for Literary and Cultural Studies* (ed. David Downing).

THE POLITICS
OF ENGLISH

1

AGAINST ENGLISH
AS IT WAS

THEORY AND THE
POLITICS OF THE DISCIPLINE

Over the past century a series of cowbird eggs have been laid in the capacious university nest. A cowbird puts its egg in the nest of some other species. Being stronger and more aggressive than the other nestlings, the young cowbirds get more of the worms, grow faster, and may shove the other nestlings out of the nest or cause them to starve.

—David Perkins, "The Future of Keats Studies"

In the literature curriculum, Perkins allows, the nestlings that have been starving and are nearly dead are the canonical works of English literature. In each new cowbird invasion, a body of theory has not only demanded space for itself but also helped plant new and brutally opportunistic textual eggs in the true nest. A series of nonnative species has filled our good English trees. First it was modern philosophy and literature displacing classical studies; then in the 1930s Marxism helped clear the way for American literature. More recently, feminism, multiculturalism, and gay studies have laid their eggs in the nest; now John Keats is starving on the forest floor. The shorthand term for the force that has done all this recent damage is "theory." Has it actually undermined the discipline, as Perkins believes, or has it kept it adaptable and enabled it to survive?

There is no question that admitting new texts or theories into the discipline has consequences. You admit Saussure or Freud, for example, and before too long you've got Derrida and Lacan on your hands. In other words, new admissions bring with them intellectual traditions that continue to develop or, in the nestling metaphor, grow and take up more space. Yet the discipline's ability to adapt and to absorb new species has also kept it alive when other fields, more resistant to cultural change, have seen themselves diminish in size and influence. But disciplinary opportunism has not always led to admirable introspection or to social responsibility. Theory's role here has been more mixed.

I want to open *Manifesto* by asking how theory has helped bring us to where we are in literary studies, and by suggesting that it has done both more and less to fulfill its promise than we might have guessed thirty years ago at the start of the theory revolution. While I cannot share Perkins's nostalgia for a past that I consider racist, sexist, reactionary, and substantially anti-intellectual, I will grant the claim that provoked his search for avian infiltrators: Keats and the traditional canon may not be headed for extinction but they do occupy a lot less of our attention than they did a few decades ago.

If the brutally selective canon we studied then were merely a function of concern for quality or value, as Perkins believes, then a pervasive sense of loss might be justified. Yet I have no doubt whatsoever that this was not the case. As a literature major from 1963 to 1967—at Antioch College, arguably the most progressive college in the country—I read not a single work by an African American writer in any course and only a few works by women. I can in fact only remember being assigned Jane Austen and Virginia Woolf. A number of us read other things on our own, but that was the extent of our assigned readings by women and minorities. Antioch did have a highly successful Black Students Association at the time, but its members focused on other issues. Even the black students themselves knew so little about the Afro-American literary heritage that they saw no reason to place any pressure on the literature curriculum. As for feminism, the contemporary movement did not begin to have an impact on the curriculum until the mid- to late 1970s.

My anecdotal evidence is supported by research Michael Bérubé reports in his *Marginal Forces / Cultural Centers* (1992). Except for some presentations on "Negro folk songs" delivered in the 1920s and 1930s, the Modern Language Association's annual convention offered no papers on African American writing until one delivered in 1953; a decade passed before another such paper was presented. Similarly, by 1950 the annual MLA bibliography listed only two contemporary studies of African American writers, both being books on the poet Paul Lawrence Dunbar (43–44). As late as the 1960s the mainstream anthologies published by Norton gave virtually no space to African American writers. So it is not surprising that African American writers were not widely taught in white institutions or that they received only narrow attention even in historically black colleges. Indeed, the hostility toward their work voiced by some of the New Critics, such as Cleanth Brooks's dismissal of Langston Hughes in his 1939 *Modern Poetry and the Tradition,* reinforced widespread institutional racism. I will have more to say about race and the curriculum both in this chapter and in chapter 5. For now, suffice it to say that the past some reactionary critics evoke nostalgically is not a past to which many Americans would eagerly return.

Yet the role of theory in provoking canonical expansion has actually been somewhat limited. Certainly there are many more theory courses than there were as recently as the 1970s, and feminist theory has successfully pressed academics to read and teach much more widely in forgotten works by women. Although political and social theory about racism has helped press the academy to begin reforming itself, literary and interpretive theory cannot take much credit for the gradual inclusion of works by minority writers in scholarship and teaching. Indeed we did not really even see theoretically inflected studies of minority writers until the 1980s, and American resistance to sophisticated theoretical reflection about the social construction of race remains very strong in the 1990s; our culture's instinctive view of race remains essentialist. Further-more, the rapid growth of the theory industry—which has dominated literary scholarship for over twenty years—has produced numerous theoretical subfields whose advocates no longer attempt to remain current across the whole spectrum of theory. Thus many American theorists avoid reading the anti-essentialist race theory that would teach them much about themselves and their country. That is not, however, to offer anti-essentialism unqualified praise. Reading Derrida alone will not fill the cultural need I am addressing. Americans might, for example, read the anti-essentialist race theory growing out of the British cultural studies tradition and then ask how it can be rearticulated to the specifities of American history.[1]

In an intellectual environment where different versions of feminism, Marxism, psychoanalysis, poststructuralism, and cultural studies intersect and compete for our commitment, therefore, does the unitary term "theory" have any meaning? As a reactive way of collapsing the whole range of theoretical discourses into a single (and thereby more avoidable) identity, the term may reasonably still be regarded with a degree of exasperation. Yet at the same time, teachers and scholars do continue to describe themselves as being "in theory," thereby at least situating themselves within a particular historical conjuncture, but it is increasingly difficult thereby to evoke the possibility of identifying themselves with a loose alliance of contemporary intellectual movements. Departments occasionally advertise for specialists in theory and talk of teaching courses in theory, a conversation in which phenomenology, deconstruction, narratology, postmodernism, and other bodies of theory all seem more or less interchangeable, but in the 1990s the universal category has widely been abandoned for more specific searches and courses. The collapsing of differences that was characteristic of the seventies and to some degree of the eighties clearly blocked the comprehension of theories on their own terms and made theory intellectually imaginable to some only as a generalized other. But at the same time it prevented the policing of theory by those uninterested in its specificity, leaving it altogether up to those involved to decide the content of theory courses. However simplified the global term may be, then, it has a historical existence and a certain practical power in our lives.

Especially in the 1980s several of the multiple discourses or bodies of theory have been strikingly in dialogue with one another and, as a result, have been partly defined by the process of adapting to, incorporating, rejecting, or transforming one another's insights, assumptions, and challenges. Thus there is arguably an implicit discursive field called theory, constantly in flux, that is structured by these affirmations and disputations. No individual discourse can realistically hope either to represent or wholly to occupy that field. Nor are the boundaries of the discursive field universally agreed on. What counts as theoretical and what counts as theoretically important are very much open to dispute. Some discourses may be acknowledged as theoretically inflected and informed without being widely credited as contributing to the continuing articulation of theoretical problematics. Some polemical and politically oppositional texts, on the other hand, though not engaged with the discourses that count as theoretical within the academy, nonetheless are implicitly theoretically grounded and certainly able to contribute to theoretical self-definition and critique. Some writers in the 1980s spoke of high and low theory to differentiate between what they considered more and less rhetorically sophisticated theoretical discourses or even to differentiate between theoretical writing and self-consciously stylized, deliberately chosen social practices, which might include the oppositional music, literature, rhetoric, or dress styles of particular subcultures. Others would consider such a distinction elitist or reactionary.

Are there, however, any characteristics common to all these theories and intellectual processes? At other moments in history, a theory has been taken to imply a finite set of logically related propositions. In the current historical context, with its wide disputation even within individual bodies of theory and its pervasive assumption that no theory can acquire permanent, ahistorical truth content, theory has a rather different status. For us, in the wake of the poststructuralist revolution, what probably most distinguishes theoretical from nontheoretical discourse is its tendency toward self-conscious and reflective interpretive, methodological, and rhetorical practices. This tendency, of course, is not unqualified. Self-reflection is not a condition that theory can decisively enter into and maintain. It is an intermittent element of various discursive practices, one made possible by particular historical pressures. Indeed, what is recognized and credited as genuine self-reflection will itself change over time, just as the available forms of self-reflection are themselves historically produced and constrained. Nonetheless, theoretical writing now typically assumes that meaning is not automatically given, that it must be consciously produced by a critical writing practice, that methodological, epistemological, and political choices and determinations are continually at issue in critical analysis.

From this perspective it is possible to see that a particular discursive tradition—say, New Criticism—could be genuinely theoretical at one point in its history and not at another. When a body of theory ceases to be in crisis, when it no longer has to struggle to define its enterprise and mark its similarities to and differences from other theories, when it imagines itself potentially coextensive with the discipline it addresses, when its assumptions come to seem not merely preferable but inevitable and automatic, when it is taken to be a given part of the natural world, when it can be entered into and applied almost without conscious decision, then it no longer counts as theory. Of course, entire bodies of theory do not usually change—develop or decay—all at once. Even though particular theorists can produce founding or radically transforming discourses, other individual practitioners may often seem either to lag behind the development of the discourse as a whole or to succeed in applying a theory in a largely uncritical and unreflective way, thereby perhaps anticipating the general process of normalization. Indeed, part of the comedy or, if you will, the charm of literary discourse in the academy is the survival of any number of discredited interpretive practices alongside the most recent developments in the humanities. Yet if this theoretical babel seems to evoke irresponsible disarray, it also allows for provocatively reductive deflations of what might otherwise be unchallenged claims to sophistication. Even apparently reactionary arguments can keep alive interpretive problems that have not, despite confident claims to the contrary, in fact been superseded by new theoretical moves.

After three decades of influential recent high theory in France and nearly that many in Britain and the United States, it is also time to admit that not all theory has been of the same quality and not all its practitioners have done thoughtful or impressive work. The best work, to be sure, has left the humanities and social sciences radically transformed and left many of us with distinctly different views of the world than we had before. We have come to understand the social construction of much, including gender, that we took as naturally given before. We have recognized the political character of cultural products that we once thought were above historical processes. Our new notions of language and meaning admit the reality of complex connotation in ways earlier generations consistently resisted. Yet the rapid movement of the life of theory has also produced a lemming-like effect, where opportunistic scholars rush after every new development in hopes of making a name for themselves. If the broader movements have not been faddish, some of their advocates have been. We need to admit this despite the tendency to overreact in defending ourselves against those who burlesque the theory revolution, from Walter Jackson Bate to David Perkins.[2] It is time to ask what theory has and has not done for us, indeed time to ask more of it than we have to date.

In 1970s English departments, questions about the usefulness of theory typically devolved into demonstrations that different theoretical perspectives could be productively adapted to the close reading of literary texts. But as theory placed ever more pressure on the produced, consensual, libidinal, or political nature of signification, texts themselves began to become increasingly indeterminate phenomena. More traditional scholars were often anxious about this, though others took pains to reassure them that the task of interpretation was in no way jeopardized by its potentially infinite character. As Paul de Man was fond of saying in the early days of deconstruction, when some thought such an unstable or conflicted view of meaning would momentarily bring the sky down over their heads, "but it does not block discourse." In other words, far from inhibiting interpretation—the universal business of the humanities—deconstruction, like other bodies of theory, would actually open more opportunities for interpretation. Thus, in what may seem a curious paradox to those in other disciplines, academics in English have come to accept (in practice if not openly) that the meaning of a literary text is, as it were, wholly up for grabs, while the sacred character of the text itself is indisputable. In this dynamic, I would argue, it has never been the sacredness of the text that has been at issue. The literary text is defended so as to distract attention from the real object to be protected—the profession of literary studies.

There is nothing necessarily illicit about the use of deconstruction (or most other bodies of theory) for various kinds of immanent textual analysis. With the rise of cultural studies, to be sure, as I shall suggest in chapter 4, immanent textual analysis appropriately became suspect. Until then, the key problem with the interpretation of individual texts arose when a depoliticized and radically decontextualized version of immanent analysis became a transcendent moral value, as often happens in English studies. When Derrida, for example, practices close textual analysis, the status of the text as an object of veneration or doubt is always open to question. Moreover, he generally reads individual texts to raise larger critical and social issues. Following Derrida, we may, then, analyze a literary narrative so as to address the issue of the general social demand that we narrate our subjectivity. However, under the leadership of what was once the Yale school, deconstruction in America restored the text to a venerated position and militantly dropped any consideration of larger social questions. Textual contradictions became merely rhetorical occasions for ecstasy or despair.

In this respect, though, literary deconstruction was merely following the pattern of other bodies of theory in the United States. Most bodies of theory, in fact, have characteristically compromised their claims to self-reflection and social or professional criticism in order to gain a place in the modern academic establishment. In other words, the object of interpretation and the content of interpretive discourse are considered appropriate subjects for discussion and scrutiny, but the interests of the interpreter and the discipline and society he or she serves are not. This restriction has produced a number of contradictory, almost schizophrenic, theoretical practices: until recently, psychoanalytic critics have typically been unable to examine either how their own interpretive activity or the aims and assumptions of their academic disciplines are libidinally determined; Marxist critics have frequently been reluctant or unable to analyze how their own projects are historically positioned and produced; and American deconstructive critics rarely examine the logic of their disciplines with the same rigor that they apply to constitutive contradictions in literary texts.

Lest this observation seem to score a distinctive blow against such contemporary theory, let me state clearly that in this respect most theorists behave like almost everyone else. They do not challenge the territorialization of university intellectual activity or in any way risk undermining the status and core beliefs of their fields. The difference, for theorists, is that this blindness or reluctance often contradicts the intellectual imperatives of the very theories they espouse. Indeed, only a theorized discipline can be an effective site for a general social critique— that is, a discipline actively engaged in self-criticism, a discipline that is a locus for struggle, a discipline that renews and revises its awareness of its history, a discipline that inquires into its differential relations with other academic fields, and a discipline that examines its place in the social formation and is willing to adapt its writing practices to suit different social functions.

To make these claims, to be sure, is to recognize that the conditions blocking this kind of inquiry are beginning to change. Indeed I would not be empowered to see the institutionalized blindness of theory within academic departments if the discipline of literary studies were not already somewhat open to this kind of self-criticism. As a discipline, perhaps we should now call on the example of the 1960s, when we were at least willing to interrupt the transmission of the canon of English literature to talk about the Vietnam War. If the general 1960s politicization of the university did not produce a real theorizing of academic disciplines, it did place the university's social responsibilities on the academic agenda. Feminism has done so as well at moments, and Afro-American studies has repeatedly attempted to do so against resistance.

Yet neither feminism nor Afro-American studies is now well positioned to initiate a general critique of academia's social mission. Both have been partly isolated by being institutionalized within separate programs. But that is not an insurmountable difficulty and indeed being outside traditional disciplines has an advantage for critique. The more serious problems include some that are internal. In two versions, cultural feminism and Afro-centrism, these movements have fallen under the spell of American exceptionalism and mounted fantasmatic claims to unique redemptive powers. This has made them intolerant of differences of opinion within their own ranks and thus ill suited for dialogue with other versions of feminism and Afro-American studies, let alone other bodies of theory. For these and other reasons, some of which I will note shortly, both bodies of theory have failed to realize their potential for a thoroughgoing analysis of academia's place in society.

Of course there have been at least isolated instances of serious and theoretically grounded disciplinary critique for some time, beginning with Richard Ohmann's *English in America: A Radical View of the Profession* (1976), but the more general phenomenon is more recent. Here one would begin by citing the publications of GRIP (the Group for Research on the Institutionalization and Professionalization of Literary Study) in this country and such British works as Chris Baldick's *The Social Mission of English Criticism* (1983); Terry Eagleton's *The Function of Criticism* (1984); and Janet Batsleer, Tony Davies, Rebecca O'Rourke, and Chris Weedon's *Rewriting English: Cultural Politics of Gender and Class* (1985). More recently, Evan Watkins, Gerald Graff, Terry Caesar, James Sosnoski, John Guillory, and others have begun to rethink the discipline's history and practices. This shift in emphasis, moreover, has real, not merely imagined, risks for the existing infrastructure of universities, even for their economy. As we shall see more specifically in the last four essays in *Manifesto*, when theory casts its gaze on departments and universities as we know them, they can be shown partly to inhibit intellectual work and even to function as reactionary forces within the larger society.

It is apparent that both disciplinary critique and a larger critique of academia—enterprises that I believe to be the inescapable destiny of the logic of theory, though not necessarily the inevitable direction of its social practice—will produce both stress within departments and a certain backlash against theory. That seems to be one underlying cause for statements like Stanley Fish's "theory's day is dying," a statement that may reflect Fish's continuing resistance—from the 1980s through his 1995 *Professional Correctness: Literary Studies and Political Change*—to the more politically and socially self-critical turn to recent theory and to the new willingness to view the profession of literary studies with some distance. For Fish's earlier work had largely emptied the text of any intrinsic meaning and instead sacralized the profession of literary studies as the guarantor of consensus and the source of a humanistic tradition. As the attention of theory began at least marginally to shift from how to interpret literature to how the discipline of literary studies is constituted and what its social effects are, the discipline came under a distinctly different and more threatening kind of intellectual pressure.

But literary studies for decades had used twin strategies for containing threats to its core politics of interpretation. The first was to harness theory primarily to immanent textual analysis. The second was to turn any body of theory with broad and unsettling disciplinary implications into a subspecialization cut off from any general dialogue with the discipline. A series of potentially revolutionary theories had been tamed in this way, and the analysis of disciplinarity itself would prove no different. Soon it became a field, an isolated area of research, a specialization with, paradoxically, no pressing claims on the discipline's general attention. Gerald Graff warns against the intellectual containment built into mutually exclusive subspecializations. For all practical purposes his own warning, however, has itself been contained, classified within the subspecialization of disciplinary history.

Similar fates had befallen most of the radical skepticisms with potential to throw the discipline into serious self-scrutiny. The first modern body of theory to be contained in this way was psychoanalysis, which in the 1950s traded disciplinary accommodation for any potential to challenge the false and unreflective rationality that still pervaded professionalized interpretation. In effect, psychoanalytic critics agreed to act like experts in a specialized method with no psychodynamic claims about how literary interpreters practiced their craft. They gave up at once their theory's inherent potential for self-analysis and for general disciplinary analysis and critique. Many also found ways to accommodate notions of unconscious motivation with sacralized models of the literary text.

Beginning in the previous decade and mounting with furor in the 1950s, the other existing body of theory with similarly disruptive structural potential—Marxism—was scandalized and largely cast out of the American university. But it would eventually establish among its warring traditions its own ways to revere literariness and thus accommodate much of its interpretive practice to disciplinary norms. Its larger politics, however, would remain a threat, so Marxism would be ruthlessly marginalized until the 1970s. As for its capacity for self-reflection and self-critique, Marxism would have to abandon its fantasmatic claims to scientificity before serious self-scrutiny could become wide-spread.

In the 1970s, however, another body of theory arrived with greater purchase on the American academy. I refer of course to contemporary feminism, which spread from the public sphere to academia in the mid- to late 1970s and became massively influential in the 1980s. Out of necessity, feminism kept literary studies and the institutions of academia at a distance in its first years. Its early focus on exposing the patriarchal bias in canonical writers prevented it from sacralizing literary texts. Meanwhile, discrimination against women meant that feminists had to fight to find academic employment; that maintained disciplinary critique as a high priority. But by the mid-1980s those patterns had begun to change. Feminists had begun the long and immensely fruitful rediscovery and reinterpretation of forgotten texts by women; that has been tremendously beneficial to the discipline and the culture, but an unexpected side effect has been to install in feminism its own version of literary reverence. Simultaneously, the number of women gaining academic employment began to reach a critical mass in many departments. Though not wholly co-opted, feminism by the early 1990s was securely institutionalized in many places, from departments to publishers' lists. It was no longer a place to look for foundational critiques of academic institutions that would extend beyond gender to the whole range of their constitutive discourses and practices.

Meanwhile, through all these changes, traditional scholars had a place to retreat to, a conceptual and methodological ground they could call their own in the face of theory's multiple onslaughts. That place was history, literary history to be specific, and it was more or less what everyone else claimed to be doing while theories multiplied and gained adherents. By the late 1980s, however, this last redoubt began to crumble. History, long little more than an unreflective site on which to stage period-based literary idealization, began to be theorized. Unproblematic and generous in its rewards for decades, history began to be a site for theoretical reflection. Those who resisted the theory revolution now had no presentable territory to call their own, so they retreated into exceptionalist platitudes about the transcendence of art.

The increasing theorizing of history was an overdetermined change. The reverberations of the expanded canon—pressed by feminists, Afro-Americanists, and scholars on the Left—had a cumulative effect on our confidence in a belief that cultural memory could be disinterested and comprehensive. Textuality, a nervous site of uncontainable meanings, began to encompass all sorts of purportedly nonliterary historical documents. Fresh enterprises like the New Historicism, initially centered in Renaissance studies, came to have wider influence. And the field of theory of history, contained by its own larger discipline in much the same way as literary studies contained its threatening subspecializations, slowly attracted readers in other departments. Meanwhile, fields like anthropology and sociology were undergoing their own crises of confidence. For all these reasons literary historiography could no longer protect itself from the ravages of theory.

By the late 1980s, therefore, a new development in English studies had coalesced enough to have a name—the return to history. Volatile and changeable for two decades, the discipline—or at least a portion of it—was making yet another foray into a new identity and set of commitments. This time, however, the change was heralded by many as a return to an earlier preoccupation. And so the name stuck, at least for a time. I remember some of my older colleagues remarking with satisfaction (and wary camaraderie) my own return to history. No doubt similar conversations and moments of unexpected recognition across a generational divide took place elsewhere in the country.

By the mid-1990s, however, history's handshake could not so easily be extended across the abandoned battlefields of the profession. In its new incarnation, the older generation began to realize, history as they knew it was pretty much spoiled. For years, history, not patriotism, had been the last refuge of the discipline's antitheoretical scoundrels. It was what they did, what they stood for, the rich, material ground they invoked against the lemming-like rush from theorist to theorist that seemed to mark the enthusiasms of the young.

There were counterclaims for history from theorists in those days, but they remained atypical. "Always historicize," cried Fredric Jameson in *The Political Unconscious* in one of the 1980s' most famous opening salvos. Oddly enough, to the extent he believed in Marxism's predictive powers, he partly meant to invoke principles that a Catholic bishop might have welcomed—focus on mankind's ultimate destiny in interpreting a mutable world; ask where all of us are (and should be) heading; what telos is hidden in the trials of local time? Of course Jameson and the prelate would have different stories to tell about history's trends and ultimate meaning, but both would prove equally principled and confident in their application. What Jameson did *not* mean by asking us always to historicize was to seek a contextualization so radical and relative that no universal generalizations about human history could be made.

A decade later it was clear the return to history had gone back to the past without any guarantees about its meaning. Now history was as slippery as textuality, and that was not what traditional literary historians had in mind. "History" indeed seemed yet one more phase in the shape-changing story of contemporary theory. Of course it was more than that for many; its materiality was elaborately recovered and treasured by many involved in the return to history. But that was not enough to relieve the burden of a history without guarantees.

AGAINST ENGLISH AS IT WAS

One final turn of the wheel of theory delivered the possibility of an end to literary studies as we knew it—the belated arrival of cultural studies on the American scene. For cultural studies threatened to import into the English curriculum a whole range of objects not only outside literariness but also outside any plausible account of the aesthetic. The underlying basis of literary studies' high cultural prestige might be lost. Moreover, that was not the only threat. The whole notion of a discipline with consensual boundaries was in doubt. Unrepresentable in their entirety in any single department, the range of new objects attracting interpretive interest in cultural studies might simply overwhelm the study of literary texts.

One interesting result of these two developments—the arrival of a self-consciously theorized historiography and the rise of cultural studies in America—was the appearance of reactionary professional organizations devoted to traditional idealization. The Modern Language Association found itself under attack for the only *good* thing it had done in thirty years—opening its closed shop to a whole range of new interests and constituencies. Rather than throw out the old and bring in the new, the MLA simply multiplied the sessions at its annual conference and gave everyone programs matching their commitments. But that was not enough to keep the literary Right in the fold. Simply having Spenser and Amiri Baraka sessions in adjoining rooms made them furious. They began to resign and form their own organizations where uncomfortable questions would not be asked.

One of the ironies of literary studies in the 1990s is that this conservative fraction of the profession saw no alternative but to revive the aesthetic faith of still earlier generations. That put this group of literary scholars—often liberals according to their self-image—in an implicit alliance with the political Right in the culture wars. English professors and conservative journalists alike could then stand in front of the symbolic schoolhouse to defend the eternal verities of the humanities. One-time English professor liberals were now for all practical purposes in league with William Bennett. Not that these people had any fondness for one another, but a political realignment had taken place in the humanities, and it would begin to have consequences when the university faced challenging questions about its mission and its employment practices.

Now the key question—still unanswered today—could be posed succinctly: would literary studies, and the humanities in general, become more fully reflective, self-critical enterprises? Would they learn to examine their practices and social effects with more than opportunistic self-interest? Meanwhile the potential social costs of an unreflective discipline—housed in unreflective institutions of higher education—began to mount. Theory had successfully opened the problematics of literary meaning, but it had not put the discipline or the institutions of higher education under comparable scrutiny. As a result, as will be clear in the final essays in the book, neither the disciplines nor the institutions were prepared for the new economic pressures higher education faced in the 1990s and beyond.

To begin to theorize the discipline of English studies, I must emphasize, does not mean that the notion of literariness as a separate cultural domain would simply disappear. The notion of literariness has a history that needs to be studied. But it also needs to be studied in relation to other cultural domains and in closer relation to social and political history, things that English departments are presently disinclined and often ill equipped to do. And the social function of English as a discipline needs to be theorized and deeply rethought.

As I suggested above, the black studies movement of the 1960s had the potential to force a radical reexamination of literary history, the hierarchizing opposition between high culture and popular culture, the ideological construction of the notion of literariness, and the social effects of the English curriculum. But the black studies protests did not produce an influential general critique of the field, in part because a whole range of social and institutional forces helped to protect most literature departments from any serious self-criticism. Black studies programs argued for a separate role because freestanding programs gave them their only guarantee of self-determination and because they wanted, in effect, to emphasize black consciousness-raising. At the same time, traditional disciplines were happy to locate the problem of race elsewhere. As a result, nonblack students avoided courses in black culture and literary studies remained largely unchanged. It is now possible to argue that the choice between separation from and integration into the regular discipline and curriculum is a false one. We need both opportunities for concentrated study of coherent individual traditions and pervasive mainstreaming of those traditions into general pedagogy and scholarship.

But the time has come—especially as some elements of the far Right become entrenched in American society through the end of the century, the increasingly conservative federal judiciary being a prime example—to begin to think and theorize about the social meaning of a specialization in literary studies and to extend that reflection to education more generally. Indeed, this kind of reference to contemporary American society, which some may feel is irrelevant to literary history, is itself therefore necessarily informed by theory. For I do not believe that one writes or teaches or interprets or theorizes in relation only to the eternal verities of the imagination, as literature departments have chosen to believe. We work in our own time; the students we train will live in this historical moment.

Questions like this led me, in the mid-1980s, to begin reviewing anthologies of American literature and course offerings in English departments to see how well writings by women and minorities were represented. By then women's poetry and fiction were being given broader representation in some anthologies, but African American writing was present with but a few token texts. We could ask, as I did, what kind of message the English curriculum of the previous decades sent to students? When a curriculum requires a course in Shakespeare, as virtually every English department did, but not a course in Afro-American literature, as virtually no departments did, what message does it give students about black people, what message about the cultural traditions that are valuable and those that are expendable? Are the students we graduate from such programs as likely to see racial justice in their own country as important? The confidence that such values will be dependably if obliquely encouraged by the eternal truths of the literature we do require is an evasive fiction. The point is that the way we construct and communicate any academic discipline, including the study of literature, has interpretable social meaning and possible real social consequences; to pretend otherwise is merely to lie to ourselves.

There is no disputing that the United States is a substantially racist society. In this historical context, therefore, it is potentially a powerful and dangerous seduction to offer students literariness as something they can identify with, as a subject position they can occupy, while constructing it as an ideology that transcends such passing material trivialities as racial justice. In a fundamentally racist society, choosing to marginalize or ignore the study of minority literature, as English departments did throughout their history until the 1990s, articulates literary study to racism.

To entice students into making a significant commitment to the study of literature, we often display its place in our own lives, telling them, in effect, that literature is one of the finer things on earth, that it exhibits at once a powerful realism about the human condition and a visionary synthesis of its highest ambitions. But what does it mean to attach this whole program for transcendence to the experience of only one race, one sex, a restricted set of class fractions within a few national cultures? What does it mean that the experiences of most of the world's peoples are obliterated in the "humanism" of the English curriculum? As the authors of *Rewriting English* put it: "Beneath the disinterested procedures of literary judgment and discrimination can be discerned the outlines of other, harsher words: exclusion, subordination, dispossession" (Batsleer et al., 30). These are not issues of coverage—this term, which apparently encapsulates the whole thoughtfulness of our model of the English major, suggests a comparison between the depth of our disciplinary model and the claims of a brand of paint—but rather issues of the social effects of disciplinary specialization.

By the mid-1990s anthologies had changed radically, with wide representation of women and minority writers. Here and there around the country a few instructors refuse to teach these texts. But it is now very difficult for an undergraduate to take survey courses in literature and not encounter a far more diverse canon than we have taught throughout our history. Yet the depth of thoughtfulness attending this new pedagogy remains doubtful. Faculty members are certainly persuaded that our meaningful literary history was far more diverse than we believed for decades, but narrow issues of coverage and representation still dominate discussions of the curriculum. As I will argue in the next chapter, the work of conceptualizing and teaching anthologies involves wider political and social issues and responsibilities than many in the discipline are comfortable in acknowledging.

Just as students now encounter works by women and minorities regularly, many of them also take courses in interpretive theory. But neither the students nor the faculty who teach them feel much inclined to challenge the social meaning of the discipline as a result. We need, for example, to recognize that literary idealization is necessarily in dialogue with, and embedded in, all the other idealizations by which our culture sustains and justifies itself. Studying literature in a self-reflexive and culturally aware fashion entails asking how the available forms of idealization feed into and relate to one another. These forms are the idealized subject positions offered to us (and from which, to some degree, we choose)—from the subject position of one who loves literature to the subject position of one who loves his or her country, from the idealization of poetry to the idealization of national power.

Many devotees of literature would assume they have no necessary common ground with devotees of the nation state, but the record suggests otherwise. First, the worldwide curricular and scholarly privileging of national literatures—so deeply embedded in our assumptions that it seems a fact of nature—not only disguises other ways of conceptualizing the field but also links literary studies to every exceptionalist narrative of national destiny, grants institutional literary study part of its social rationale, and underwrites the economic basis of the profession. As recent materialist scholarship has shown, the teaching of Shakespeare helps socialize people into their national identity.

However marginalized literary study may be in the United States, therefore, it is nonetheless implicated in an overdetermined field of privileged social roles and admired cultural domains. Indeed, there are differential relations of mutual dependency between the various idealizations that structure and facilitate the ideologies of our moment. Negotiations between and among those differential relations make possible not only our academic specializations but also our governmental policies. We need to draw a map of the relations between literature and our other valorized and devalued domains and discourses. We need to inquire how and why certain concepts—like "literature" or "freedom"—have their inner contradictions precipitated out and become elevated to a transcendent status within the social formation. For it is not the same to teach English when our economy is impoverishing millions of our citizens. It is not irrelevant to the study of literature that members of Congress are trying to reverse the civil rights gains of the last thirty years. The connotative effects of the ideals of the whole history of literature become quite different in such changing social contexts. And the social function and impact of the classroom become quite different as well.

A liberal reading of the curriculum presupposes that a universal decency, fairness, and empathy are somehow encouraged by the values promoted within a limited textual corpus.[3] To press such matters further is to ask, with what some may feel is an unseemly focus on current events rather than on the transcendent values of the discipline, what an English professor's role might be in educating students to participate in a democracy. But the question of whether the privileged forms of idealization in the West—privileged again in the discipline of English studies—will necessarily produce either a national or an international sense of multiracial community has already been answered negatively. The historically empowered configuration of the discourses of Western humanism has repeatedly failed. To see it as our job merely to praise that tradition in its present form is to be certain to perpetuate that failure. This is not to say that there are no resources in the tradition. I use those resources throughout this book; its discourses about the rights of workers underwrites *Manifesto*'s whole last section. It is rather to say that the tradition needs to be rethought, critically theorized, significantly restructured, and realigned in relation to other discourses.

What I am calling for, therefore, is not merely a culturally expanded discipline, something we have substantially achieved in the last decade, but a theoretically self-critical and reflective one, something we still lack. If I am against English as it was, then, I am far from an unqualified fan of English as it is, and I have little confidence in what English will be five or ten years from now. Having recovered from an unbroken history of sexism and become barely aware of our long night of racism, we are rapidly descending into a gulag labor program. On the other hand, the theory revolution of the last three decades has given us the intellectual resources we need to reform ourselves, to theorize our disciplinary practices and our relations to the larger culture. It has given us the terms, categories, vantage points, and modes of analysis we need to see ourselves more clearly. That is the larger promise of the unitary term "theory," and it is a promise, as I hope to demonstrate in what follows, that we ignore at our certain peril.

2

MULTICULTURALISM WITHOUT GUARANTEES

FROM ANTHOLOGIES TO THE SOCIAL TEXT

The alien is the nation, nothing more or less. . . .
The alien is the nation. Nothing else.
—Genevieve Taggard, "Ode in Time of Crisis"

I want to take up the question of multiculturalism by addressing the subject of anthologies, not only because they are one of the major ways of bringing together texts from a variety of cultural traditions but also because anthologies that are explicitly multicultural—as anthologies of American literature are increasingly tending to be—are also a means of constructing in miniature textual versions of a larger multicultural society.[1] Anthologies are, in a significant way, representations of the wider social text, figurations of the body politic; their compilation and use is thus fraught with social and political meaning and responsibility. What conservatives see as the illegitimate contamination of anthologies and the literature classroom with other (justly or unjustly) analogous structures is neither hypothetical nor improbable. It is one of the immediate effects of putting the anthology form to use and it may well be one of the few effects to have a long, complex, and indirect life, a life that continues to reverberate long after students may have forgotten many of the texts they actually read in class.

Both here and in the second section of the book, therefore, I part company with John Guillory's often persuasive *Cultural Capital.* Unlike Guillory, I believe the content of the curriculum matters a great deal and that changes in widely used texts can have significant social impact. I also think it matters what kinds of knowledge count as cultural capital and that when repressed or marginalized traditions achieve that status other changes may open up as a result. While canonical representation does not map directly onto social representation, the two are complexly related, and the wider nets cast by comprehensive anthologies can create powerful simulacra of social formations. That is not to diminish the importance of who has access to education but rather to grant equal importance to what they are taught. Here I take that issue up in relation to anthologies.

The anthology as a single bound book, of course, has parallels with a similar structure that all college teachers assemble—the semester's syllabus or reading list. The book has higher visibility and a wider audience, but the same issues of inclusion or exclusion obtain; in that sense, then, all teachers are anthologists. In both cases the priority placed on multicultural representation in the classroom helps persuade students about the priority of multicultural representation on the faculty and in the student body. The admissions policy embodied in the anthology makes an implicit comment on the admissions policy appropriate to the institution as a whole. Nor is it much of a leap to make a connection with the nation's admission policy—its immigration statutes and their mixed and still politically contentious history of openness and racism in the 1990s. The problems of ethnic, racial, and gender representation in an anthology devoted to a nation's history or its literature—anthologies that are common not only in the United States but in other countries as well—speak quite directly to questions about representation in public debate and in legislative bodies. Anthologies empower students to make these connections, whether or not teachers choose to make them explicit. As I began to argue in the previous chapter, these effects are part of the cultural work anthologies and curricula do even if we pretend they are not.

Inclusion in an anthology is not equivalent to wielding effective political power, but neither are discursive and political representation in these different domains wholly discontinuous cultural processes. Literary and historical anthologies are not, to be sure, appropriate mechanisms for detailed social engineering; their use and impact is too unpredictable and their relation to detailed policy questions in other arenas entirely too oblique.[2] But their role in promoting core values that are exclusionary or inclusive, in valuing or devaluing minority and working-class cultures, in familiarizing readers with different traditions, and in imaging a multicultural body politic can be significant. The fact that anthologies and other educational practices cannot guarantee social change does not justify ignoring their role in promoting or discouraging it.

The cultural power wielded by anthologies used by large numbers of secondary or college students should not, therefore, be underestimated. They succeed to a significant degree in representing not only the kind of society we have been but also the sort of society we are now and have the potential to become in the future. There is no escaping those effects; the option of simply collecting texts from the past in a neutral fashion does not exist. Every choice about what to include or exclude not only grants or denies those individual texts wide visibility but also puts each included text in a dialogue with the other texts in the anthology, a dialogue that gives readers a chance to test possible class or intercultural relations and a dialogue that would otherwise not take place. Anthologies figure not only the material facts of history but also the active process of remembering and reconstructing it. They offer a reading of past social relationships and put forward opportunities for new social relations in the future. Far more is at stake, therefore, than just the already significant power to propel a poem, story, or historical document from obscurity to renown, though that is obviously among an anthology's powers as well, especially when a little-known small press publication thereby suddenly gains a much larger audience. But anthologies do not only have radical effects on texts. They also work to recreate *their readers* by repositioning them in relation to a remembered past, a lived present, and an imagined future. Anthologies are hardly the only force acting in that capacity, but they are not trivial, and they will, once again, have those effects whether their editors admit it or not.

Editing an anthology of American literature is thus not only an aesthetic but also a social and political project. One must decide which racial, ethnic, and social groups to include, how much space to grant them, and whether to mix them up or group them together. A historical anthology can grant not only past but also present agency to various constituencies and political parties. One has to decide not only how such groups represent their own history but also how they represent *other* races, ethnicities, and political groups and indeed how they represent the nation's various acts, ideals, and institutions. No past conversation recreated over such issues can fail to speak to the present. And nothing but the most benighted notion of evaluation would lead us to conclude that all these matters would be settled by judgments of quality or historical importance alone.[3] For notions of quality change when different styles and forms of literary expression enter the picture, just as what counts as historically important changes when a focus on diplomatic, military, and dominant political history is broadened to include dissident groups and everyday life. Nor does the recognition that inclusion in anthologies can help to empower gendered, ethnic, racial, and political groups settle the problem of which sorts of texts get in and which stay out. The anthologist has to decide what sort of national history he or she wants us to remember and how the relations between different groups of people have helped shape that history. It is not merely a question of whether black or white or red or yellow perspectives matter, but rather a question about what sort of voices they will have within what is necessarily a very selective frame.

An anthologist working with modern American poems must, for example, decide whether to limit the selection of Langston Hughes's poems to his more humanistic affirmations of black identity, as most anthologists do, or to include his concise attacks on white racism and on Christian hypocrisy. Does one focus, like most anthologists, on Claude McKay's most abstract protest poems or include the poems of explicit anguish about racial identity and rage at white America? In anthologizing the contemporary Mesquakie poet Ray Young Bear, do you include only his more affirmative poems focused on Native American culture, like "The Personification of a Name," or pick more overtly troubled poems like "The Significance of a Water Animal" or "It Is the Fish-Faced Boy Who Struggles," or even his towering poem of protest and indictment, "In Viewpoint: Poem for 14 Catfish and the Town of Tama, Iowa"? Does one ignore the many powerful poems protesting racism written by white Americans, instead anthologizing poems on less troubling topics? Does one include (or at least cite) some of the *racist* poems by major and minor white poets to show that poetry exemplified the same struggles typical of the rest of the culture or instead, again like most anthologists, allow readers to believe poets remained focused on more easily idealized subjects?

The dominant pattern for many years for general anthologies of American literature has been to seek minority poems that can be read as affirming the poet's culture but not mounting major challenges to white readers. One of Ray Young Bear's most regularly anthologized poems, "Grandmother," may seem not even to have been written by a Native American when it is taken out of the context of the rest of his work. It is also, to be sure, not just a question of the nature of the poem at issue but of our reading practices, interests, and assumptions and what interpretations they are most likely to produce. But that is something an anthologist can influence. Just how much of African American history seems to be invoked by Hughes's widely anthologized "The Negro Speaks of Rivers" will depend in part on how much knowledge the reader brings to the poem and how much of that knowledge is put in play and amplified by the other poems in the anthology, especially other poems by Hughes himself.

Simply placing "The Negro Speaks of Rivers" ("I've known rivers ancient as the world and older than the flow of human veins") next to Hughes's "The Bitter River" ("I've drunk of the bitter river . . . Mixed with the blood of the lynched boys") will increase the likelihood that the earlier poem, with its references to Lincoln and the Mississippi, will carry more complex historical freight. Young Bear's remarkable "It Is the Fish-Faced Boy Who Struggles," in which the people come together at the end to observe ceremonies they had long forgotten, will be more marked by the history of white repression if it is read along with "In Viewpoint: Poem for 14 Catfish and the Town of Tama, Iowa." The latter poem, moreover, is about how the genocidal mentality of the frontier survives today, so its challenge to contemporary readers is especially pointed. The poem opens by asking "in whose world do we go on living?" and proceeds to detail the ways white abuse of the Mesquakie permeates every element of daily life, from the louts who dream of bludgeoning Native Americans on a weekend to the town newspaper that dramatizes every Mesquakie offense and relegates every positive story about the tribe to the back pages.

Once editors find the courage to include more antagonistic texts, as most do not, the issues at stake become more complex and the works available richer and more varied. An anthology that aims to present multicultural history relationally and interactively, indeed, is not limited to literary works that divide easily into affirmative and negative groups. One can, for example, include white poets writing empathically, reflectively, or awkwardly about African American or Native American culture. And an accurately representative record of multicultural literary and historical relations will show that not only minority identities but also the dominant white identities come under scrutiny. One answer to the recurrent question of how to make *whiteness* visible in our history is simply to reprint the works that seek to do just that. In the 1920s and the 1930s, a period when writers from a variety of cultures regularly took up questions of race, that would include some of the poems I assigned in the course I will describe in chapter 5, such as Aqua Laluah's "Lullaby," Anne Spencer's "White Things," Claude McKay's "To the White Fiends," and Kenneth Patchen's "Nice Day for a Lynching."

"I'm looking for a house," Hughes announces in a 1931 poem, "where white shadows/ Will not fall." "There is no such house," he answers, "No such house at all."[4] What does it mean, modern poets repeatedly ask, to bear on one's body the sign of that history—white skin—the figure for a cultural dominance so omnipresent it was, like a white shadow, as though invisible? It is a question relatively few white Americans have felt impelled to ask in the eighties and nineties, though it is a question anthologists may be able to help put in play again, as Langston Hughes and Arna Bontemps did in their important 1949 anthology *The Poetry of the Negro,* which included a section of poems by white poets. In her 1929 poem "Lullaby," Laluah warns a black child not to wish for whiteness, lest he become "a shade in human draperies," out of touch with his family and in love with death. Spencer's 1923 "White Things" had put forward similar notions, suggesting that agents of a valorized whiteness have taken a multicolored world and "blanched [it] with their wand of power." Lucia Trent's 1929 poem "A White Woman Speaks" responds by declaring herself "ashamed of being white," but Kenneth Patchen instead claims "I know that one of my hands / Is black, and one white." What becomes clear in all these poems, perhaps because of their very dichotomous figuration, is that racial difference is relational, that its meanings are historically produced, and that one burden of our mutual history is that we are bound together in any future we can imagine. There is no way of being white in America except in relation to what it has meant to be black, no way of being black in America, in turn, except in relation to the history of whiteness.

The same year that Hughes published his poem expressing the impossible wish to be free of the presence of white shadows, he also wrote and published "Union," in which he calls out to "the whole oppressed / Poor world, / White and black," and urges all to "put their hands with mine" to undermine false beliefs and entrenched powers. Many have assumed "White Shadows" and "Union" to represent opposing and irreconcilable points of view rather than related (and perhaps equally necessary) perspectives growing out of the same general history. Extended beyond white/black relations to the whole multicultural field, this constructed notion of contradiction suggests that antagonism and alliance are wholly incompatible and that a multicultural anthology or society must choose one or the other. Conservative writers often argue that any recognition of class, racial, or ethnic antagonism automatically increases their power over the culture and decreases opportunities for resolution. In fact, these views can coexist in individuals just as they do in the culture. Alliances can recognize and distinguish between warranted and unwarranted antagonisms and either work through them or build them into the terms of their negotiations. A multicultural anthology can inhibit or facilitate this present and future process by virtue of how fully it represents the historical record and how successfully it facilitates comparison and contrast between different positions. Then we can not only teach the conflicts, as Gerald Graff has helpfully argued, but also work with our students to find grounds for negotiation and mutual accommodation.

Kenneth Warren has recently warned in "The Problem of Anthologies" that anthologies foster the illusion that we can easily imagine a utopia where every race and gender can amiably rub elbows together. That seems to me, however, to be less a risk inherent in the anthology form than an effect of the kinds of anthologies cautiously liberal or politically conservative academic anthologists have assembled in recent decades, which tend to suggest that mutual tolerance is either a given or a readily achievable end. Anthologies that foreground the social conflicts American writers have struggled with would leave quite a different impression—that shared interests exist but that real differences and difficulties which must be worked on stand in the way of any alliances we might want to form. Such anthologies would also show that American poets and novelists have been passionately involved in articulating those differences. Warren also argues that newer, more racially diverse anthologies manage not so much to suggest that the kingdom of heaven has been taken by storm but rather that the meek have inherited the earth. That seems to me exactly right as a judgment about mainstream academic culture, but again it is the result of the *selection* academics usually make from minority and other writers. That selection, moreover, is governed not only by liberal fear of social antagonism but also by a desire to sustain a transcendentalizing version of literariness. It is more difficult to confer an aura of timeless, uncontested, universal value on a collection of works in obvious conflict with one another. Unfortunately, that means that the transhistorical values put forward by texts making aggressive attacks on injustice and urging revolutionary change get excluded from the ruling notions of literariness.

For more than a decade now, moreover, from Ronald Reagan to George Bush, from William Bennett to Lynne Cheney, from the increasingly conservative judiciary to the Republican Congress of the mid-nineties, the social imaging anthologies can do has been either directly or implicitly entangled with a broad spectrum of political issues and finally with state power itself. As our anthologies have become more multicultural, the chairs of the National Endowment for the Humanities during Republican presidencies have repeatedly insisted that there is a right and a wrong way to do multiculturalism. The right way, from Lynne Cheney's perspective, for example, is very clear—happy family multiculturalism, with selections celebrating cultural traditions but de-emphasizing an often anguished historical record, refraining from negative comments about other groups, and avoiding attacks on the nation-state. Conservative multiculturalism, then, would grant the impossibility of a melting pot and settle instead for a cookbook of recipes for unchallenged coexistence. It is not easy to create a multicultural literary or historical anthology that wholly honors that harmonious ideal but it is possible to come surprisingly close to doing so. In the process, we lose not only a sense of the real struggles that have shaped (and continue to shape) our history but also the terrain that must be negotiated for relations in the future.

We also lose the capacity to understand the relational nature of both past and present identities. Identity comes into existence relationally and sustains or redefines itself the same way. When the subject positions that racial, ethnic, gendered, or class identities offer us begin to change, they do not change simply as a result of some exclusive, inner mutation; they change as part of continuing renegotiation and competition with, appeals to and resistance against, incorporations of and rejections of, other identities and cultural forces. When Ray Young Bear gave a poetry reading at the University of Illinois in 1991 and his wife Stella joined him on stage to play the drum, he noted that her decision to do so was somewhat controversial, since drum playing had traditionally been reserved for the men in his tribe. This change is hardly purely internal to Native American cultures; it takes place in response to contemporary American feminism. What we are historically is partly a function of what we did and said and what was done and said to and about us, along with how we responded to a host of other cultural representations. Groups define themselves in relation to other groups; their identity cannot be extricated from that comparative process. When identity is reinforced by a sense of group solidarity, that too remains relational. The textual history of a subculture typically embodies those negotiations. The students in our classes embody the current state of those opportunities and conflicts. There is little reason to hope we can change without acknowledging both that complex history and its current products.

One aim of happy family multiculturalism is, of course, to maintain the status quo, to preserve as long as possible the present uneven distribution of wealth, prestige, and power. Hiding past and present inequities, injustices, and antagonisms decreases the chance that they will be redressed now or ever. That is the obvious dark side of Cheney's histrionic sermonizing. But the briefs for happy family multiculturalism also speak to another kind of fear that is more mutually warranted and thus shared by some of those who would anthologize both multiculturalism's inner triumphs and its outwardly directed antagonisms—the fear of a balkanized body politic. To bring forward either our targeted anger or our phantasmatic misrepresentations, it is feared, would only further polarize an already fragmented cultural terrain, making relations between groups still more antagonistic.

Of course we have lived with intermittent cultural warfare across differently constituted lines of class, race, gender, and ethnicity throughout our history. And deep if still unstably articulated social antagonisms obviously remain with us today. Allowing for some notable exceptions, however, most groups seek at least temporary working alliances across battle lines when self-interest seems to argue for them. And few broadly multicultural anthologists are likely to view their enterprise as the first step in arming their constituencies for open warfare. Indeed, in a democratic society most of us need some vision of possible grounds for improved social relations to justify our present work; except for the far Right, few in a society not literally at war can adopt organized murder as a way of dealing with diversity.

If we begin by taking a conflicted and substantially unjust present as a given, then, the question is how we might move to something better and how, in a minor way, an anthology might contribute to such a process. For the happy family folks the answer is simple—repress past and present antagonisms immediately. Indeed, they take such willed forgetfulness to be a condition for even entering into negotiations, and they would enforce those conditions with all the power available to them. Those groups that refuse to forget, say, a genocidal history and a present, at the very least, of lived inequities, are to be cast out of the social contract. Their family membership is canceled. In effect, the happy family multiculturalists have in mind an exclusionary and repressive body politic, despite their success at times in evoking a false and disingenuous liberalism based on an ideologically restricted inclusiveness. We have seen that kind of liberalism at work during the great purge of the Left in the 1950s and we know something of the monolithic right-wing culture to which it too readily capitulates. It is in fact not multiculturalism at all, but rather a monoculture in varied dress.

Such confident solutions are not available to a multiculturalism that wishes to maintain both more full historical knowledge and a greater frankness about present tensions. Reading a multicultural anthology compiled with such aims can involve powerful moments of epiphanic identification across cultural differences; it can also produce moments when difference is treasured for the sense of partially irreducible variety that is one of its pleasures. A more fully multicultural anthology will also provoke moments of self-interrogation and historical anguish. Yet such multicultural anthologies give us more still than recovered pain and ecstasy within inviolable cultural boundaries. They give us workbooks of discourses for rearticulation, texts for comparison, contrast, and realignment. They give us a discursive space in which to compare histories and test possible filiations and alliances. Properly assembled, multicultural anthologies mix utopian longings with a historical review of the fate such longings have often met in the past. They indicate some of the bases for strategic alliances across different cultures in the future, while giving voice to the forces that will resist and undermine those same alliances. They thus promote realism and vision in the context of historical reflection, empowering progressive work without simply reinforcing readers' self-images.

There is no way of assuring that readers will put anthologies to use in that fashion, just as there is no way of suturing a multicultural society in advance of its emergence. Much like individual texts, anthologies acquire different meanings in different contexts. Competing constituencies will construe their intertextual implications in diverse and contradictory ways. This is, to borrow a phrase Stuart Hall has put to good use, a multiculturalism "without guarantees."[5] That is the most we can ask for now, and it is better than the alternatives—misery, mayhem, and Republican right-wing extremism.

In moving from anthologies to political reflection on multiculturalism we need to accept the fact that there can be no secure social text to hold in view, let alone any renegotiated social space whose character can be guaranteed in advance. Despite what the Right wants to believe, the future cannot be guaranteed; all we can do is to educate ourselves about our diverse cultural traditions and try to maximize good will, while recognizing that even those ground rules will not be universally valued. What can be guaranteed, however, is that multicultural negotiations carried on in ignorance of one another's history and traditions will be permeated with bad faith. It is also probably inevitable that the social forms that can structure such negotiations will themselves change under pressure from competing and distinctive cultural traditions. While the Right has willfully conflated culture and society, maliciously implying thereby that cultural diversity necessarily threatens the *existence* of any consensually maintained social institutions, there is reason to assume that cultural differences will prompt changes that cut broadly across social life. Indeed, there is sound basis to conclude that has always been the case. There is no part of social life which can be wholly protected from cultural pressures. It may not be necessary, however, that the center hold, nor even that the spaces of recognized social articulation be conceived of *as* exclusively central, nor even that everyone suddenly be miraculously invested in caring about our intercultural exchanges. There has not been universal, continuous engagement in public life in the past, and there is no reason to suppose we can expect it in the future. Our "common" culture, moreover, has never been common in the sense of meaning the same thing to every constituency and subculture. Nor have its elements penetrated every area of cultural life nor penetrated it to the same degree. It may be sufficient to agree that there need to be such spaces, including institutions in which power is shared, contracts and meanings are negotiated, contact is maintained, and common enterprises are agreed upon. Such spaces include our public schools and our legislatures. Those are among the places capable of producing some level of multicultural exchange; we do not need to be identical with one another and we do not need to forget our history for those institutions to function. They may even function better if we refuse to repress the past.

3

RELATIVISM, POLITICS, AND ETHICS

WRITING LITERARY HISTORY IN THE SHADOW OF POSTSTRUCTURALISM

How else could we entitle that word "history," now, except in speech-marks, under the sign of vocative instability, outside any assumed consensus? As perhaps the most over-employed item in the vocabulary of literary-critical and cultural analysis, "history" may well also be the least decisive. We return to history, work toward history, and espouse a historical method, but few of us can say exactly what we mean by history, except in the most gestural way. Those of us who worry about it at all find ourselves necessarily mired in complex theoretical retractions and modifications, bewildering enough to sponsor some fairly radical insecurities. Others, sensing a probable dead end street, run for the cover of the kind of "new historicism" that looks to history as to a safe and approved harbor, a place where one may sleep peacefully, lulled by anecdotal stories, after tossing on the stormy seas of deconstructive and theoretical Marxist uncertainty.
— David Simpson, "Raymond Williams"

The entire development of contemporary epistemology has established that there is no fact that allows its meaning to be read transparently.
— Ernesto Laclau and Chantal Mouffe,
"Post-Marxism without Guarantees"

In the current critical climate one may easily find proclamations of a "return to history" sharing disciplinary contemporaneity with declarations that objective historical knowledge is impossible. Given the far-reaching and apparently opposite nature of these claims, it is not surprising that many see them not only as irreconcilable but also as competing moral, epistemological, professional, and cultural agendas. They represent, or so we are often urged to conclude, radically different ways of thinking about both historiography and the world itself. I would not want to argue that it is possible to synthesize certainty and doubt as they are embodied in these positions, but rather, as I will argue, that there is reason to take up their relationship as a problematic.

Among the recent developments in literary studies to be most welcomed, I believe, are some that make such a negotiation possible, especially the increasingly close relationships between the discourses of theory and the discourses of minority scholarship and canonical critique. Through the 1960s and 1970s theory, or what was widely recognized as theory, largely stayed away from these projects of cultural recovery and critique. As I suggested in the opening chapter, what has in some quarters in recent years been variously hailed or mourned as the *death* of theory in fact represents theory's productive engagement with and rearticulation to these material social projects. It may be, then, that theory conceived as an abstract, transhistorical metadiscourse has died. If so, I am not persuaded that its death is necessarily to be regretted. Theory that cannot be pursued with an Olympian disdain for its social contexts and effects is in many ways theory that can do more, rather than less, productive work both in academic disciplines and in the public sphere. That this is not obvious to English professors says more about the discipline than it says about the nature of theory.

I am interested in addressing one particular terrain within this general phenomenon—the mutual articulation of theory and the efforts to open up the canon in literary studies. My focus will be on one of my own contributions to this project, *Repression and Recovery: Modern American Poetry and the Politics of Cultural Memory, 1910–1945* (1989). The effects research for this and subsequent books and essays had on my teaching will be the subject of my fifth chapter, "Progressive Pedagogy without Apologies." Here I want instead to focus on the book's general cultural aims, but I want to begin not so much by reflecting on what I did and did not accomplish in that book but rather by laying out some of the intersecting theoretical and practical forces that made the book possible. I also hope thereby to disentangle some of the competing aims in the book, the countervailing pressures that shaped numerous tactical decisions made in the process of composition. Finally, by making those tactical decisions more explicit here than I did in the book itself, I may be able to make both my writing strategies and the broader issues that surround them more available to other critics.

I came to this project with two strong commitments representing what had until recently been quite divergent traditions. I was first of all committed to the necessity of wide reading in the literary past and to the recovery of many forgotten writers whose work I found of great power and interest. At the same time I was also committed to a poststructuralist doubt about the possibility of actually and literally *recovering* anything. Neither history itself nor the individual text, I believed, had any meaning apart from the effort to reinterpret them within contemporary historical, social, and intellectual contexts. In the current critical scene it was beginning to be possible to experience these two commitments partly—but only partly—as enjoyably and productively competing, rather than as merely impossibly contradictory. But that has not always been the case.

Until recently, many people engaged in recovering forgotten authors might easily see themselves as doing real, productive, material work that made high theory seem hopelessly self-indulgent or useless. And theorists, in turn, might see themselves as engaged in settling far more universal and intellectually ambitious problems than literary historians were willing to consider. The project of opening up the canon often seemed intellectually and methodologically unreflective and largely untheorized. And indeed for the profession as a whole, to take a simple but rather indicative example, it seemed impossible to imagine someone interested in theory working in a rare book room or a literary archive. While this kind of self-aggrandizing mutual disdain is not flattering to either position, it does not follow that these two traditions could easily be placed in dialogue with one another, let alone combined in any given project. For there were real adjustments to be made and real losses to sustain in viewing either tradition from the vantage point of the other.

Moreover, ingrained defenses and compensations let each tradition seem self-sufficient to its practitioners. From the perspective of a 1960s feminism or a classical Marxism, the project of opening up the canon might seem already sufficiently theorized. The larger narrative into which individual projects might fit was already written in the metanarratives of class or gender oppression. Those narratives would become more persuasive by being proven in local circumstances, and they would as well continue to produce more detailed new accounts of local historical conditions, but neither their capacity to contain further knowledge nor the validity of the narratives themselves were in doubt. Continued elaborate theorizing was to some degree considered either irrelevant or counterproductive. Conversely, high theory had its own convincing social and material investments. It was engaged in rereading either literary or critical texts (and thus disseminating its discourses) and in efforts to terrorize traditional academic disciplines. Its real-world investments thus appeared to be as important as any projects a polemical and self-assured feminism or Marxism could define.

Through the 1960s and 1970s, then, efforts to expand the canon could continue without much interaction with the more abstract enterprise of pure theory. This situation persisted despite the fact that sophisticated doubt about the objectivity of both textual and historical knowledge was apparent in some quarters as of the late 1960s. By the mid-1970s—as poststructuralism began to replace structuralism; as linguistically experimental French feminism began to be disseminated in the United States; as some British and American feminists began to argue for more complex analyses of the social construction of gender; and as the new Marxism abandoned an unquestioning belief in the master narratives of its predecessors—the certainty that earlier texts could be recovered with their meaning intact became more difficult to sustain. People of course continued to write as if these developments had not taken place, but only by either repressing their responses to the current state of theory or by actively attacking the new theory. There ensued, for example, the regrettable phenomenon of feminists or Marxists committed to historical certainty attacking other feminists or Marxists who were reflecting on the overdetermination of all knowledge.

The spread of a poststructuralist doubt throughout much of contemporary theory should not, however, be taken as successfully superseding everything that preceded it. Theory develops and changes through its own debates and in response to a whole range of historical forces. But conscious or unconscious allusion to a myth of progress in theory is best avoided, not so much because of the truth or falsity of such a myth but because of its effects: its tendency to block self-reflection and critique, to cover over patterns of difference and repression, and to encourage disinterest in the social consequences of theorizing. Other narratives may also simplify but can also do progressive work. Some of the more polemical feminisms of the 1960s and 1970s, including narratives of victimization that effectively (if unintentionally) de-emphasized the need to read women's writing differentially and in detail, provided exactly what was politically necessary at that moment in time; moreover, these critical works often remain vital today. They are part of the necessary cultural underpinning to feminist work of the 1980s and 1990s. The only serious problem arises when people try to write now as though the last twenty years of intellectual history had not taken place. It is not possible simply to *be* a 1960s feminist, Marxist, or, for that matter, a 1960s literary historian, without writing a partly reactive prose highlighted with signal resistances, silences, evasions, and anxieties. The certainties of an earlier moment cannot simply be imitated today. Again, it is not that theory has *progressed* in any straightforward way but rather that it has developed out of its continuing internal dialogue and its negotiation with changing historical conditions. It has not ceased to be blind, but its blindness is differently constituted and serves different strategic ends.

These in any case were some of the issues that seemed relevant to me as I began a study of the modern poetry canon several years ago. The result, paradoxically, is a book that insists on the mediated and constructed (rather than preexisting) nature of all historical knowledge, while setting about on an extensive project of recovering forgotten poems and magazines. Indeed, I was concerned to recover as well a number of material features of the literature of the first half of the century: book jackets and pamphlet covers, illustrated poems from books and magazines, and covers to song sheets and magazines. I frequently urge people to think about what social uses poetry has served in earlier periods, uses that are often different from those it serves in our own. And finally I include seventy pages of footnotes, some devoted to continuing theoretical reflection but many devoted to recovering forgotten information about the lives and careers of the poets I discuss. The index lists about eighty entries devoted to "bio-bibliographical notes." In short, for a book that argues that texts have no intrinsic meaning, that all history is reconstructed to meet contemporary needs, and that interpretive certainty is unachievable, there seem to be quite a few facts assembled for the reader. That no doubt explains why one reader described the book as "at once postmodern and decidedly old-fashioned."

Not every reader will recognize this situation as partly paradoxical. Some will recognize no contradiction. Others will see the copresence of historical recovery with poststructuralist doubt as thoroughly disabling, a kind of continual betrayal of one impulse by the other.[1] It will not ameliorate but rather exacerbate the problem to acknowledge (as I insist on doing) my own sense that I had to struggle to keep these somewhat competing aims responsive to one another. For the issue remains to decide what status the "facts" I assemble are finally to have. That is not an issue I address directly in the book, though my answer is implicit in my arguments about the interested construction of history and interpretation of texts. I argue at one point that there is no possibility of access to an uninterpreted level of textuality. We cannot jettison our cultural and disciplinary assumptions and psychological needs to perceive some level of sheer uninterpreted textual materiality. If we could do so, the text "in itself," to echo Derrida, would be nothing more than black marks on a white page. An uninterpreted text would have no meaning at all. The same thing, as Hayden White's work suggests, is true of the facts historians sometimes see themselves as assembling.[2]

Facts, of course, are often embedded in interested narratives, but even the decision to assemble a mere list of seemingly neutral facts about an author—birth and death dates, lists of publications—embodies numerous assumptions about how to organize information about the past, what is worth remembering, and what cultural uses people are likely to find for these facts once they are disseminated again. So such facts are in many ways already interpreted when we first see them. The selection and presentation of facts typically embodies implicit narratives about their cultural meaning and value. There are no innocent facts, self-contained and awaiting collection. Facts are icons for cultural investment, an index for what we consider important and worth remembering, a guide to how we organize and categorize the past. They are thus already meaningful, already embedded in relational structures. A sheer uninterpreted fact would have no meaning at all; it is also, one might argue, a largely hypothetical entity.

I suppose that an author's birth and death dates would represent something

RELATIVISM, POLITICS, AND ETHICS

like the zero degree of facticity, an almost material facticity that seems outside any interpretive practice. Yet the effort to retain those dates in current historiography, the belief that a particular writer's birth and death merits repeated reciting, carries considerable baggage with it, a sense of why that writer's work mattered then and why it matters to us now. Yeats died in 1939, and for some critics modern literature effectively came to an end at that moment as well. Moreover, that was the year the Second World War began, so Yeats's death can also be dramatized by narrating it in company with other watershed moments of historical change. (In this case, of course, the relationship between the dates is merely coincidental and the linkage thereby purely symbolic. But it helps suggest that we need always to ask what criteria lead us to conclude that one historical fact stands in an anchoring relation to another.) Similarly, to recite T. S. Eliot's birth and death dates is to commemorate one of the poets in whom modernism (and our identification with modernism) is most fully invested. Those dates evoke the pathos of that cultural and disciplinary investment. The poet H. H. Lewis's birth and death dates, on the other hand, suggest little more than the irrelevant detritus of lived time to most modern poetry scholars. Those dates do not matter in the same way; they do not resonate as T. S. Eliot's do in modern literary culture, though of course H. H. Lewis's birth and death dates do matter to me. He serves in *Repression and Recovery* as the most extreme case of a political poet well known in his time but wholly outside any taste a New Critical sensibility could underwrite.[3] On the other hand, the very difficulty of establishing Melvin Tolson's or Zora Neale Hurston's birth dates resonates with the exclusions of the canon and the pathos of their rediscovery. So if the abstract notion of birth and death dates appears to suggest a realm of neutral data with no complex semiotic effects, reflection on actual material dates suggests otherwise. We encounter them variously embedded in and thus also variously constituted by webs of meaning or the denial of meaning. Thus we must overcome the notion that the dates themselves are neutral but that our discursive operations convert them from facts into ideological constructs. Their material existence depends on the work of ideology.

Since this issue is so readily misunderstood, let me press it further. Yeats's birth and death dates may mean somewhat different things to an Irish nationalist than they do to a literary critic. An Irish nationalist might well take 1916 as the key modern date and see Yeats's dates only in relation to it. Ezra Pound's birth and death dates signify rather differently within a literary paean to his lyrical genius and a legal brief against his fascist radio broadcasts over Italian radio during the Second World War. Of course our sense of history is generally punctuated with dates whose importance is continually reinterpreted and reconstructed. Assuming such dates are not in dispute, the argument, then, is not over *whether* such facts exist but over what they mean. Moreover, if they are only available either in consciousness or within some discursive practice, then they do not effectively exist apart from one or another interpretive framework, a framework which even places in doubt the material boundary of a fact. Traditional literary historians often throw up their hands in exasperation at poststructuralist doubt, thinking that it denies the existence of historical fact. If poststructuralism did make such claims, it could then, in effect, be employed by the sort of pseudo-historians who imagine the Holocaust did not take place. What poststructuralism places in doubt, however, is not the existence but the meaning of the Holocaust. Pressed far enough, poststructuralism suggests that facts have no inherent meaning and that they can never be extricated from systems of meaning and apprehended on their own.

Extending this perspective to the problem of writing literary history, and recognizing that there is no innocent information, at one point I actually considered trying to write *Repression and Recovery* without authors' names, since I was interested in part in discursive patterns in the poetry of the period, and I felt organizing poetry by author blocked recognition of verbal parallels that cut across the categories in which we habitually place individual authors. Moreover, there were numerous points in the modern period—including the Harlem Renaissance and the Great Depression—when poetry was clearly being written as part of a collective, partly dialogic cultural process, not as the wholly isolated creative effort of individuals. At these times there was, in effect, a chorus of overlapping and divergent voices that took up images, themes, slogans, arguments, and forms in a continual registering of similarity and difference. Poetry in the process became a different kind of social activity than it had been before.

I was prepared to read the poetry in this way by a number of theoretical developments. Marxism had long struggled to define the social and economic determination of art. Poststructuralism, on the other hand, had in other ways broken the links between the image of an organically unified text and a comparably coherent human subject; indeed, it gave us many reasons to stop thinking of people as consistent and unified subjects at all. Postcolonial theory has since taken our sense of the fragmented, conflicted nature of subjectivity still further. Detaching poets' names from poems helps us recognize as well that many of the discursive elements of poems reflect and contribute to diverse cultural processes. Linking poems with their authors, conversely, sustains a romanticized notion of individual creativity that a wider sense of texts published in a given period tends to undermine. More importantly, to be confronted with texts that are no longer taken to be vehicles of self-expression is to be drawn to consider what other cultural functions poetry may have served.

It is this effort to rethink the social meaning of poetry that required the most elaborate negotiation of multiple theoretical traditions. Combining in particular the poststructuralism of Derrida and the Marxist cultural studies of critics like Hall and Laclau and Mouffe, I tried to work out a position that I think of as a kind of politicized Saussurianism. From the poststructuralist radicalization of Saussure I drew a semiotics that is differential but also mobile and partly unpredictable. From Marxist cultural studies I drew the recognition that differences are a site of political contestation, that various interests compete to gain power over images and meanings and integrate them into a common persuasive enterprise. The politicized Saussurianism that results is one in which meanings are recognized to come not from inherent and essential identity but from a structured and differential field of struggle. A politicized Saussurianism recognizes the linguisticality of the cultural field but tracks meaning as a discursive struggle involving the continual rearticulation of all discursive domains to one another. Literature, politics, religion, law, all struggle over the limits of a relative autonomy in which all these discursive domains are defined in relation to one another and in which potential social functions are both lost and recaptured. Not only the meaning of poems but also the meaning and social functions of the notion of literariness and the genre of poetry are constructed, I argue, by this sort of cultural process. Far from a book that simply adds a number of poets to the ongoing conversation of the profession, then, *Repression and Recovery* argues for a reconsideration of the shifting, unstable, and contested meaning of poetry.

In the end, while pursuing that wider inquiry into the social meaning of poetry, I decided to retain authors' names and to present biographical information about them. I did so in part because the sheer quantity of unfamiliar poets cited in the book can, on its own, persuade people that the narrow story of modern poetry we constructed and now repeatedly retell is wholly inadequate. Moreover, the citation of this wide range of interesting modern poets suggests that the slow process of reevaluating individual poets for possible recovery is insufficient; we need as well a more thorough critique of our cultural memory and of the role literary scholarship plays in constructing and maintaining it. Finally, authors' names remain one of the major ways we select and recover texts of interest from the almost overwhelming number of texts actually published. Tracking an author through journals, books, and archives was one of the major ways I worked, so I preserved that structure for the reader. But that is not a disinterested decision, and I still feel the project of writing about modern poetry—and about literature in general—without authors' names remains unfinished.

How to realize that goal, however, remains quite another matter. I gave a draft of the book that excluded poets' names to a few friends to read, and all of them found it intolerable to read large numbers of quotes unmoored to any writer's identity. A year or so later I wrote an essay on 1930s political poetry without any authors' names linked to the quotes and had the same results. The sense of literary discourse as inherently and necessarily *authored* is so strong now that people are generally unwilling to process it in any other way. For a critic to withhold a writer's name is, in any case, clearly an affront, one for which I have not yet found a way to gain a hearing.

Some other deliberate aims and strategies were probably more successful. One of these was to make it clear that this historiography could never actually contain or fully represent the history it engaged. The actual literary history of the times would remain elsewhere, outside our grasp. I was not, therefore, aiming to invoke the familiar claim that texts are primary and commentary secondary. Neither in any historical reconstruction nor in the original poems would we find the lived time of history. It is no longer available to us. Conventional literary histories often aim for a confident sense that history is effectively relived within their narratives. I wanted to make it clear that I consider that goal impossible and that effect of narration either illicit or misleading.

One simple way to register the inadequacy of the presence of history in my narratives, I decided, was to limit most of my quotations to fragments, rather than complete poems. For the most part, the texts I discuss are always elsewhere, sometimes in an elsewhere difficult to recover, since many of them are out of print. That was frustrating to some readers, but it had partly the disabling effect I wanted. My book would thus always display a certain lack.

Another deliberate strategy was to be inconsistent about what kinds of information and what sort of prose I placed in the text and the notes. I once read a reader's report on someone else's manuscript that expressed annoyance that the text and notes were not devoted to different kinds of writing and different categories of knowledge. A reader has a right to know, the report argued, what to expect in the main body of the book versus what to expect in the notes. I wanted to take that "right" away, to overturn the implicit hierarchical relation between text and notes. I did not want the sort of confident relationship of mastery between these textual domains that prevails in most academic writing. So while I did put most bibliographic information in the notes I also deliberately saved some particularly enjoyable stories for the notes and included in the text information about some authors that in other cases was relegated to notes. Some reviewers have found this frustrating; others have recognized what I was doing. One recognized that my decision to place one illustration in the notes was a way of signaling my intentions about their status. In any case, the overall aim was not to deny the presence of hierarchized domains of knowledge but to put them into question in terms of both the book's argument and its structure.

A more complex historiographical strategy was built into my decision not to break the book into chapters and to mix chronology with a spatial presentation of different texts and styles. In part this reflects my conclusions about the diverse and often distinctly nonlinear nature of literary influence during the modern period. Modern poetry, in other words, did not develop in a clear progressive fashion. Some of its most radical innovations—notably in Gertrude Stein's poetry—came almost immediately and took decades to gain wide influence. All its familiar traditions and styles overlapped and interpenetrated. There were, moreover, recoveries of earlier styles under new names and conservative count-erreactions along with unexpected experiments. Dividing literary history into chapters tends to segregate discursive impulses that should be seen relationally. When the resulting categories—minority poetry, women's poetry, imagism, political poetry—become mutually exclusive, the effects are both political and discriminatory. Eliminating chapters and mixing chronological narration with cultural and stylistic groupings spanning several decades made all our descriptive categories unstable and subject to contemporary critical intervention. Nothing was to be taken as given to us unproblematically.

In some cases, I chose both to imitate and undermine standard critical structures. The decision to have notes at all, while making them distinctly textual, was one choice of that sort. Another was the choice to include an introduction but let the separation between the introduction and the main body of the text be somewhat arbitrary. Though physically divided, the introduction and the main body of the text in fact flow together. None of these decisions, however, carries with it a moral or political imprimatur for future work. These may be exemplary strategies, but they are chosen within history and in response to immediate professional and cultural needs. They have no inflexible warrant over other peoples' work or my own work in the future. I feel free to abandon these strategies myself; while I hope other people find them suggestive, I do not offer them as models to be imitated uncritically. The style and structure of the book, I would hope, match the provisional nature of its interpretive claims.

So I do not, in summary, see the facts assembled about numerous writers in the text and in the notes as neutral, innocent, or uninterpreted. A similar recognition informs my readings of poems and poets throughout the book. While I try to make persuasive claims about how we might read these poets and why we might value their work, my readings make no pretense to be permanent and decisive statements. From feminism, Marxism, and poststructuralism I have learned that criticism is an interested, politically implicated, strategically positioned, and historically specific activity. My readings are efforts to influence how we might read these poets now; I am not interested in the fantasy of commentary that pretends it may last for all time. From time to time I comment on how readings of particular poets have shifted to meet contemporary interests. To avoid being tiresomely repetitive, I decided not to repeat that argument continuously, so not all my analyses are framed in those terms. But the general claim, I hope, will remain implicit throughout: When I make a strong assertion about a poem, it is not a claim about the poem's essential nature but rather an urgent claim on the interests and commitments of contemporary readers.

Some would argue that poststructuralism's insistence on the undecidability of texts makes such strategically designed readings either impossible or fraudulent. And it is true that one current in poststructuralism is an ecstatic assertion that texts can mean anything, that texts are polymorphously inventive and perverse. But the claim that texts can mean anything does not necessarily imply that they can mean anything here and now. There are too many constraints on how we see texts and too many constraints on how we can imagine using them for an infinite range of meanings to be immediately available. This claim for unlimited potential meaning is often balanced within poststructuralism by a commitment to trying to understand the nature of the interpretive inducements and constraints in both our own and other periods. It is that strain within poststructuralism that I have adopted and tried to put to use. That sense of variable but positioned and multiply determined meaning to some degree opens up a potential to argue for interpretations that are designed for a contemporary audience and that are responsible to the current social environment. Indeed, if a text has no inherent, immutable meaning, then the struggle over what kinds of meanings will be important is all that is left. To say that poststructuralism denies that possibility is to collapse a series of positions disingenuously into a single spectacle of excess.

That is not to say, however, that my belief in the undecidability of texts and the ultimate impossibility of historical knowledge places no strain on a project of recovering forgotten texts. When recovering texts that have clearly been repressed or marginalized for political reasons or because of the culture's history of racism and sexism, there is a strong desire not only to disseminate the texts again but also to come to understand the experience of their authors and even to imagine that disseminating these texts gives their authors a voice in the culture and an opportunity to communicate again. Thus, when people first began to recover slave narratives, they wanted to believe the texts were reliably representational, that they gave us secure access to the experiences of their authors and the communities of which they were a part. In this commendable desire to compensate for a century of cultural repression, the well-known unreliability of language's mediations was forgotten. Forgotten too was the knowledge that authors often have purposes other than straightforward communication or representation when they write. And not so much forgotten as unthought

RELATIVISM, POLITICS, AND ETHICS

was the still more knotty problem of our own historically determined interests and perspectives, interests that can never be fully cast aside. These are interests, moreover, that we cannot even expect entirely to recognize.

In the end we need to admit that we will never know for certain what it was like to live in an earlier period. Of course we need the kind of empathy that allows us to construct a simulacra of access, but the experience of gaining full access to another author's consciousness is a fantasy. And the histories we devise are constructed in the service of our own needs, compulsions, plans, and interests. That is not to say, however, that the desire to make repressed and forgotten traditions visible again, or to give them special moral and ethical claims on the present, is illicit. But the process of recovery is as much a process of current cultural critique as it is one of restoration. And what we "recover" in many ways will never have existed before. Nor is it inappropriate to try to understand the dynamics of an earlier period. It is merely that we will never finally distinguish ourselves from them, and we will never have in hand a set of unmediated facts that are clearly of the past and not of the present.

In writing *Repression and Recovery* I confronted these issues as a problematic, as an arena of work rather than as a problem to be solved. A partly Marxist recognition of my own social and economic positioning and the necessarily historically determined nature of my own interests was frequently in tension with an older and admirably passionate Marxism that aimed straightforwardly to give voice to what our culture had repressed. A poststructuralist doubt about what can be known was in conflict with a desire to know and often with a sensation of having gained access to a past we had quite forgotten. Not infrequently I was dealing with letters and diaries and poems that were not only unpublished but unread. At times an unpublished, unheard tape or record of an author's voice was available. As historians will agree, it is hard to imagine circumstances in which a sense of recovering the past would be much stronger. I did not try to resolve these conflicts but rather to play them off against one another. At times, indeed, my book is a record of self-correction and theoretical counterpointing, as these aims and recognitions reflect on one another. At other times, succumbing to a certain will to power, to a wish to persuade and provoke change, I write over the seams between doubt and certainty, in a prose of advocacy and conviction.

This tonal instability seems to me to reflect the mix of relativism and commitment appropriate to an informed and responsible engagement with history. Once we realize that history's meaning is always open to dispute, the work of interpretation and persuasion becomes crucial, not irrelevant. The situation is exactly parallel with relativism's impact on moral and ethical standards, a subject continually exploited by the political Right over the last decade.

The New Right's attacks on relativism have made calm, serious discussion of this important issue nearly impossible. When academics argue that the world exists but is in some ways unknowable—a position with a credible history dating back to Kant—conservatives counter that we are clowns who believe there is no external reality. When poststructuralists point out that we have no unmediated access to material reality—that all sensation is interpreted, mediated, organized, and made meaningful by language—conservatives shout again that we believe the world does not exist. When we warn that moral values are not transcendent and guaranteed—that they must be continually rearticulated, defended, and relearned in context—reactionary commentators wail that we have opened the door to barbarism.

If we concede that there are no universally guaranteed human values—that being human can mean *anything* at various times and places, as our century has repeatedly proven—then the work of winning consent to certain judgments about history and to certain standards of behavior becomes more, not less, urgent. History shows us that human beings are capable of anything. Knowing that does not empty values of meaning but rather grants them the only meaning they have ever had—contingent meaning that is open to negotiation, transformation, and dispute.

We cannot plausibly argue for transhistorical values but we can argue on behalf of the purchase particular values should have on our own time. That is actually the only power we have ever had in such matters. Conservative critics have claimed to the contrary that poststructuralism—and particularly its deconstructive incarnation—makes all moral argument empty. And indeed American deconstructive critics like Paul de Man were inclined to avoid larger moral issues. But Jacques Derrida, the founder of deconstruction, has for years regularly written cultural and political essays of clear moral urgency; he has written about apartheid, nuclear war, racism, and the politics of academia. Recognizing how fragile and contingent both moral and historical consensus is only increases the need for advocacy and interpretation. The lesson is admittedly a painful one, especially when we see how quickly historical events that matter to us can be emptied of the meaning we thought was guaranteed. The interpretive claims need to be made anew for each generation; the work never ends. False certainty about the permanence or historically transcendent status of what are actually vulnerable local assertions is no substitute for the work of rearticulating meanings to new cultural contexts. Thus I argue for the purchase these forgotten poems should have on our lives, indeed for the moral value inherent in recovering repressed traditions, but I can do so only for my own time.

RELATIVISM, POLITICS, AND ETHICS

4

ALWAYS ALREADY CULTURAL STUDIES

ACADEMIC CONFERENCES AND A MANIFESTO

The rapidly increasing visibility of cultural studies in the United States over the past few years gives us an opportunity to see how an emerging body of theory is realized politically and professionally, to reflect on its articulation to existing institutions *in medias res,* before those articulations are fixed for any period of time. One of those institutions is the large academic conference, two of which took place within a few months of each other, "Cultural Studies Now and in the Future" at the University of Illinois in April of 1990, a conference I helped to organize, and "Crossing the Disciplines: Cultural Studies in the 1990s" at the University of Oklahoma in October of 1990, a conference organized by Robert Con Davis and Ron Schlieffer where I presented an earlier version of this chapter. Cultural studies has also recently been the subject of special sessions at regional and national meetings of the Modern Language Association, all of which events together give a fairly good indication of what the future of cultural studies—especially in English—is likely to be. Though cultural studies has a much longer and very different, if still contested, history in U.S. Communications departments, it is on its very recent commodification in English that I want to focus here.

I might begin by posing a single strategic question: what does it mean that Robert Con Davis and Ron Schlieffer, in the papers they gave at the Oklahoma conference quite properly felt it appropriate and necessary to refer to the work of the Centre for Contemporary Cultural Studies at the University of Birmingham in Britain and Hillis Miller, presenting the keynote talk at the opening of the same conference, gave no evidence of knowing anything about it and yet felt fully empowered to define both the history and future of cultural studies? I suppose in the broadest sense it means that the spread of American power and American culture across the globe has led some Americans to believe Disneyland is the origin of the world. I have the uneasy feeling that if one told Miller he ought to find out about the Birmingham tradition he'd reply that he didn't know such interesting work had gone on in Alabama.

At a regional MLA conference in 1988 I argued that people who claim to be commenting on or "doing" cultural studies ought at least to familiarize themselves with the British cultural studies tradition, beginning with Raymond Williams and Richard Hoggart and moving through Birmingham and beyond. I must emphasize, however, that almost nothing in this tradition is simply transferable to the United States. Williams was partly concerned with defining a distinctly British heritage. The interdisciplinary work at Birmingham was often deeply ollaborative, a style that has little chance of succeeding in American depart\. \ts and little chance of surviving the American academic system of rewards. But the struggle to shape the field in Britain has lessons we can learn much from, and British cultural studies achieved theoretical advances that are immensely useful in an American context. So that would be part of my answer to the question Jonathan Culler posed, with an air of whimsical hopelessness, in Oklahoma: "What is a professor of cultural studies supposed to know?" A professor of cultural studies might, in other words, be expected to know the history of the field. Professors of cultural studies need not agree with or emulate all the imperatives of British cultural studies, but they do have a responsibility to take a position on a tradition whose name they are borrowing. Moreover, people with strong disciplinary training who are now feeling their way toward cultural studies have something to gain from encounters with others who have already made such journeys. Leaving open what it will mean to establish cultural studies in America, British cultural studies nonetheless illustrates some of what is at stake in theorizing culture in any historical moment.

Immediately after my 1988 talk, my friend Vincent Leitch, who ought to know better, stood up in the audience, waving his arms as he scaled some Bunker Hill of the imagination, and declared that he "thought we had thrown off the yoke of the British two hundred years ago." At an Indiana University of Pennsylvania conference on theory and pedagogy in September of 1990, I heard James Berlin prophesy, with a solemnity nowhere cognizant that he was predicting coals would be brought to Newcastle, that he was simply giving critical theory a new name, that cultural studies would miraculously turn our attention toward "textuality in all its forms." The claim of course was hardly new; indeed, this heralded revolution had already taken place under another name. In November of 1990, a panel on cultural studies at the Pacific Coast Philological Association unself-consciously offered two models of cultural studies: as an opportunistic umbrella for English professors who want to study film or the graphic arts, and as a terrain of vague, metonymic sliding between all the competing theories on the contemporary scene. Cultural studies in that context was considered interchangeable with semiotics, the New Historicism, and other recent bodies of theory. And at an October 1990 University of Illinois panel on "The Frontiers of Eighteenth-Century Studies" John Richetti, preening himself in the manner of a disciplinary cockatoo, announced with satisfaction that "eighteenth-century people had been doing cultural studies all along."

I could add other anecdotes. But these are enough to introduce the first points I want to make: of all the intellectual movements that have swept the humanities in America over the last twenty years, none will be taken up so shallowly, so opportunistically, so unreflectively, and so ahistorically as cultural studies. It is becoming the perfect paradigm for a people with no sense of history—born yesterday and born on the make. A concept with a long history of struggle over its definition, a concept born in class consciousness and in critique of the academy, a concept with a skeptical relationship with its own theoretical advances, is often for English in America little more than a way of repackaging what we were already doing. Of course nothing can prevent the term "cultural studies" from coming to mean something very different in another time and place. But the casual dismissal of its history needs to be seen for what it is—an interested effort to depoliticize a concept whose whole prior history has been preeminently political and oppositional. The depoliticizing of cultural studies will no doubt pay off, making it more palatable at once to granting agencies and to conservative colleagues, administrators, and politicians, but only at the cost of blocking cultural studies from having any critical purchase on American social life.

People interested in theory have often been universally accused by the Right of facile opportunism. As I argued in the opening chapter, there is certainly an element of thoughtless opportunism in the way people flock to the most recent turns in theory, but the historical record actually suggests a very different and much more difficult pattern of struggle and mutual transformation for many of those committed to the major bodies of interpretive theory. Consider the deep personal transformation, the institutional changes, the wholesale reorientation of social understanding that accompanied the feminist revolution and its extension into the academy. Compare the various times this century when taking up Marxism has meant a comparable reorientation of one's whole understanding of society. Even a body of theory like psychoanalysis, which in its academic incarnations has avoided many of its imperatives toward personal and institutional change, has entailed a good deal more than adopting a special vocabulary; even for academics, psychoanalysis has meant accepting a view of human agency that isolates them from their traditionally rationalist colleagues. In Britain and Australia taking up cultural studies has followed the more radical pattern among these alternatives. But not for most disciplines in the United States.

The conference in Oklahoma was part of that repackaging effort. Its joint sponsorship by the Semiotic Society of America suggested as well that semiotics could get new life by being recycled as cultural studies. One also hears graduate students and faculty members talk frankly about repackaging themselves as cultural studies people. The disastrous academic job market, to be sure, along with most of the daily messages consumer capitalism sends us, encourages that sort of anxious cynicism about how one markets oneself. The large number of young people who presented papers at Oklahoma—many of them willing to pay a $95 registration fee and endure the humiliation of potentially tiny audiences at multiple sessions (there were seventeen simultaneous sessions on Sunday morning at 8:30)—testifies to the sense that putting a "Cultural Studies in the 1990s" label on your vita is worth an investment in exploitation and alienation.

I do not mean to belittle the impulse behind the willingness to cooperate with that kind of structure. The unpredictable realities of the job market are terrifying enough to more than explain graduate students and young faculty members signing on for the odd honorific anonymity that being on a large conference program entails. But I also think there's good reason to bring these realities into the open and subject them to critique.

Indeed, the job market in cultural studies—at least in English—gives a pretty good indication of how the discipline is going to take up this new paradigm. In 1989 a graduate student at Illinois—a specialist in feminist cultural studies with a degree in communications—interviewed for cultural studies positions at MLA. It was quite clear that many departments hadn't the faintest idea what cultural studies was. It was a way to ask the dean for new money by pointing out an area where they needed to catch up and a way for interviewers to make a display of ignorance look like canny interrogation: "So what is all this cultural studies stuff about anyway?" What better way to ask uninformed questions than in the role of job interviewer? Who cares what serious cultural studies job candidates might think? The search committee has the power and the money. If the answers are confusing or slightly threatening, the candidate will be out of the room in twenty minutes anyway. The committee, of course, has the only last word that counts—the authority to recommend who gets offered the job. Some departments in effect conducted fake, exploratory cultural studies searches as a lazy way of finding out between cocktails a little bit about what the young people are up to these days. As the Illinois student found out, it all comes down to the final question: but can you fill in when we need someone to do the Milton course?

Although the excruciating ironies of the job market will be the special focus of the entire third section of *Manifesto,* it is important here to take note of the special circumstances of cultural studies candidates. What is now permissible, at least for many doctoral committees supervising graduate students, is very broad indeed. But few English departments have faculty positions for people working outside literature or film. The job market, not the dissertation committee or the promotion committee, now serves as the discipline's de facto arbiter of the possible and the permissible. Indeed, whatever intellectual largesse underwrites the regulation of dissertation topics is virtually rendered moot by the job market, since a dissertation committee cannot effectively police entry into a discipline that has no jobs. Hostility to new developments like cultural studies is thus more likely to be mobilized at the critical point of entry into the discipline—the hiring process.

In the publishing world, as it happens, boundaries are more fluid. For many young cultural studies students, inspired by the more freewheeling world of publishing, animated by what they read, the links between disciplines and their traditional objects of study are increasingly irrelevant. The job market, especially in an extended era of fiscal crisis, is another matter. For in a time of budget cuts and retrenchment many departments look first to protect their more traditional investments and object choices. It is hardly news that the leading edges of a discipline are not necessarily replicated in the recidivist reaches of every reactionary department. But the current situation in cultural studies, in which disciplinary cultural studies degree recipients and departmental hiring committees march to such different drummers, is distinctive and alarming. It presents young intellectuals with impossible and equally hopeless alternatives—abandon your passions in order to become more palatable, or devote yourself to what matters whatever the consequences.

If one rationale for young people paying to give talks at a cultural studies conference is understandable, then, the lineup of senior speakers at plenary sessions (the only times when no concurrent sessions were scheduled) at the Oklahoma conference was less clear: J. Hillis Miller, Jonathan Culler, Robert Scholes, and Gayatri Spivak. Since only Gayatri Spivak has a history of talking about cultural studies, it is safe to conclude that seniority in the broader area of theory in English controlled the choice of speakers. But even in America, Lynne Cheney and company notwithstanding, theory in general and cultural studies are not yet interchangeable.

I had an uneasy sense that the Oklahoma conference might as well have been called "The 1980s: An MLA Reunion." Perhaps that's all right. Perhaps not. But there were differences to be marked. They were especially clear in Hillis Miller's talk, which I will concentrate on for several reasons. Scholes addressed cultural studies not at all, though it is possible he believes his sexist presentation ("In the Brothel of Modernism: Picasso and Joyce") was an example of cultural analysis. Culler dealt with cultural studies only as part of a general survey of contemporary theory, and Spivak, finally, gave an informal talk, not a coherent paper. It was only Miller among the plenary speakers who made a full effort to define the project of cultural studies.

As someone who respects and admires much of Hillis Miller's early work, especially his elegant phenomenological readings of literary texts, I must in this context, however, nonetheless say that I just do not see its productive relation to the cultural studies tradition. A concern with ethics on the other hand, central in his recent publications, is not the same as the long cultural studies engagement with Left politics. And the internationalization of technology, which was at the center of his Oklahoma talk "The Work of Cultural Criticism in the Age of Digital Reproduction," in fact points to the importance of global politics and economics, the global dissemination and subsequent localization of cultural power, issues that Miller thinks will be swept aside in a McLuhanesque spread of technology creating a common global culture. Indeed, it is only blindness to economics and power and cultural differences that made it possible for Miller to present as an argument his fantasy that everyone in the world will have a personal computer within a few years. Had he no sense of what life is like in South Central Los Angeles, let alone in Bangladesh or Somalia? I take this as the limit case of false cultural studies—a warrant for privileged American academics who are used to juggling theories to begin making claims about the material world as well—without ever looking at it. Miller's expected deadline has now long passed, and his prediction remains unfulfilled.

The effect of Miller's appearance at the first plenary session at Oklahoma was to give the program an opening benediction, a benediction warranting a humanized, "transnational," confidently democratized version of cultural studies as the new American world order. His key role in depoliticizing deconstruction was apparently to be repeated for cultural studies. Indeed, the plenary sessions deferred the centrally political mission of cultural studies until Gayatri Spivak spoke in the final session. Despite their inclusion in many smaller sessions throughout, race, class, and gender were all thus symbolically marginalized or deferred, excluded from the sessions at which everyone was expected to be present, until the end, the last instance that we reach but have no time to discuss.

And in this regard I think it is worth recalling that Hillis Miller once cosigned a letter in the MLA *Newsletter* warning that an official Modern Language Association position against the undeclared Vietnam War might make all thirty thousand MLA members liable to a charge of treason. I bring this up not to question his position on a war long ended but because the letter insisted on the separation between academic and political life, a separation that cultural studies has sought to overcome. What is at stake here is a definition of the nature and limits of cultural studies. Both in the letter and in his efforts to limit deconstruction to a depoliticized version of textual analysis, he has more than once had something to say about the cultural role of English studies. Those views are very much at odds with the heritage of cultural studies. They may well come to dominate the Americanization of cultural studies, but this is not a process that should proceed unremarked.

Of course the definition and disciplinary mission of cultural studies are precisely what is at stake here. As it happens, I was invited to speak at the Oklahoma conference because I helped organize the Illinois cultural studies conference a few months earlier. That conference gave high visibility to the several strands of the British and Australian cultural studies traditions, along with people whose work we thought could gain from being heard in the context of those traditions. Although a number of people attended both conferences, there was no overlap between the speakers at the two events. That alone is remarkable. I don't think it would be true of the other major bodies of theory on the scene today. A large conference on Marxism, feminism, psychoanalysis, or poststructuralism—a conference on gender, race, or class in the humanities— a conference on New Historicism: all these would either have overlapping speakers or at least draw from a pool of people with similar commitments or traditions clearly in dialogue with each other.

Perhaps only in cultural studies as English professors conceive it could two massive conferences have almost no points of correspondence. In this context I do not think an uncritical argument for liberal diversity has much value. Welcoming the opening of the cultural studies field need not necessitate abandoning a debate about what enterprises do and do not deserve to use the cultural studies name, about what commitments cultural studies entails, about what cultural studies projects seem most productive and urgent in the current context. That is not to say I think either the British or the Americans and Australians and Canadians who have learned from them can police the field. In fact I think the more open, generous, democratic—but less critical—shape of the Oklahoma conference will likely win the day. This much more inclusive vision probably *is* the future of cultural studies in America. I am merely trying to offer a challenge to that enterprise, even if it is a challenge likely to be swept aside by events.

At a paper presented at the annual MLA meeting in December of 1991, Janice Radway argued that attempts to define cultural studies and police its borders risk turning it into a "ghostly discipline." I would argue that cultural studies has always been exactly that—a ghostly discipline with shifting borders and unstable contents—and that it needs to continue being so. It is an ongoing set of traditions, a body of work whose contributors are in dialogue and debate with one another. Attempts to define its aims and limits, regularly overthrown, have been part of its history from the outset. It is also in significant ways antidisciplinary; that is, it responds critically to the exclusive parceling out of objects of study to individual disciplines, to the way academic disciplines divide up the field of knowledge, and to the social impact of much academic work. To some degree it puts forward its own contradisciplinary forms of knowledge. Yet none of these stances comes into being in a universe free of disciplinary histories and constraints. Cultural studies defines its enterprise in part by positioning itself in relation to more traditional disciplines; in the process it becomes something like a cluster of disciplines under erasure. Its own ghostly disciplinarity unsettles all other humanities and social science disciplines; that ghostly disciplinarity is thus a condition to be welcomed rather than feared.

Notably, most cultural sudies work is done by people in traditional disciplines, often with an ambivalent relation to the discipline but not necessarily in full rejection of its historical commitments. Some want cultural studies to transform their discipline. Others, as I argue in the introduction to *Disciplinarity and Dissent in Cultural Studies,* have largely left disciplinarity behind. Yet most remain housed in traditional departments nonetheless. Cultural studies itself has shown relatively little drive to found its own degree-granting units. Better economic times might have given us actual cultural studies departments by now, but the anti-institutional tenor of cultural studies culture still leaves many wary about departmental authority.

Indeed, the resistance to *any* effort to define cultural studies—a resistance unique to its Americanization—reflects a widespread and quite warranted dissatisfaction with the constraints of disciplinary knowledge. Especially for students and faculty in reactionary departments, cultural studies seems to offer the only realistic solution to a repressive work environment—literally overthrowing disciplinary knowledge. For cultural studies then to occupy itself with defining its boundaries and deciding which activities should and should not be included under its umbrella seems a betrayal of the emotional needs cultural studies was counted on to meet. Some people think of cultural studies as a kind of polymorphously free zone for any and all intellectual investments. That some individual or collaborative cultural studies work comes to be more widely recognized or valued than others seems in that context a violation of the undifferentiated zone of permission cultural studies was imagined to be. Indeed, for some people to defend their particular practices passionately seems equally suspect.

One can begin to see why some students were distressed at the presence of cultural studies "stars" on stage at Illinois. It suggests a field hierarchized by reputation and achievement in much the way traditional disciplines are. But is there any alternative? Actually, there is, but only one: wholesale anti-intellectualism. Some ordinarily canny cultural studies scholars are willing to appeal to just that anti-intellectual strain in American cultural studies. Thus Gayatri Spivak was cheered when she opened her Oklahoma talk by disingenuously declaring how relieved she was to be presenting a lecture that was not destined to be immortalized in a book. Would she be even more relieved to have that state of affairs persist for a few years? Similarly, Radway met with applause when she declared at MLA that the definition of cultural studies should be expanded to include a whole range of political activities. Presumably one could be "in" cultural studies by virtue of joining campus demonstrations. Obviously cultural studies allies itself with and helps to theorize political action. Cultural studies writers both inside and outside the academy are often involved in politics and concerned with the contribution their work makes to political action. But political action and cultural studies are not interchangeable. It should not be necessary to say this, but apparently it is: cultural studies is a set of writing and teaching practices; it is a discursive, analytic, interpretive tradition.

Meanwhile, as an intellectual enterprise cultural studies will inevitably have some people of greater achievement and influence associated with it. Those who would urge us to ignore such a hierarchy—based on accomplishment and impact—are simply being foolish and irrational. Given the chance to hear Stuart Hall or just about anybody else, I'll opt to hear Hall, as will virtually anyone else in cultural studies. You leave a Hall talk feeling energized for perhaps the next month; it's not easy to forgo such opportunities. And he is the perfect example, because he has never given any indication that hierarchy or personal achievement has any part in his self-image. They are features rather of other people's evaluation of his work. But some in cultural studies manage at once to admire him and to resent, not him, but their own admiration. Cultural studies for them is to be a place where no one is more equal than anyone else, a leveling utopia of free inquiry, a status it can only maintain if no one attempts to say what it is.

Though none of the above was acknowledged openly at Oklahoma, these values churned under the surface. This helps explain the absence of references to the history of cultural studies from more than a few of the talks, and it may also explain the relative absence of well-known cultural studies scholars from the program. Of course it is possible that those organizing the Oklahoma conference invited scholars long associated with cultural studies—Stuart Hall, Dick Hebdige, Donna Haraway, or others—and that those people declined the invitation. The Oklahoma conference in fact followed what is now the common practice in academia and offered some of its plenary speakers expenses plus a $1,000 honorarium. But many people won't come for the money. They'll come if the event has an intellectual and political shape and mission that seems important; if it does, they'll come without an honorarium. In fact, only one person refused Illinois' invitation to speak because of the lack of an honorarium.

Actually, the Oklahoma conference did have an implicit but unstated mission. Although some people were invited to participate, most of the papers were given by people who answered an open invitation to submit topics. Essentially everyone who volunteered to give a talk was placed on the program. The result was about 350 papers given in 100 sessions over three days. So the conference, in effect, said here's a self-selected group of North Americans who declare themselves to be doing cultural studies. Let's see where they stand. That's an interesting and potentially important mission, though its value was limited by being undeclared and thus never an explicit subject of discussion during the conference itself.

Incidentally, by current standards Oklahoma's honoraria are quite modest. The annual conference on twentieth-century literature at the University of Louisville gives honoraria of about $1,500 each to its two keynote speakers, and a recent conference on poststructuralism and New Historicism at Texas A&M University had sliding scales of honoraria up to $3,000. So Oklahoma can be credited with resisting inflation. I am not, by the way, faulting people for accepting honoraria. I've never demanded one when asked to speak at a conference, but I've certainly taken them when offered, and I *have* asked that my expenses be covered. Since that was my status at Oklahoma—expenses paid but no honorarium—I am implicated in the structure I now want to question. A somewhat rude way of putting the issue would be to say that the contemporary North American conference at which a few stars are paid large sums to create the illusion that something is happening at a given campus risks being rather empty. It has now become one standard model of the high-visibility conference on campuses in the United States, and I think it deserves frank commentary. People's accomplishments inevitably bring them higher salaries and other benefits. But I do not think the economic hierarchies of the profession need to be maintained at conferences. If they are, we should acknowledge them openly, which most conference organizers are reluctant to do. But it may be better to take the time to conceive a meeting that some key people will feel they cannot miss.

No matter how conferences are organized, they are expensive, and registration fees often make some contribution to the cost. Most everyone would agree that registration fees should be kept as low as possible. I would add that it is best not to charge registration fees at all to people who are presenting papers. In collecting nearly $30,000 in fees from people who were presenting papers Oklahoma was, I believe, pushing the economics of large conferences in a regrettable direction. I found myself quite uncomfortable with the idea that other people presenting papers were, in effect, paying honoraria and expenses for a few high-visibility speakers. Since most of the keynote speakers had little or no credibility in cultural studies, I drew attention to this problem by making a rather subversive suggestion: that those who had not yet paid their fee save the university administrative staff a lot of bother by simply passing the money on somewhat more directly. Perhaps, I suggested, they might take a trip to a local shopping mall, purchase $95 worth of videos, CDs, T-shirts, or other examples of popular culture and give them directly to whichever plenary speaker they thought most needed them. He or she would then be better informed about cultural studies next time around.

Unfortunately, the economics of academic conferences are more and more commonly becoming exploitive, with any paper topic submitted being accepted as long as the presenter can pay a registration fee. In the spring of 1996 one of my graduate students received a call about a conference co-sponsored by two Iowa campuses; he had submitted a proposal, which had been accepted, but they had not heard back from him. Was he coming? The caller was fairly aggressive in pushing the conference, and my student suddenly realized he was probably not talking to a graduate student or faculty member but rather to some Iowa conference telemarketer. Look, the caller argued, "if you want to come here just to present your paper and then leave, we'll only charge you a $200 fee." No doubt some students are desperate enough to go ahead and effectively purchase a line on their vitas; my student declined. And people wonder why academia is losing some of its luster. Cultural studies might want to turn its attention to practices like these.

From my perspective, a good deal of what was presented at Oklahoma simply did not qualify as cultural studies. But then the Oklahoma and Illinois conferences represented substantially different views of the state of cultural studies in America. The Oklahoma conference was organized to take advantage of an intellectual and economic opportunity. The Illinois conference was organized partly out of our sense that remarkable new cultural studies work was going on both here and abroad. But we were also responding to a sense of the dissolution and depoliticization of cultural studies in the United States.

Many people came to Illinois out of a need to share what might be left of their common ground and debate the nature of the cultural studies enterprise. Yet the level and nature of debate that resulted was quite different from that at the Marxism and the Interpretation of Culture conference that I helped organize at Illinois in 1983. Marxism then was perceived as simultaneously in crisis and in a heyday of expansion, somewhat as cultural studies is now. But the lines for Marxist criticism were more clearly drawn, and people's allegiances were marked in advance. Thus positions about what did and did not qualify as Marxism were argued forcefully. Fred Jameson could thus announce that he felt like a dinosaur, like the last true Marxist on earth, in arguing for a traditional revolutionary teleology. Ernesto Laclau and Chantal Mouffe on the other hand could argue that one role for Marxism now was to call on democratic societies to realize the full radical potential of the beliefs they supposedly espoused.

The situation of cultural studies is rather different; it is in a period of testing the viability of potential alliances. People may hold strong beliefs about the limits of cultural studies but are often cautious about expressing them. It is a body of thought that now sometimes destabilizes and de-essentializes categories of race, class, gender, and nationality while simultaneously keeping them at the foreground of debate and definition. Moreover, cultural studies can forge problematic allegiances that transgress and realign the subject positions historically produced in terms of those categories. In practical terms this meant that people at the Illinois conference mapped out their models of cultural studies affirmatively, frequently without overtly marking their differences with others claiming title to its terrain until pressed to do so in the discussion periods.

Despite the uncertainties created by this reticence, the experience of the Illinois conference—together with teaching seminars in cultural studies and writing a book that tried to map out a cultural studies model of a literary genre—leads me to believe some generalizations about the cultural studies enterprise can and must be put forward. I think it is important to try to say both what cultural studies is and what it is not; keeping in mind the well-known series of definitional articles throughout the history of cultural studies,[1] I would like to do so in the form of a series of numbered points, one version of a cultural studies manifesto:

1. Cultural studies is not simply the close analysis of objects other than literary texts. Some English departments would like to believe that their transportable methods of close reading can make them cultural studies departments as soon as they expand the range of cultural objects they habitually study. Indeed, cultural studies is usually sold to English departments as part of the manifest destiny of the discipline. Our skills at close reading need to be extended to other cultural domains, it is often argued, lest these domains be left to the dubious care of student subcultures or the imprecise attention of lesser disciplines like speech communication. Similarly, some scholars like the sense of theoretical prestige that an unspecified cultural studies umbrella gives their close readings of nontraditional objects. Indeed, cultural studies often arrives in English departments in the form of an easy alliance between debased textuality and recent theory. But the immanent formal, thematic, or semiotic analysis of films, paintings, songs, romance novels, comic books, or clothing styles does not in itself constitute cultural studies.

2. Cultural studies does not, as some people believe, require that every project involve the study of artifacts of popular culture. On the other hand, people with ingrained contempt for popular culture can never fully understand the cultural studies project. In part that is because cultural studies has traditionally been deeply concerned with how all cultural production is sustained and determined by (and in turn influences) the broad terrain of popular common sense. Thus no properly historicized cultural studies can cut itself off from that sense of "the popular."

3. Cultural studies also does not mean that we have to abandon the study of what have been historically identified as the domains of high culture, though it does challenge us to study them in radically new ways. Since every cultural practice has a degree of relative autonomy, every cultural practice potentially merits focused attention. But we need to recognize that autonomy is not a function of intrinsic merit and it is never fixed and never more than relative. The notion of relative autonomy, of course, makes it properly impossible to repeat traditional claims that some cultural production transcends history.

4. Cultural studies is not simply the neutral study of semiotic systems, no matter how mobile and flexible those systems are made to be. There can be a semiotic component to cultural studies, but cultural studies and semiotics

are not interchangeable. Cultural studies is not satisfied with mapping sign systems. It is concerned with the struggles over meaning that reshape and define the terrain of culture. It is devoted, among other things, to studying the politics of signification.

5. Cultural studies is committed to studying the production, reception, and varied use of texts, not merely their internal characteristics. This is one of the reasons why cultural studies work is more difficult in periods when the historical record is either fragmentary or highly restrictive in class terms. So long as the difficulties are foregrounded, however, limited but ambitious and important cultural studies projects can be carried out for earlier periods of history.

6. Cultural studies conceives culture relationally. Thus the analysis of an individual text, discourse, behavior, ritual, style, genre, or subculture does not constitute cultural studies unless the thing analyzed is considered in terms of its competitive, reinforcing, and determining relations with other objects and cultural forces. This task is also, it should be noted, an impossible one to complete in any given instance. But unless the constitutive and dissolving cultural relations are taken as a primary concern the work is not properly considered cultural studies.

   This relational understanding of culture was one of cultural studies' earliest defining goals. Yet just what is meant by the relational study of culture has changed and evolved and abruptly shifted throughout the history of cultural studies, from Williams's efforts to describe culture as a whole way of life, to the effort by Hall and others to adapt Gramsci's notion of a war of position, to discursive and political analyses of contemporary Britain. One could in fact write the history of cultural studies in terms of how it conceives relationality and puts it into practice.

7. Cultural studies is not a fixed, repeatable methodology that can be learned and thereafter applied to any given cultural domain. It is the social and textual history of varying efforts to take up the problematic of the politics and meaning of culture. Its history mixes founding moments with transformative challenges and disputations. To do cultural studies is to take a place within that history.

8. Taking a place within that history means thinking of one's work in relation to cultural studies work on the politics of race. It means taking seriously the way feminism radically transformed cultural studies in the 1980s. And it also means positioning one's work in relation to the long, complex, and often contentious history of cultural studies' engagements with Marxism, from Raymond Williams to Stuart Hall. To treat that history of engagements with Marxism as irrelevant, as many Americans do, is to abandon

cultural studies for a fake practice that merely borrows its name. None of this is meant to suggest that current cultural studies scholars need to *emulate* these traditions, any more than they need to emulate British cultural studies. They do, however, need to be familiar with them and mark their relationship to them.

9. Cultural studies is concerned with the social and political meaning and effects of its own analyses. It assumes that scholarly writing can and does do meaningful cultural work. To avoid facing this challenge and retreat into academic modesty (asserting that interpretive writing is impotent or irrelevant) or claims of disinterested scholarship (protesting that political commitments vitiate scholarly objectivity) is to hide from cultural studies' historical mission. A poststructuralist academic liberalism might lead one to argue that, since the political effects of discourse are indeterminate and unpredictable, scholarship and politics are best kept separate. Cultural studies might counter by arguing that such arguments do not free us from responsibility for the political meaning of scholarly work. Cultural studies typically accepts the notion that scholarship entails an engagement with and commitment to your own historical context. The choice of what scholarly writing to do involves a decision about what your most effective intervention can be.

10. In much the same way it must be emphasized that cultural studies does not simply offer students a liberal cornucopia of free choices. Cultural studies seeks to empower students to understand the social and political meaning of what they learn throughout the university. It urges them to reflect on the social meaning of disciplinary work and to decide what kinds of projects the culture needs most. A cultural studies pedagogy thus encourages a more critical relationship to cultural and political life. One small but necessary implication in this is that current debates and social practices need to be a far more pervasive element of many more courses than is now the case. Fields like history and literature that often teach pure period courses need to make detailed and specific analogies to present conditions. It is not enough to establish contexts for and relationships between discourses in earlier periods on the assumption that students will make the contemporary connections and work out the contemporary differences on their own. The Taylorized curriculum needs to be thoroughly undermined with the aim of gaining critical purchase on contemporary life.

11. Cultural studies has a responsibility to continue interrogating and reflecting on its own commitments. In fulfilling this task, however, cultural studies has inevitably had a history that is far from perfect. It needs now to critique its investment in what has been called the Left's "mantra of race, class, and gender," categories that are properly considered both in relation to one

another and to the culture as a whole. It needs as well to question its recent fetishizing of fandom. A ritualized, unreflective confession of fandom has become almost a requirement in some American cultural studies circles. Being a fan is not a prerequisite for doing cultural analysis. Invoking fandom without describing or specifying its conditions and its cultural construction has little intellectual value. Being a fan gives potential access to important insights; the challenge is to reflect on fandom and articulate what you learn from it.

12. Cultural studies is not required to approve a struggle for dominance among the disenfranchised. Multiculturalism in America sometimes degenerates into a competitive form of identity politics in which oppressed and marginalized groups work to sort themselves out into a hierarchy based on their record of historical suffering. Cultural studies is not, however, simply a neutral field in which people can give free reign to their inclinations to play identity politics. Cultural studies is properly an enterprise in which people can explore their race, ethnicity, or gender and articulate its relations with the larger culture. A properly relational and historical analysis suggests that no one group can claim the ultimate site of oppression. The progressive alliances we now need require us to avoid using previously marginalized identities to suppress debate and criticism. At the other end of the spectrum multiculturalism restricts itself to an unrealistic liberal ideal of diversity and difference without conflict. Cultural studies needs to maintain a critical relation to both these tendencies. Cultural studies may thus establish alliances with multiculturalism but should resist being absorbed by it. Similarly, if multicultural work is to claim a place within cultural studies it cannot ignore all the innovative work other cultural studies scholars have done on race, gender, and ethnicity.

Much of this work suggests that race, gender, and ethnicity are always constructed, never given and guaranteed in advance. Furthermore they change and adapt to new circumstances. New "races" or "ethnicities" can emerge and be produced and already existing ones be radically transformed so as to become far more visible and influential. Cultural studies may well want to facilitate such developments in particular cases. Yet cultural studies is pressed by many of its historic theoretical commitments to take up an anti-essentialist position. Thus cultural studies must recognize that such identities are never pure; they are always hybrid, constructed, impure, and their social power should thus never be constituted on grounds of purity.

13. The historicizing impulse in cultural studies is properly in dialogue with an awareness of the contemporary rearticulation of earlier texts, contexts, and social practices. In literary studies, New Historicism may sometimes suc-

cumb to an illusion of being able to address only the earlier historical period being analyzed but cultural studies properly does not. Being historically and politically here and there—then and now—is part of the continuing and thus necessarily newly theorized burden of cultural studies. Nothing we rescue from forgetfulness or distortion stays the same. To study the present or the past is inevitably to rearticulate it to current interests; that is a problem and an opportunity to take up consciously, not to repress or regret. Cultural studies can never be a simple program of recovery; properly speaking, such programs are not cultural studies. Indeed, a conservative tendency to categorize every limited project of cultural recovery as cultural studies usually signals a high cultural contempt for the things being recovered. The tendency, for example, to classify efforts to recover minority literatures as cultural studies sometimes reflects an assumption that these literatures are inherently inferior or that they lack the aesthetic importance of the traditional canon.

14. In its projects of historical and contemporary analysis, cultural studies is often concerned as well with intervening in the present and with encouraging certain possible futures rather than others. Thus as cultural studies people reflect on the simultaneously undermined and reinforced status of the nation-state in different parts of the world they are often also concerned with the future status of nationhood. An interest in how high technology has changed our lives may be combined with an effort to shape its future impact. The opportunities offered by fragmented postmodern identities are not only to be studied but exploited. A study of the multiple meanings of gender in a given moment may lead to reflection on how our lives may be gendered in the future. For many scholars outside cultural studies such double investments are to be avoided. In cultural studies they can be at the center of the enterprise.

15. Cultural studies accepts the notion that the work of theorizing its enterprise is inescapably grounded in contemporary life and current politics. New social and political realities require fresh reflection and debate on the cultural studies enterprise, no matter what historical period one is studying. Although it is possible to overstate the phenomenon of a local theorizing grounded in current social realities, since such a process involves a rearticulation of previously existing theories, it is nonetheless true that major changes in cultural studies have regularly come from an effort to understand and intervene in new historical conditions. From a cultural studies perspective, then, one never imagines that it is possible to theorize for all times and places. Not only our interpretations but also our theories are produced for the world in which we live.

16. Cultural studies within the academy is inescapably concerned with and critical of the politics of disciplinary knowledge. It is not simply interdisciplinary in the model of liberal diversity and idealized communication. This means that the nontrivial institutionalization of cultural studies within traditional academic disciplines is impossible unless those disciplines dismantle themselves. A first step, for a discipline like English, is to make a commitment to hiring faculty members who do not have degrees from English departments. Otherwise there is little chance that English departments will even admit that literature does not acquire its meaning primarily from its own autonomous traditions, let alone take up the general problematics of culture. Yet while English departments have much to gain from expanding their enterprises to include cultural studies, it is less clear what cultural studies has to gain from being institutionalized in English departments. If it is to be institutionalized at all, cultural studies might be better served by a variety of programs outside traditional departments.

Not every individual cultural studies book or essay can fulfill all the conditions in these sixteen points. But a successful cultural studies project should position itself in relation to many of these concerns. When it does not take them on directly, they should be implicit in the project's interests, terms, and references. These, it seems to me, represent some of the key aims and imperatives growing out of thirty years of cultural work. These points, I would argue, are effectively part of the cultural studies paradigm and part of the cultural studies challenge to the contemporary world. Since they are focused on the ways cultural studies has and is likely to continue to change and develop, they are less rigid than the form of a numbered manifesto may lead some readers to think.[2] Indeed, to take up these points is to write in such a way as to engage in a continual interrogation of what cultural studies is and can be. Thus I have articulated this manifesto at a level of theoretical generality that does not totalize and synthesize all cultural studies projects. These principles do not attempt to anticipate the specific work of local theorizing. To place yourself in relation to the history of cultural studies is precisely to recognize that the practices of cultural studies are not given in advance. They are always to be rethought, rearticulated to contemporary conditions. That imperative to continuing political renewal and struggle is part of what cultural studies has bequeathed to us.

My sixteen points also do not cover all areas of weakness and grounds for improvement in cultural studies. I believe, for example, that cultural studies for much of its history has suffered from the lack of a strong comparativist tradition. It is often difficult to recognize what a cultural practice means if you have no idea what alternatives there might be to it, or what an apparently similar practice means in different times and cultures. Some of the problems inherent in immanent textual analysis get transferred in this way to the analysis of whole historical conjunctures. It would represent a major change in both cultural studies' pedagogy and its scholarship for it to become more comparative, but that seems one of the few ways of limiting cultural and disciplinary bias.

It was priorities like these and a sense that, although a great deal of interesting new cultural studies work was being done both here and abroad, the core commitments described above were at risk in the Americanization of cultural studies that led Larry Grossberg, Paula Treichler, and me to organize a large international conference at Illinois in April of 1990. The conference gathered together thirty-three speakers who gave thirty-one long papers offering either their sense of the priorities in cultural studies or a model of cultural studies analysis. There were no concurrent sessions because we wanted the sense of momentum and shared experience that could come from staying together for sixteen sessions spread out over much of five days. Extensive discussions of about forty-five minutes concluded each session. Microphones in the audience relayed all questions, comments, and statements through a public address system, giving them as much presence as comments from the stage. We taped and transcribed the discussions for inclusion in the book based on the conference, as we had with *Marxism and the Interpretation of Culture.* The book, *Cultural Studies,* was published by Routledge in 1992. Although the speakers were all invited, the audience thus had a certain democratic access to the floor and to publication of their comments.

Past experience led us to anticipate that empowering the audience in this way—giving them the basis for shared experience and access to an effective public address system—would also empower discontent. Conferences with large numbers of simultaneous sessions inevitably scatter critique and block people from organizing themselves. Some people felt that the conference model was hierarchical, which indeed it was, though many of the people on stage—two-thirds of whom were women or minorities—were very much on the margins of the academy. Some had lost academic jobs or found them only after years of searching. Most (though not all) were stars in terms of their reputations among cultural studies people but few were stars, say, in terms of their salaries. Another problem came from the sheer size of the audience. As many as six hundred people attended some of the sessions, and this was predictably intimidating to some people, especially those attending their first conference.

It also proved true that our priorities, though shared by many of the speakers and audience members, were not shared by everyone. An audience of over six hundred people in an auditorium was better suited for people committed to a clear intellectual project than for people who were uncertain of their direction and therefore wanted intimate consultation and support. We were interested in establishing models for the discourses of cultural studies, whereas some of the younger people in the audience wanted sessions devoted to their career problems—finding jobs, teaching cultural studies within traditional disciplines. Those are valid concerns, and in retrospect I wish we had taken them up formally. Some, as I suggested above, arrived so disenchanted with academia that the very format of speakers addressing an audience seemed intolerably oppressive and hierarchical; they felt that the traditional conference structure—with its division between speakers and audience—should be abandoned. For us it seemed ironic that this structure should be slated for demolition at the very moment that disenfranchised populations were finally gaining access to the stage. But many people felt cultural studies should be more reflexive and self-critical about its institutional forms, which is clearly a sound argument. In fact I would agree that intimate conferences with a maximum attendance of fifty are often the most satisfying. But if you are going to advertize a conference with Stuart Hall, Meaghan Morris, Paul Gilroy, Catherine Hall, Simon Frith, Homi Bhabha, Tony Bennett, and other people whom American audiences don't often hear in person, then a large audience is inevitable.

The crisis came, as we knew it would because it happened in 1983 as well, when someone in the audience proposed that the conference be disbanded and the time and space used for free discussion. Larry and I came on stage to remind people that an attractive and comfortable alternative space was available for those who did not want to hear the talks. Of course it did not represent much fun or much of a victory to attend free discussions elsewhere. The only gratifying symbolism would be to take over the main stage. But the job of the conference organizers in such a situation is to ensure that speakers get the chance to read their papers and that those who have come long distances to hear them be able to do so. In fact, though in the spirit of the moment's solidarity, many in the audience will cheer the revolutionary fervor of those who call for the conference to be disbanded, the overwhelming majority want the conference to go on largely as planned. So we played our role as sympathetic heavies and got the program going again. We gained several things as a result: an opportunity for people to hear and discuss a wide range of reflective and politically committed papers on cultural studies, material for a large book that has the potential to be a major intervention in the field, and a more self-conscious awareness of cultural studies as a force within the academy.

We had invited as speakers not only those long identified with cultural studies but also people whose work we thought gave them a potential relationship to the cultural studies tradition, a relationship we hoped the conference might draw out and establish. The three of us debated over many names before agreeing on a few. That debate was often heated, as we discussed similarities and differences and potential alliances with cultural studies. Some people looking at the 1990 conference schedule half a decade later concluded it was *all* made up of stars. Actually, in 1988 and 1989, when we were inviting participants, many of these people were just beginning their careers; some were still not widely known when the conference took place. Most of them have since become influential. Indeed the book itself, which has now sold nearly twenty-five thousand copies worldwide, has helped give some of its contributors an audience they did not have beforehand.

Since the book adds a number of essays by people who attended the conference but did not present papers there, it is broader and more open still. Not everything that we gained, however, will be viewed positively even now. For the most obvious result of the conference is the oversized eight-hundred-page book it produced. From the perspective of the editors, the book is, if anything, overly generous in its presentation of the field. It includes a number of essays that one or more of us feel represent not yet fully realized cultural studies projects. Thus we see the book as opening up diverse possibilities for cultural studies work. But its sheer size, its title, and its appearance on the hitherto wholly uncodified American cultural studies scene will make some feel it is a hurdle they must pass over before they can present themselves as cultural studies people. Varied as the book is, it still suggests that cultural studies entails written work subject to commentary and evaluation, inclusion and exclusion, high and low visibility, success and failure. The fact that the book is there and has to be contended with undercuts the illusion that cultural studies is a zone of free permission. For some, the challenge to write an essay that might be worth including in such a book is already a challenge that spoils whatever lure the field first had.

The Oklahoma conference went a different route. It was an open admissions cultural studies conference, and even though many of the papers had nothing to do with cultural studies, there was much to be gained from listening to them and trying to decide where they stood. Such a process of negotiation and debate over what is and is not cultural studies has to take place if cultural studies is to have any intellectual power and political effectivity. Wider alliances need to be formed, but not every alliance is worth the potential price in dissolution and compromise.

Perhaps I sound like a Third Period Stalinist who is not ready to accept the Popular Front coalition of the late 1930s. But we need to remember that the broad, inclusive alliance of the Popular Front had a political mission and a political reason for the compromises it made—the struggle against fascism. Those on the Left in America and those committed to progressive projects in humanities departments in universities have a related mission today—the struggle against the global inequities following upon the Reagan–Bush era, the struggle against the Allan Bloom–Lynne Cheney consensus about American education and American culture, the growing articulation of discomfort and anger over racism and sexism as universities' efforts to become more "culturally diverse" take hold. It is our task to make American institutions nervous about cultural studies. One boundary worth drawing around the cultural studies alliance is between those who will and those who will not join that struggle. The price of depoliticizing cultural studies is not a price we should be willing to pay. There are alliances worth making and alliances too costly to make. If the bargain is that we may have cultural studies so long as we do not criticize the government in our classrooms, we should reject it. Cultural studies does not need to render unto Caesar what Caesar thinks belongs to him.

Caesar, however, is in the midst of having his say in any case. Over the last two years or so the phrase "cultural studies" has been taken up by journalists and politicians of the New Right in America as one of a cluster of scare terms — the others include "multiculturalism" and "deconstruction" — that have been articulated together to signal a crisis in higher education and American intellectual life generally. One fair response for cultural studies people would be to work to disarticulate these terms, already effectively welded together in popular understanding. Cultural studies is not multiculturalism and is not deconstruction, we might argue, though cultural studies welcomes some versions of multiculturalism and shares with deconstruction sympathies for the general project of poststructuralism. Unfortunately, it seems likely that the qualifications in the second half of the sentence pretty much undo any useful work the denials in the first half of the sentence might do in the public arena. These are distinctions we need to draw for our students and colleagues, but we are unlikely to be able to do so successfully for the media or the public. These are different intellectual traditions, but their points of partial correspondence are sufficient to convince people they are part of the same general cultural pattern. Our audiences, in other words, will smell a rat. Since we can do little now to resist that moment of recognition, it might be better to welcome it. Cultural studies, in other words, might well set out to *be that rat*.

The creature I have in mind is a largely urban animal who is wary, focused on local conditions, and willing to eat almost anything—an animal, in short, very much like cultural studies. He or she is, in other words, a political animal attuned to assuring the survival of his or her interests. Now that recent theory as a whole has been accused of being politicized—something many theorists of the last two decades would themselves be hard put to demonstrate—cultural studies can willingly occupy the site of theory as politics. Now that efforts to open up the canon and efforts to expand the cultural reach of academia's field of vision have been scandalized for abandoning the transcendent and eternal standards of Western high culture—something not everyone involved in canon revision or multiculturalism would want to embrace—cultural studies can cheerfully occupy the site of standard-free omnivorousness. Everyone else may choose to respond to the Right's assault by filling and backsliding and denying they are now or ever have been political in their aims or interests. Cultural studies can step in and be the very thing the Right loves to hate. Indeed, those cultural studies professors who are tenured should do their best to attract the bulk of the criticism about politicized pedagogy and scholarship.

Cultural studies has never meant only one thing, and it is unlikely to mean only one thing in the future. It may, then, be necessary for individuals to adopt different cultural studies identities in different contexts. When strategically useful, they can be deconstructionists or multiculturalists. All the while, however, they should be reiterating that the real villain is cultural studies. That should certainly thin the ranks of cultural studies' fair-weather friends. More importantly, it should focus on a body of work (cultural studies) as well as the political responsibilities and effects the field has traditionally worked to understand.

For the time has come when the political meaning of teaching and scholarship can no longer be avoided. Attacks on feminist, minority, multicultural, and theoretical research in the academy are helping to discredit those values and constituencies in the general culture as well. A delegitimated university thus does double duty: it oversees its own increasingly curtailed and embattled mission while serving as an object lesson that undermines progressive thought throughout the culture. Meanwhile, the heyday of free time for research in the humanities and social sciences has past. It was a spin-off of the cold war, and the cold war has ended. If the New Right in America has its way, the only time available for research will be that funded by industry. If universities give up their role of social critique, only conservative think tanks will remain to fund social critique over the long term. At the same time, access to higher education will be steadily restricted to wealthier families. Public elementary and secondary education, increasingly vocational, will be reserved for the poor. A divisive struggle for power among minorities will only facilitate that agenda. We need relational analyses of the political meaning of the work all of us do, we need careful disarticulations of the elements the Right has joined to win popular consent, and we need unsentimental readings of the possibilities for alliances amongst those with the most to lose spiritually and economically. That is a task historically appropriate for a politicized cultural studies that devotes itself to the kinds of cultural analysis the society needs.

THE ACADEMY
AND THE CULTURE DEBATES

5

PROGRESSIVE PEDAGOGY
WITHOUT APOLOGIES

THE CULTURAL WORK OF
TEACHING NONCANONICAL POETRY

I want to ground this chapter's remarks about theory and social responsibility in undergraduate teaching in a specific material context—a course
in modern poetry that I taught recently. I was returning to the undergraduate
literature classroom after several years' absence, having done mostly courses and
seminars in theory. Because I wanted my students to treat critical books and
essays as texts, rather than as mere exportable systems of ideas (and because no
one else in my department was teaching courses in pure theory at the time), I
considered it important to exclude literary texts from my theory courses and to
require students to write directly about theory, not to apply it to literature. That
was a requirement I maintained for both graduate and undergraduate students.
Except for a graduate seminar in contemporary poetry, I thus had not taught

literature at all for some time. But now I was writing the book about modern poetry that I discussed in chapter 3, *Repression and Recovery: Modern American Poetry and the Politics of Cultural Memory, 1910–1945,* and I did not want it to be impoverished by lack of contact with student opinions and reactions. Moreover, I had acquired a sense of mission about overturning the modern poetry canon and giving new cultural life to dozens of forgotten poets; it was time to share that mission with our undergraduates. In exchange, they would counteract the hermeticism to which all solitary intellectual projects are subject.

My long sabbatical from literature meant that it was time to begin thinking seriously about what I thought a literature class might do in the late 1980s. In a way I had no choice. The texts I had used years earlier were either out of print or so narrow in their representations of women and minorities as to be totally alienating. The most obvious new anthologies—such as the current revisions of the *Norton Anthology of Poetry* (Allison) or the *Norton Anthology of Modern Poetry* (Ellmann and O'Clair) could hardly have been less generous in their representations of the expanded canon; as I note in chapter 1, a number of other anthologies had by then been updated, but Norton's modern poetry anthology remains to this day highly conservative. I no longer really remembered the details of the modern poetry courses I had taught years ago, and I didn't want to think about the effort that would be required to find any of my old syllabi. And indeed literature itself—in a classroom—seemed a foreign and uneasy prospect. Having spent years trying to persuade students who had never read anything *other* than literature in an English class that they ought to stop reading it for a time, I was now required to reverse motion. Little remained of the inertial energy that so often shapes our plans for our literature classes.

But I felt a good deal of motivating energy of other sorts, from convictions about the centrality of theory in literary studies to nearly a decade of frustration with the Reagan–Bush era. A series of contexts (local, national, disciplinary)—along with my own research commitments—colored what I thought it necessary and appropriate to do. With the Left in retreat across much of the postindustrialized world and with the Right—short of economic collapse—increasingly in control of American institutions, a critical and subversive alternative pedagogy seemed essential. I did not expect to be able entirely to change my students' lives; I did not imagine this course to be one step toward ushering in a utopia. I did expect to be able to acquaint them with historical perspectives they might not have known beforehand. One way to provide students with models of a more critical relationship to American culture and American political life, I concluded, was simply to acquaint them with the Left literary traditions excluded from their more canonically oriented courses. There is a substantial tradition of progressive resistance to the dominant culture in modern American poetry, and I wanted my students to learn about that tradition and reflect on what it said about their culture and what it might mean in their own lives. Learning about these traditions, I believed, would not only lend Left commitments increased credibility but also help students disarticulate the elements of the popular common sense that ruled their lives. Though I do not want to exaggerate what can be accomplished in one course, I also do not want to ignore or trivialize what one course can do. Certainly it is not unusual for one course to help shape several students' intellectual interests for the rest of their careers. Many other students would at least leave the course not only with a very different sense of our literary heritage, but also with a considerably expanded notion of the social functions poetry can serve and with a more self-conscious and critical relation to the discipline of English and perhaps other humanities disciplines as well.

This course, moreover, was part of a pattern of research and teaching commitments that eventually affected quite a few people's lives. I was also teaching graduate seminars in modern poetry, and some of those graduate students were writing dissertations on radical poetry and teaching their own noncanonical undergraduate poetry courses. Other people around the country meanwhile were continuing to teach courses in an expanded canon incorporating research they, I, and others had done. It is worth noting in this context how well integrated teaching and research in noncanonical literature can be. The forgotten or unpublished poem that I find in a library or an archive one semester can be part of a course syllabus that semester or the next one. My classes in turn give me a realistic sense of whether a poem can find a new audience today and what impact it might have. With noncanonical texts, moreover, where little previous scholarship exists, the classroom provides the only forum for detailed dialogue about individual works. Finally, essays like this one give me the opportunity to share the results with still other readers. The cultural work done in the course extends into the work this chapter may do. In the light of all of this, the clichés we all hear about the inherent conflicts—some would say complete incompatibility—between research and teaching seem wholly insupportable. At least for those who have the freedom to choose and design their own courses—which not everyone does—research and teaching can be substantially intertwined and more than mutually supportive and corrective.

What I was not particularly interested in doing, I might point out, however, was letting the course be shaped primarily by an effort to honor my students' initial sense of their own needs. I was interested in learning what they hoped to get out of a poetry class, but I was not about to be constrained by it. I had an agenda of discovery and political consciousness-raising for them, an agenda determined by my sense of where the country and the profession were culturally and politically, an agenda shaped by the cultural work I thought it was most useful for me to do as a teacher. I was prepared to adjust and redirect my plans as the semester proceeded, especially as I found what texts and issues did and did not excite them, but even though the class spent most of its time in discussion, the course was clearly shaped by my agenda, not theirs. Some, it turned out, responded enthusiastically; others resisted. A few have since told me or my colleagues it was one of the two or three best courses they took here; on the other hand, the evaluation form that complained "if this was to be a left-wing indoctrination course we should have been warned" no doubt captured some other students' views as well. For they had no choice about going along with the general program, which was a product of the readings I assigned and the topics I raised. Indeed, though it was essential that they talk through the poems and the theoretical issues at stake, this process was important not so much for the virtues of self-articulation but so that the class could become a theater of contesting interpretations and so that the values I was encouraging could be drawn out of discussion rather than simply be articulated from above.

I realize, of course, that many faculty members are immensely uncomfortable with this sort of unashamed advocacy. The course I am describing, moreover, is in many ways exactly the sort of course the New Right has worked to scandalize. This chapter may give people like Roger Kimball and Dinesh D'Souza notably more substantive evidence than they usually have available to make their case against radical teaching. But I believe there is more to be gained by describing the aims and substance of my teaching practices accurately than by retreating; that is, by filling and backsliding and denying my interests. In fact many of my colleagues use the classroom to promote their own values—from religious beliefs to political disengagement to patriotism—while maintaining a mask of disinterested objectivity. I prefer to let my students know where I stand.

Like other literature professors, I assign many texts whose values and concerns I share. To a considerable extent, then, the topics we take up in class are *promoted by the texts themselves*—promoted in my course by poems by women, minorities, and writers on the Left. In responding to a course like mine, it is at least impossible to claim I am *imposing* radical politics on the poetry. One could argue in objection, I suppose, that these poems should not be read because they are not as good as the poems in the canon, that expanded historical knowledge of this sort is of no use if it means lowering the quality of the texts we know well as a result. To a considerable extent, that's exactly how the argument has been put, though generally by scholars who have not actually read the progressive poetry they reject as inferior. So it is possible to win a hearing by calling for reevaluations of texts on an individual basis, though my own position is that a major phase of our literary history needs to be remembered, whether or not we admire the texts it produced.

There is another alternative, however, another route the Right takes to scandalize progressive pedagogy. It is articulated succinctly in a 1996 attack on affirmative action by National Association of Scholars officials Stephen Balch and Peter Warren: "To the extent that scholars allow theories of social justice to drive their decision making, they forfeit their special claim to insulation from the political process and hence to academic freedom. And this is especially true when these theories embody concepts such as group rights, which are conspicuously at odds with evaluating the intellectual merits of individual students, scholars, and ideas."[1] This strikingly broad statement might lead us to doubt that the Holocaust could be described as unjust, since objections to genocide involve issues of group history, identity, and rights; the injustice, then, would only be the murder of individuals. But are we to teach World War II in so neutral a fashion as to give no hint that we thought it better that one side won rather than the other? Are we to avoid letting "theories of social justice" influence our decision making about how to teach slavery or apartheid? What, precisely, are faculty members whose research and teaching are focused on theories of social justice supposed to do? Offer no opinions about any of the theories they teach? "Theories of social justice" indeed underlie the whole expanded academy of the postwar years, but then the Right finds that development unsavory as well, despite the fact that the Right promotes its own odious theories of social justice and individual rights. Perhaps it is no accident that this NAS principle is articulated in a piece that complains about the high percentage of registered Democrats in humanities departments; one wonders if their cause would seem so compelling were the political balance reversed—not that students will miss hearing conservative faculty when they take business, political science, or engineering courses.

In any case, despite the fact that value-driven academic decision making is inevitable and perhaps sometimes laudable in a democracy, the NAS folks hope to scandalize it and even suggest those engaged in it have given up their right to basic freedoms. They want to create the impression that only progressive advocacy really counts as advocacy, that progressive advocacy is a problem we must solve. The issue I raise, of giving history its due, of giving full treatment to the political beliefs that dominated 1930s poetry and fiction, might not get a hearing from the NAS. It is essential that they deny the inescapable connections between art and politics at many cultural moments, that they make these connections seem superfluous impositions. Progressive artists were of course often concerned about group rights; you empty their work of part of its meaning if you rule such issues inappropriate for discussion or curricular planning. This pattern is hardly unique to American poetry; it recurs throughout socially conscious art, literature, and nonfiction. It is the NAS, in effect, that seeks to curtail free speech rights.

There appears to be an emerging New Right consensus about the need to restrict academic freedom in universities. The argument goes something like this: these radicals are abusing their free speech privileges; they've thus given up their right to them. Academic freedom, in other words, is valid as long as you do not exercise it. The attacks on progressive pedagogy, the attacks on tenure, the effort to defund higher education: all these come into play over this issue; all seek to curtail higher education's critical presence in American culture.

The extreme conservatism of the NAS and the cultural Right in the United States makes negotiating of these matters with them difficult. But the historical claims behind some progressive teaching—the claim that forgotten subcultures are being revived for renewed discussion and analysis—could win tolerance from many who might otherwise have their doubts. In the case of my course at least, it is worth noting that, if the course content was unconventional, the format was not. Except for performing a lot of poetry orally—sometimes individually, sometimes in chorus, and sometimes with the class divided in half and reading successive passages alternately—there was nothing surprising about the classroom structure. Many of these students were students of rather unreflective prosperity, unaware that their privileges were class specific and unaware that education might serve other—and more critical—functions than those associated with facilitating careers. Under the influence of the 1960s and 1970s, some faculty members still believe that simple changes in the classroom structure can revolutionize education by dissolving hierarchies and empowering students to take control of their own education. But that faith in self-determination is actually underwritten by faculty members' confidence in students' basic values. I admired some of my students' values but not others. For some of the students of the 1980s and 1990s, sitting in a circle and taking charge of the class might represent an opportunity to talk about how to invest the money they hoped to earn after graduation. That is less true of a poetry class, to be sure, than of many other subjects, but it is nonetheless fair to say that these students are rather less critically engaged with American culture and their place in it than students were when I began teaching in the midst of the Vietnam War twenty-some years ago.

As to the poems the students would have chosen to read, those who knew anything about modern poetry knew only the conventional canon. Some of the students—especially women and minority students—were more than ready to read outside the canon, but they would not have been able to name many modern poets to meet that need. Those women who had an interest in feminist poetry knew only the work of a few poets who came to prominence after the

Second World War; some knew only Adrienne Rich. Once they had been through the bulk of the course, the students would be able to define their own special interests within noncanonical modern poetry. Even after half way through the course they could with help design a semester's research project. But the students needed me to guide them toward material and research techniques they had never heard of and issues they had never discussed in the classes they had taken to date.

As it happens, I was teaching two sections of the course to what turned out to be very different audiences—freshmen and upper-class undergraduates. The differences were at once cheering and depressing. The first-year students were much more open to an unconventional reading list. Most of them saw nothing wrong with a course in which the white male canon occupied less than half their time. Yet these students also knew little or nothing about modern poetry. Many of the students who had been on campus a few years, however, were quite anxious about the course. Not merely resistant to noncanonical poetry, they were often puzzled and frightened by it. The idea that poetry could be pervaded by social issues rather than by speculations about the imagination and such supposedly transhistorical issues as death and mutability undermined the investments they had made in the study of literature. And they were flatly uncomfortable with the large number of women and minorities in the syllabus. While this pattern made the prospect of teaching beginning students appealing, it offered little reason to be happy about the socialization process in either the department or the university.

Twenty years earlier a theorized classroom had meant in part an experimental classroom, where participants tried multiple different formats, met away from the university, and followed agendas in part set by the students. I had taught such classes in answer to the politics of those days. But today's students are not the students of twenty years ago. There was a time when Left teaching meant collaborating with a sense of cultural, political, and educational necessity shared by a majority of the students. Now I was fighting a different action; I was doing resistance teaching in a largely conservative department under a reactionary government. That meant that I was sometimes working against my students' assumptions, prejudices, and sense of priorities. I had allies among the students, to be sure, including some who were extremely happy finally to be reading poems that had more direct bearing on their lives. But I did not have the kind of Left consensus that was possible in the 1960s and early 1970s, a consensus that made structural changes in the classroom environment both possible and helpful. Although I made certain that all students could air their views and frequently helped articulate positions with which I disagreed, it was generally clear where I stood and clear as well that I was politically allied with some students and not others. For some of the students, therefore, I was a figure to resist or reject. I could live with the resulting tensions more easily than I could live with suppressing my values in the classroom, but I nonetheless definitely preferred the class section where more of the students were sympathetic.

As it happened, however, the class composed mostly of first-year students not only had more students open to reading noncanonical poetry; it also had more conservative students who strongly objected to the politics of many of the poems we read. I also much preferred this open rebellion to silent resentment. It made for better debates and it demonstrated clearly that people bring social and political values to the literature classroom, that those values shape their reading of literary texts. Unfamiliar with the ritualized indirection of literary profession-alism, the first-year students simply assumed that all their social investments were at issue in reading poems. Within a few years they would learn to suppress that knowledge. Then they would be good literature majors. In the meantime they might learn something useful about the politics of reading and the politics of canonization; they could learn it in part by seeing it in one another's behavior. The older students in the other section were another matter. Most would not admit that their reactions were historically, culturally, and politically grounded. I was never really successful in getting them to see how cultural investments in race, class, and gender affected the way they evaluated poems. In neither class, however, did I have anything like the sort of Left consensus possible during the Vietnam War.

That our culture has changed and thus requires different pedagogical strate-gies does not, however, render the politics of an earlier moment meaningless. Nor is it a sign of defeat that we have to adapt to different political contexts. The notion that politically relevant teaching will always take the same form does not survive historical analysis and reflection. The attempt—not only by some radical faculty members but also by faculty members influenced by various traditional humanisms—to impose one politically correct form of teaching on all of us is the tyranny of an empty idealism, not any plausible real-world politics. Even at one moment in history there are likely to be a variety of classroom structures appropriate to different material conditions. Now the con-tent of the course and the cultural purposes I articulated for it seemed far more important than a critique of classroom hierarchy. The students would go through the experience whether they wanted to or not. Thus they would be required to write essays about race or gender, essays about poems on working-class experience, whether or not they shared these concerns. They need not come to conclusions I agreed with, they need not even be sympathetic, but they had to take on these issues.

Having encouraged all the students to express themselves as openly as they could, it would hardly have been appropriate for me to penalize them once they did so. Some students, to be sure, made appallingly sexist or racist remarks in class. I still remember with embarrassment the day when a basically liberal student was led by a poem written in a black woman's voice to begin generalizing about black people's physique and sexuality. On those occasions, I did my best to wait for others to object before stating my own views. That was not always easy, but it was sometimes rewarded. In the first case above, the students were too embarrassed to speak, so I had to intervene. On the other hand, the student who responded to one of Countee Cullen's concise poems about racism by complaining irrelevantly about "welfare cheats" was resoundingly reeducated by his peers. The poem, they pointed out, was about racism, not about government programs that did not exist when the poem was written. Similarly, a student who reacted to a series of poems about workers being exploited or injured in factories by launching into an attack on unions may not have understood what this connection revealed about him and his culture, but a number of the other students made it clear that they did. On the other hand, all these comments, both those from the Left and the Right, were valuable examples of the way people read poems from the vantage point of their social positioning. The more professionally acculturated students might have the same reactions, but they would never admit to them in class.

The problem of how to deal with papers was somewhat different. Since the papers were essentially private communications to me, I did not have to be so concerned with their public impact, but I also lacked the advantage of group reeducation. In the end I decided that students should know I would comment on objectionable remarks in papers but not downgrade people for them. Thus a witty and outrageously reactionary student knew he could write what he pleased and still get an "A" in the course as long as his paper was coherent and included the required detailed analyses of individual poems. None of these strategies left me altogether comfortable, but they were the best I could devise. My aim, after all, was to expose students to alternative literary traditions and to explore what kind of role those traditions might play now in our conflicted culture, not to demand a false conformity that would have vanished once the course was over in any case. Quite apart from the ethical implications of trying simply to impose values on students, the fact is that we cannot do so successfully anyway. Unlike some faculty members, I do not believe that penalizing students for racism or sexism will cure them of those biases.

I also had a theoretical agenda that directed my comments about our readings. In fact, although the course was called "Modern American Poetry," I'm not sure whether it was really a course in theory or in poetry. Our readings were all poems, in part because the particular theoretical texts that informed my lectures—such as Ernesto Laclau and Chantal Mouffe's *Hegemony and Socialist Strategy*—were too difficult for beginning undergraduates and in part because teaching them to read contemporary theory would require a course of its own. Contrary, however, to the widespread beliefs of the 1970s, undergraduates *can* read abstract theory, but not every undergraduate can handle the most difficult texts. Certainly a theory course for juniors and seniors can deal with a quite wide range of recent theoretical texts. I have taught Roland Barthes's *S/Z* in an undergraduate honors seminar by going through portions of the book sentence by sentence and explicating it, but I have not attempted Derrida's *Of Grammatology* with the same group. I have also read essays by Michel Foucault, Luce Irigaray, Georges Poulet, Hayden White, and Raymond Williams with undergraduates, but I would not assign them all of Foucault's *The Order of Things*. For this course, moreover, some of the most pertinent work was quite far from literary analysis. Rather than read, say, Stuart Hall on Thatcherism, summarize the history of cultural studies, and then explain how Hall offers a model of discursive politics that can illuminate the history of modern poetry, I chose simply to use his concepts to talk about cultural processes and about the texts we were reading.

Teaching theory only by way of lecture and discussion meant largely betraying my own commitment to critical textuality. Yet in some ways that was less troubling than the realization that the students had no awareness that theoretical concepts and problems come with their own intellectual and political history. Both classes—not only the first-year students but also the juniors and seniors—were inclined to assume that ideas exist in a freely accessible space of contemporaneity. No one ever asked what critics or what disciplines had developed notions like "relative autonomy" or "rearticulation" that I was using in my lectures. I supplied some of this background because I felt it was irresponsible not to, but I would never have been asked for it. This was also the only area where I consistently felt uneasy about my authority in the classroom, not simply because none of the students felt empowered to resist my intellectual categories but because none of them imagined it was necessary or possible to do so. The students were quite willing to criticize my arguments about the profession and about the canon, and they continually offered inventive alternative readings of the poetry we discussed. But they were in no way inclined or prepared to contest the effects of the theoretical concepts I used. That was a limitation in their acculturation I never overcame.

Nonetheless, a good deal of class time was spent at the blackboard writing down theoretical terms and defining them. Twenty-minute lectures on theoretical issues were frequent and some entire class periods were spent that way. That the class was generically unstable, a hybrid of theory and literature, seemed to me one of its strengths. Indeed, I think it is fair to say that the theory and the poetry had shifting relations of priority; neither consistently served the other. Sometimes an overview of cultural issues introduced a discussion of poetry; on other occasions the poems served as sources of theoretical concerns.

Part of what this demonstrates, I think, is that what counts as "theory" and what cultural functions we understand theory to serve vary historically. Through the 1950s and 1960s—and into the early 1970s—theory came in discreet units like psychoanalysis, Marxism, or feminism that could be learned and applied to literary texts. In the course of the 1970s, however, these theories began to define themselves more energetically in relation to one another. At the same time we began to realize that taking up theory entailed taking up certain writing practices as well. But theory, it seemed, could still be studied without putting intense pressure on the social and political institutions of which it was a part. In the course of the 1980s, however, it became increasingly impossible for me to teach theory without also reflecting on and theorizing the social mission of English studies. Consequently I could not now imagine teaching an introductory litera- ture course that would not also introduce students to current debates in English and to the politics and social positioning of the discipline. I was as concerned to get them thinking about what it meant to study poetry as I was to familiarize them with the poetry itself. From this I hoped that they would begin to be able to understand the social and political meaning of what they learned in other classes and to reflect more generally on the social impact of intellectual work.

The mutual implication or contamination of poetry, theory, and politics was made apparent on the first day. I distributed photocopies of five improbable modern American poems: Mike Quin's "The Glorious Fourth," Irene Paull's "Ballad of a Lumberjack," Lucia Trent's "Parade the Narrow Turrets," Henry Tichenor's version of "Onward, Christian Soldiers" from his *Rhymes of the Revolution,* and Kenneth Fearing's "Dirge." There is a good chance that none of these texts would open other modern poetry courses; indeed they would proba- bly fall into a nervous, degenerate academic category that some of my colleagues call "occasional verse." They are all explicitly political and all satiric, but their form and style varies. Quin's 1941 poem, nine stanzas long, describes a hollow, opportunistic, reactionary politician:

> Senator Screwball would nearly die
> If he couldn't make a speech on the Fourth of July;
> If he couldn't stand up there beside Old Glory
> And blow off his mouth like a damned old tory.

I told the students that they could, if they liked, think of it as a prophetic poem about Dan Quayle. Trent's 1929 poem is an attack on academic escapism: "What do you care if blacks are lynched beneath a withering sky? / What do you care if two men burn to death in a great steel chair"—"Thumb over your well-worn classics with clammy and accurate eyes, / Teach freshman to scan Homer and Horace and look wise." Fearing, in the distinctive frenetic rhythms he adopted during the Great Depression, takes on a modern businessman destroyed by the commodified culture he serves: "O executive type, would you like to drive a floating-power, / knee-action, silk-upholstered six? Wed a Hollywood star?" Tichenor's "Onward, Christian Soldiers" straddles poetry and song in an international economic lesson that is no less pertinent now than it was in 1914:

> Big Business is behind you
> In your fight for kingdom come—
> It is sailing with its cargoes
> Of Gatling guns and rum—
> Just fill the heathen with your creeds
> To keep them out of hell—
> And tell them of the shoddy goods
> Big
>   Business
>   Has
>   To
>   Sell.

Taken together, these poems amount to an irreverent critique of American culture, an uncivil burlesque of the high modernist canon, and, with Trent's poem, a witty but savage attack on the English profession, a convenient way of making the politics of literary study an unavoidable topic. The poems were also thoroughly accessible, and thus the students formed opinions about them immediately. I announced that we would have a vote to determine which was the poem that seemed most and least "literary" or "poetic." After that, I asked people to discuss the reasons for their votes, having deliberately made no effort to define what I meant by literariness. Some opinions were predictable. The few students with sensibilities shaped by experimental modernism thought Fearing's poem the most literary. On the other hand, although I expected Irene Paull's "Ballad of a Lumberjack" to rate low, I did not anticipate that it would receive not a single vote. Originally included in a leaflet distributed during the 1937

Timber Workers strike, its seven stanzas lay out the realities of industrial exploitation:

> We told 'em the blankets were crummy
> And they said that we like 'em that way.
> We told 'em that skunks couldn't smell like our bunks,
> But they said that our bunks were okey.

I cast my vote for this orphaned text and prepared to defend it.

Although the students did not quite have a category for "Ballad of a Lumberjack" they were pretty sure it wasn't poetry; it just wasn't respectable enough. So I asked the key question: would the workers who picked up the leaflet in 1937 have been likely to think it was poetry? There was a moment of genuine surprise, followed by some sputtering, but general agreement developed: they would. Unwilling to opt for overt snobbery, most had to admit this poem might have functioned like a poem for that audience; it wouldn't do simply to assert our superiority and exile the poem to some extraliterary category. Nor was the poem quite as simple as they all initially argued it was. It condensed some fairly complex notions of class difference and rhetorical deception into commonsense language. In combination with the overall spread of votes—which differed in the two sections I was teaching—it became clear that literariness was not self-evidently inherent in poems. Literariness was to a degree a quality the culture invented and reinforced in various selective ways. I talked for a while about the different kinds of cultural work poems might do at different times. And I concluded by talking about the canon and about why none of these poems were in it. It would be a course, it was clear, not only about modern poetry but also about the English profession, about key issues in current theoretical debates, and about the varying cultural roles poetry has played in our history. In the end it was a course in cultural studies, with poetry granted only a relative autonomy, a relative autonomy in which poems were variously reinforced and challenged by other cultural forces. It was also, as discussion about some of the working-class poems made clear, a setting in which students' own cultural heritage and class positioning became more evident, since intimate knowledge about working-class life was hardly universal.

In the light of these five poems, the next poems we discussed, though also largely forgotten, would seem almost conventionally poetic. It was also a strategy I would use in my book: exposure to a series of more bluntly rhetorical political poems would win tolerance for poems where the language was more recognizably and appealingly "literary." We dealt with a series of depression-era poems on working conditions amongst the working class. Included were Edwin Rolfe's "Asbestos" and Tillie Olsen's "I Want You Women Up North to Know." If the students had doubts about whether we needed to remember Irene Paull, they had no doubts about the value of remembering these metaphorically inventive poems. Olsen calls on women in the north to recognize

> how those dainty children's dresses you buy
> > at macy's, wannamaker's, gimbels, marshall fields
> are dyed in blood . . .

She asks them to think of women like "Maria Vasquez, spinster, emptiness, emptiness / flaming with dresses for children she can never fondle." Rolfe's "Asbestos" tells us in a chilling conceit how a dying worker's body becomes his deathbed:

> John's deathbed is a curious affair:
> the posts are made of bone, the spring of nerves,
> the mattress bleeding flesh. Infinite air,
> compressed from dizzy altitudes, now serves
> his skullface as a pillow.

The only plausible reasons for eliminating these poems from literary histories and anthologies were ideological. The class began to feel a sense of injustice about the profession's selective memory; it was a feeling I had wanted them to have, but I was still surprised by its intensity. Working-class experience and economic exploitation were apparently not acceptable poetic subjects for the profession. Olsen's poem is based on a letter to *New Masses;* comparing the poem and its source also gave us an opportunity to develop the earlier discussion about literariness.

The students were now involved in looking at the broader range of texts from which the modern poetry canon was selected; they were beginning to be in a position to evaluate and critique the discipline's politics and its sense of social mission. They were helped by the fact that poems about the dangers of factory life were no longer dated. After years of indifference to reporting Reagan's failure to enforce job safety laws, newspapers were beginning to carry stories about the people being injured and killed in the workplace. These poems thus seemed highly relevant again. And it seemed appropriate that the values they espoused have a place in the sometimes rarified domain of the "poetic."

From there on the syllabus was structured as a dialogue between the canon and its alternatives. In fact I had ended up assigning the *Norton Anthology of Modern Poetry,* along with my own 300-page photocopied selection of noncanonical poems, though I also gave them the table of contents of the previous edition of the Norton so they could see how little progress it had made in expanding the canon. Thus it was a course with two texts in explicit competition. About half of the poems we read were well known; the others were not. We were also therefore shuttling back and forth between rereadings of canonical poems and readings of poems that were now out of print. Neither of these commitments, it seems to me, would be sufficient on its own. We need to teach the traditional canon because we cannot otherwise understand either our profession or the place of literature in the dominant culture. The shaping of the exclusionary modern canon is a part of our history that we need to know. But the modern American poetry canon—which now emphasizes Eliot, Pound, Stevens, and Williams—excludes so many important perspectives on race, class, and gender, and so many forgotten versions of modernist experimentation that it gives a quite false view of our literary history. And it offers no evidence of the cultural work women and minorities accomplished in poetry in the first half of the century. A wide range of social functions for poetry, along with an incredible variety of poetic forms and styles, is eliminated if we focus only on rereading the narrow postwar canon. Finally, the modern canon deprives women, minority, and working-class students of the full range of relevant subject positions historically available to them in modern poetry. As a result, the traditional canon distorts and impoverishes the potential meaning of poetry in their lives. It is not, therefore, condescending to argue that women and minorities deserve a chance to see how their particular interests and experiences have been taken up in poetry.

In explicitly moving back and forth between canonical and noncanonical poems, always asking why any given poem was or was not canonical, I was to a certain extent also following Gerald Graff's oft-repeated slogan to "teach the conflicts" in the profession. But I was not indulging in any fiction of liberal neutrality. Nor was I pretending that all the parties in any conflict are equally empowered. And I was also addressing a number of theoretical issues not being widely debated in literary studies, such as the competitive relations between literature and other discourses and institutions within the culture. We did not treat "poetry" as a secure and preexisting category but rather as a changing and contested cultural space. We recognized how certain topics, styles, and cultural aims were variously included in or cast out of our notions of "the poetic" at different moments. We looked repeatedly at how poetry won and lost various powers and social functions in the course of the modern period and its critical reconstitution in the decades to follow. And we worked to understand how different groups could simultaneously hold very different notions of what properly constituted poetry's texts and audiences.

The course would not have worked at all, I should point out, if I had been obsessed with the issue of coverage. I decided to leave claims about coverage to others and concern myself more with the course's intellectual aims. That is not to say that people who are concerned with coverage necessarily lack intellectual commitments, though it is to say that a focus on coverage can, at the very least, displace other issues of importance. Sometimes, moreover, people obsessed with coverage do use it as a way of avoiding dealing with more threatening theoretical and political problems. In the logic of the profession, invocations of coverage give moral cover for a faculty member's anti-intellectualism.

My own sense of what merited time and attention did not, however, always carry the day. Thus when the students were not interested in a topic I generally abandoned it. My only complete failure, I think, was my effort to win some sympathy for the more blatantly pro-Soviet revolutionary poems of the early 1930s. The choral classroom readings that worked extraordinarily well for some of the sound poems of the 1920s—turning sound poems by Harry Crosby and Eugene Jolas into ritual incantations—were no help here. Reading 1920s sound poems on their own, students considered them mere nonsense. Reading them in class—sometimes in unison and sometimes in a call and response style—they discovered uncanny power and humor in texts that first seemed meaningless. Here, for example, is Jolas's "Mountain Words" and Crosby's "Pharmacie du Soleil," the first almost a pure sound poem, the second a list of elements where the names gain poetic force from their sound when read in sequence:

> mira ool dara frim
> oasta grala drima
> os tristomeen.
>
> ala grool in rosa
> alsabrume
> lorabim
> mascaloo
> blueheart of a
>
> roolata gasta
> miralotimbana
> allatin
>
> juanilama

---

calcium iron hydrogen sodium nickel
magnesium cobalt silicon aluminum
titanium chromium strontium manganese
vanadium barium carbon scandium yttritium
zirconium molybdenum lanthanum niobium
paladium neodymium copper zinc silver
tin lead erbium potassium iridium
tantalum osmium thorium platinum tungsten
                ruthenium uranium

We read Jolas's poem in unison in fairly deep tones and read Crosby's poem by dividing the class in two with each half reading alternate words in an incantatory contest. As a result the class grew fond of the poems, but it was still quite a challenge to articulate why that was so. On the other hand, choral reading could not save many of the explicitly revolutionary proletarian poems of the 1930s. I can still remember the dull, flat sounds of thirty-five students unenthusiastically reading the line "All Power to the Soviets!" from Sol Funaroff's "What the Thunder Said: A Fire Sermon." Nor would the revolutionary communist poems of the 1930s be helped now by the fall of communism in Eastern Europe and the Soviet Union. So I cut my losses and eliminated the rest of these poems from the course.

I was learning, I think, something about the limits of my students' cultural sympathies. In a course devoted exclusively to the 1930s there would, to be sure, have been time for a much more thorough historical grounding in the realities of the depression. We would also have been reading many more depression-era poems. The line "All Power to the Soviets," we might have noted, also appears in Richard Wright's "I am a Red Slogan." That would have given us an opportunity to talk about the role of explicit, preexisting political slogans in 1930s poetry, a discursive element we usually like to think has no place in poetry whatsoever.

The one text where we made some progress with this issue was Tillie Olsen's 1934 poem "I Want You Women Up North to Know." The bulk of the poem deals with the impossible lives of Mexican American women in Texas who earn at most a few dollars a week hand-embroidering children's dresses for sale up north. It is not until about two-thirds of the way through the poem that Olsen refers to "a heaven . . . brought to earth in 1917 in Russia." The students talked enthusiastically about the poem by simply avoiding any mention of the offending line. When it did finally come up, the class fell silent, a silence which we were then able to discuss and evaluate.

On the other hand, when students wanted to spend more time with a topic we adjusted the syllabus accordingly. Thus when a week on poems about race by white authors stretched to two weeks something had to go. I looked at the syllabus and decided that Wallace Stevens was expendable. In a moment he disappeared from modernism. I felt a passing sensation of guilt, apparently, it would seem, myself still a partial victim of the very ideology I was trying to overturn, but shortly thereafter I experienced a certain bemused pleasure at Stevens's local erasure, and that emotion has happily ruled since. I was not about to eliminate the canon in its entirety, but I could survive the loss of one of its representatives.

It was while teaching poems about race that I felt the strongest sense that I was doing teaching that mattered. We had read work by Angelina Weld Grimké, Countee Cullen, Sterling Brown, Anne Spencer, and Langston Hughes and then moved on to a series of poems by white poets: Sol Funaroff's "Goin Mah Own Road," Charles Henri Ford's "Plaint," e. e. cummings's "Theys SO Alive," V. J. Jerome's "A Negro Mother to Her Child," Carl Sandburg's "Nigger," "Mammy," and "Jazz Fantasia," Kenneth Patchen's "Nice Day for a Lynching," Genevieve Taggard's "To the Negro People," and others. Especially in the 1920s and 1930s many white poets felt it important to write both poems protesting racial injustice and poems sympathetic to black culture.[2] Most remarkable of all is the fact that a surprising number of white poets tried to write poems in black dialect, something it would be difficult to imagine a white poet daring to do today. Some of these poems I find powerful and effective. In other cases, white poets trying to write positively about black culture ended up repeating offensive stereotypes. But it was sometimes difficult for all of us to agree about whether a poem was or was not racist, a shockingly fundamental matter to be so difficult to resolve. The subtle duplicities of racism in the poems, I believe, gave the students a start at thinking about racism in their own lives, as did the revealing and sometimes heated class discussions.

It was notable that opinions about these poems did not divide predictably along racial lines. The white students, for example, assumed Sandburg's "Nigger" to be an unredeemably racist poem. But one black student argued that its startling, accusatory, self-assertive conclusion could do important cultural work:

> Brooding and muttering with memories of shackles:
> I am the nigger.
> Look at me.
> I am the nigger.

The epithet we all found offensive, he argued, was after all probably the right word for that moment in history. Nervous, the white students were looking for the quick, politically correct response. The black student called them to more sustained reflection.

What was most striking overall was the students' eagerness to debate the strengths and weaknesses of these poems. In the midst of a racist culture these poems—especially the ones by white poets—enabled the class to deal openly with issues they very much needed to discuss. In some degree I had assigned the poems because I considered it part of my social responsibility to spend classroom time discussing race in America. I wanted the white students in the class to feel the special ethical pressure they would feel only if they heard white poets speaking out against racial injustice. And I wanted the "minority" students in the class to hear white poets engaged in kinds of racially reflective, committed cultural work they might not have imagined possible for members of the dominant culture. For all the students it was a revelation—about the discipline and about American culture—to hear white writers far more intricately and thoughtfully engaged in questions of race sixty years ago than they are in our supposedly more progressive contemporary culture. Sometimes the class came to a consensus about a particular poem. Other times they did not. I made no effort to impose a resolution. This was a case where theories of textual indeterminacy—theories we had often talked about in the course of the semester—had not only the most intractable material support but also quite powerful and sometimes painful social and emotional consequences. But if these students were going to live in America, then by any sane standard of what matters they needed to read these poems more than they needed to read T. S. Eliot and Wallace Stevens. That all too few of my colleagues would agree with me in a way says all one needs to say about the politics of English in America.

Since last teaching this class, my convictions about the centrality of the social mission of English have, if anything, intensified. In an America whose incredibly resistant underlying racism has been steadily strengthened by conservative politicians and commentators, it has seemed increasingly important to me to get students to talk about race and write about it in their papers. Again, I have no problem assigning such topics whether or not students would choose to write about them. Yet the model I used before had only three elements—class discussion, lectures, and individual research papers. But class discussions do not give individual students enough time to work through their feelings and articulate them in detail. And solitary research and writing are not enough to make a difference in students' attitudes, let alone their social practices. So I have now decided to give students small group research projects to work on as well. Whenever the mix of students in the class makes it possible, I would structure the groups so as to maximize racial, ethnic, and gender diversity. That is hardly the way the students would sort themselves out; indeed, if time permits, I'll let students choose their own groups for a second project. The first group, however, will be set according to my agenda—to make multiracial intellectual work and multiracial social relations part of the class experience. I believe that is something the country desperately needs. It is also a socially and politically relevant pedagogy I would challenge the Right to attack if they dare.

6

CANON
FODDER

AN EVENING WITH WILLIAM BENNETT, LYNNE CHENEY, AND DINESH D'SOUZA

O n Thursday 4 April 1991, the conservative Washington, D.C. based American Enterprise Institute held a two-hour round table with Lynne Cheney, William Bennett, and Dinesh D'Souza, author of the recently published *Illiberal Education.*[1] They were addressing an invited audience on the subject of "The Politics of Race and Sex on Campus," which is also the subtitle of D'Souza's book. Bennett and Cheney are, of course, former and present heads of the National Endowment for the Humanities, Bennett also filling in as former secretary of education and former drug czar. D'Souza is a former *Dartmouth Review* board member and was then the current darling of the New Right. Following presentations by the three speakers, there was a question and answer session with what was essentially a hand-picked and altogether friendly audience.

Both the panelists and the audience were thus well selected to speak collectively for all the moral panics the Right wants to use to consolidate its power and authority. They were also well selected to help stitch together state power and critiques of the academy, a highly visible project in America ever since the Reagan administration decided to politicize the National Endowment for the Humanities. (I learned about this politicization of NEH early on, after an NEH employee told me William Bennett had called a staff meeting to warn people that grants like two that had been just awarded to me—to direct a 1983 teaching institute and conference on Marxist cultural theory—would never get past him again.) I watched the round table event on television, courtesy of the C-Span cable network.

For the most part the panel exuded unanimity. The shared scare words of the hour were "deconstruction" and "multiculturalism," terms that have had their nefarious character steadily reinforced throughout the 1990s. "Cultural Studies," already on the academic scene but not yet visible to conservatives, was soon added to this list of intellectual misdeeds, as Cheney's 1995 *Telling the Truth* demonstrates. In the lexicon of those members of the Right concerned with research and education in the humanities, the term "deconstruction" now functions as something like a traveling suitcase that can be crammed, among other things, with every prominent theory of interpretation over the last several decades; "multiculturalism," on the other hand, serves for them as a convenient meeting ground for affirmative action efforts in hiring, along with every research or pedagogical effort to revise and rethink the dominant canon of literary texts. In the loose but effective configuration of the New Right it is apparently not necessary for everyone who cites these concepts to have any direct contact with scholarship that uses them. Once they get currency amongst conservative speakers and columnists, other journalists feel free to treat one another's inaccurate definitions as gospel. What the terms actually mean doesn't matter; what matters is what cultural and political influence can be gained by characterizing them in provocative ways.

With alliances between high theory and canon revision a rather new and tenuous feature of the critical scene, as I argued earlier, it may surprise some academics to hear that all these projects—from deconstruction's efforts to track the internal contradictions in Lévi-Strauss's anthropological writings to American colleges' efforts to hire more minority faculty—are deeply implicated in one another. It would certainly have surprised the deconstructive critics at Yale, a group that believed scholarship was apolitical and who hardly wrote a word about an author who wasn't a canonized white male. Such folks would find links between affirmative action in *hiring* and canon revision in *research* equally strange. Having to deal with people who play fast and loose with intellectual concepts, who will link any cultural phenomenon with any other if they think they can get away with it (and if it seems like it will give them a chance to warn us of yet another alarming trend in higher education) is a rather new experience for most academics.

But for our panelists the connections were indisputable. Bennett indeed referred to all these institutional, pedagogical, and scholarly developments collectively as an "infection" that had taken over higher education and had better be stopped before it contaminated elementary and secondary education as well. A questioner from the floor (someone who no doubt will not receive a return invitation) advised him to remember that deconstruction and multiculturalism were different creatures. He accepted this as a friendly amendment to his bill of new un-American particulars, especially after D'Souza volunteered to explain their relationship: deconstruction, it seemed, had provided the *philosophical* underpinning for the projects of multiculturalism by arguing that all knowledge was reducible to political struggle and that no true and permanent values exist. Thus the legions of multicultural students could rise up, philosophically brainwashed, to demand equal time for Chicano authors or black faculty members because standards for quality no longer mattered.

Just how thousands of undergraduates were supposed to have been influenced by deconstruction, a now notorious but for most of its history rather marginal theory in literary studies and continental philosophy, a theory that relatively few undergraduates would ever have encountered in a classroom, is difficult to guess. And in any case Bennett et al. felt no need to pause and tell us, though I suppose characterizing it as an "infection" allows it to spread invisibly and on its own. Nor were they interested in proving links between affirmative action or multiculturalism and, say, noncanonical research in literary history. The links are there in teaching, to some degree, but the issues in scholarship are usually framed differently. To give an example of the kind of incoherence that can result from simply collapsing different cultural domains together, instead of interrogating their complex differences and relations, I might point out that I haven't heard anyone insist on or complain about strict quota systems for who does or does not get mentioned in literary histories. On the other hand, we do now recognize that the relative absence of women and minorities from literary histories tells us more about scholars' biases than it does about history itself.

As for affirmative action in hiring or admissions, D'Souza, in another panel a few months later, one I will comment on toward the end of this chapter, put the Right's position succinctly: "the problem is that universities talk about equal opportunity but behind closed doors they practice racial preference—both in student admissions and in faculty hiring." In fact universities have every right to decide that it is part of their social mission to compensate for the *current* deplorable state of inner-city social life and education generally and admit black students to special programs that can increase the number that receive college educations. It is less a matter of answering for past inequities than of facing America's current need to move more blacks into the middle class. Affirmative action in hiring is another matter. In 1963 a woman who had just received her Ph.D. from Ohio State was one of two finalists for a job in the English department at the University of Washington. The department head there called her unabashedly to bring her up to date: "The two of you were equally qualified, so of course we offered the job to the man." Two years later a young woman who had just received her Ph.D. from Yale approached her advisers to ask if they thought she might be able to get a job at the English department at the University of Illinois, where her husband had just been hired in another department. They all gave the same answer: Illinois doesn't hire women. Actually, Illinois occasionally did, but they didn't make a habit of it. That year the Illinois English department hired twelve people, all men. These stories happen to come from two of my colleagues, but such stories are legion; they represent in miniature the world affirmative action sought to change. In fact it was not until the 1970s that jobs were even publicly announced and advertized. The pattern now is that men and women compete equally. Given roughly comparable candidates, however, it is perfectly appropriate for departments to hire women or minorities when they are underrepresented. One reason is that it is important that students not receive all their instruction from white men. Some students benefit from professorial role models of their own sex or race. All students lose if they are led to believe that only white men are capable of being professors. Are standards sometimes lowered in hiring and promotion decisions? Yes. However, based on nearly thirty years' experience in colleges and universities—experience that includes reviewing hundreds of sets of promotion papers covering almost every department that exists, from Accounting to Zoology—I can say with assurance that even now, when departments make special cases, when they bring out the crying towel and lower their standards, *in the overwhelming majority of cases it will be on behalf of a white male.* That remains the best kept secret in all discussions of affirmative action.

In fact these panelists were not concerned with describing cultural conditions with any care. They were responding to targets of opportunity. Deconstruction, for example, has been scandalized by the revelations of the late Paul de Man's Nazi past. For many of us, of course, the key figure in deconstruction remains its founder Jacques Derrida, who happens to be a Jew, not any of deconstruction's American interpreters, neither de Man nor anyone else. No matter. The media took up the de Man issue with a frenzy. Academics responded ineffectively, certainly not in ways that would work outside the university, and the battle was lost. As damaged goods, deconstruction now serves as a conveniently vulnerable figure for the whole range of critical positions, for all those "Marxists, feminists, and people who read Marvel comics instead of books," to quote Bennett again. Similarly, references to affirmative action quotas, with their air of standard-free militancy, provide a way of scandalizing every effort to study and teach a broader range of literary texts. Indeed, one of the marvels of the Right's attack is their success in some quarters at linking efforts to expand the canon of American and British literature with wholesale condemnations of the heritage of the West. Just who are these forgotten American and British women and minority writers if they are not part of the Western tradition? Intruders from outer space? The work being done to expand the canon is partly an effort to expand our memory of and knowledge about the cultural history of the West.

To charge these efforts to broaden and deepen our knowledge, say, of American literary history with being anti-Western is to assert that only the traditional white male canon is truly of the West. That would amount to a more explicit racism and sexism than even Bennett would be willing to exhibit. In any case there is no lack of white males excluded from the canon because they wrote on unacceptable subjects, so an expanded canon will increase their numbers as well. Solidified by white male critics during a period of political repression, the postwar canon excludes much literature that mounts an uncompromising critique of American culture and most work by women and minorities. Some of this work fails to meet the narrow aesthetic criteria set by these academic servants of the dominant political culture; other work—significantly—does meet those aesthetic standards but gets excluded because it treats unacceptable topics in unacceptable ways. Thus poems that urge racial harmony are fine, but poems that indict the culture as deeply racist tend not to enter the canon; that pattern is certainly confirmed by the poetry anthologies I criticize in the previous chapter and in chapter 2.

Unless we recover such work we cannot pretend to have an adequate knowledge of our cultural heritage. That is perhaps the first rebuttal to make to the New Right, since it is an argument that changes the context of the debate. For decades literary history has been both written and taught by telling flattering stories about the very tiny percentage of literary texts canonized after the Second World War. In many periods literary history has thus encompassed no general knowledge about what was being written, read, and debated. Whatever else one can call this enterprise—stories about our favorite poems and novels from the past—one cannot call it history. At the very least, literary history must try to account for the general conditions of literary production and reception in a given period of time. To study or to teach literary history thus requires us to go well beyond the selective memory embodied in the canon. Even though secure knowledge about literary history is impossible, as I argue in chapter 3, the astonishingly narrow modern poetry canon that reigned for decades barred us even from glimpsing literary history's unstable diversity.

But the Right is exercised not only over what texts are studied and taught but also over the intent behind their selection and in the attitudes displayed in changing the curriculum. All the panelists claimed support for a limited "multiculturalism" that remained positive about the existing canon but slightly expanded its reach. Cheney warned that there was both a "right" and a "wrong" way to expand the curriculum. Multiculturalism must be "generous in its spirit." What they all rejected was expanding the canon in the context of an attack on the masterpieces of the West or on the moral failures of American history. On one level their first concern can be met. There is no reason why a college or university has to attack Plato or Shakespeare in order to offer minority and third world literatures in its curriculum. One of the things the Right has done is to conflate interested attacks by small groups or individuals with far more neutral institutional changes. Thus a college that adds a course on Chicano literature can be accused of knuckling under to a few students who, in the heat of the moment, say they want to do away with all dead white males. In 1994 a cheerfully racist English department faculty member in New Haven told Yale's alumni magazine that it was time to teach the great works of the canon rather than "some novel that some Chicano wrote yesterday." This despite the fact that enrollments in traditional courses at Yale and elsewhere remain high.

The conflation of individual positions with institutional change is clearly dishonest, but the issues are not so simple for individual teachers and researchers. The canon is sustained and promulgated by an interpretive tradition that is deeply conservative and sometimes sexist and racist as well. For many people that interpretive tradition is part of the problem and needs to be acknowledged and resisted. The texts of the canon, in other words, have a history of sexist and racist use. They need critical reinterpretation if they are to serve other purposes. So a cheerful multiculturalism that ignores this history—which is what the Right seems to want—is not really intellectually sustainable. What Cheney proposes—the "happy family" multiculturalism I described in chapter 2—may be appropriate for an elementary school but hardly for a college. Rather than deal with the intellectual challenges appropriate to postsecondary education, however, the Right makes another strategic conflation—confusing efforts to reinterpret texts with efforts to *remove* them from the curriculum. It seems fair to say that the chair of NEH has no business policing *interpretations.* She can only get away with that by pretending to address the false issue of whether or not texts are taught.

D'Souza takes a somewhat cruder approach, arguing that you cannot simply add to the curriculum. "Students can read a limited and defined number of texts," he would claim in September, "if you add new works in, you've got to subtract something from the existing list, so it is a fantasy to assert that no choices have to be made, that if someone comes in, no one gets out." D'Souza has built his whole career on misleading simplifications that will sound persuasive to a popular audience. What is disturbing about him is that he knows better. Perhaps he has decided that his position is so just that any means are warranted in winning popular consent for it. Or perhaps he is not a very honorable fellow. In any case, there are at least two kinds of curricular issues being conflated here. In a departmental curriculum there is plenty of room for additions because there is substantial duplication. An English major may read Conrad's *Heart of Darkness* in an introduction to literary study course, read it again in a course on the short story, and read it yet again in a survey of modern literature. There's nothing wrong with that, but it is hard to see how Western civilization will be brought to its knees by substituting a work by a black writer on one of those occasions. If all that is at stake is a single course, then certainly only so many pages can be read. But no single survey of Western thought or survey of American literature can be complete or representative in any case; all it can be is a very partial sample. Treating a single course as the battleground for the future of civilization, as the Right has been doing, is pure demagoguery.

There is, to be sure, good reason to debate as well what a universally required core curriculum might be. Despite Bennett's and D'Souza's allegations to the contrary, many humanities students and faculty—including the campus radicals that the Right excoriates—could easily agree in principle on an expanded core curriculum that included both the traditional canon and its alternatives. At large universities the resistance to this obvious compromise is unlikely to come from campus radicals. It is likely instead to come from professional schools—Engineering, Commerce—who rightly say that their students can get jobs without studying literature, art, or philosophy. At Illinois one prominent engineer was fond of repeating his boast that he didn't see why a university needed a philosophy department in the first place. Of course the Right is not about to dwell on that reality because that would mean criticizing the ideology of American business.

People committed to the traditional canon could, however, make more productive contributions to these debates. If NEH had been willing, for example, to play a more appropriate role of negotiating between positions, it could have helped us realize that, as students and faculty begin to discover what has been excluded from their education—and excluded thereby from having an active cultural life in the present—by the narrow canon of major works, their first reactions include not only considerable excitement at the variety of texts now available to them but also a certain shock and anger at decades of effective cultural repression. That anger has been visible in the well-publicized struggles at places like Stanford, and it has simultaneously threatened the Right and given them another target of opportunity. Yet it seems unlikely that these struggles over the curriculum could have occurred without such anger, for some anger at an education that has been substantially distorted is more than warranted. Nonetheless, one finds few faculty members arguing that the traditional canon should be entirely abandoned. It too is part of our cultural history. It needs to be reread, preserved, and understood—affirmed and challenged as people see fit—both as part of a selective tradition and as part of a much wider cultural field. To seek to block any of these alternatives—as NEH did during Republican administrations and as Lynne Cheney's and Jerry Martin's National Alumni Forum now seeks to do—is to mount a basic attack on academic freedom.

At least for a time, however, all texts will be partly charged with a sense of their status in these debates, with a sense of their recent history of privilege or marginalization. That history may not be a permanent part of the baggage these texts carry with them, but it is part of the baggage they bear now. It is better to deal with that history openly (and recognize its potentially transitory character) than resent it (as the Right does) or pretend it is an eternal feature of a text's identity (as the Left tends to do). At the moment, then, we read an expanded canon either in the aftermath or the very midst of these struggles for broader cultural representation. Neither the expanded canon nor the expanded curriculum will necessarily emphasize the signs of that struggle in the future. Yet successive generations do need to learn a lesson from these debates: they too should pose for themselves those basic questions about what they are reading and why they are reading it; they too should interrogate the social meaning of the curriculum they adopt.

For some on the far Right this very self-consciousness about research and about the curriculum is unacceptable. They want faculty and students to display an unqualified patriotism and an unreflective enthusiasm about the dominant traditions in Western culture. That does not mean—as some have assumed—that the Right imagines the celebratory discourses of research and pedagogy will remain unchanged, repeated like ritual incantations down through succeeding generations. For those on the Right who realize that history changes, it is clear that scholarship and teaching must adapt as well. The task for a properly docile university is not, therefore, to say the same words decade after decade but rather to adapt its message to changing circumstances, to find the new words necessary to rationalize power and privilege in changing times. This is especially important because the young are susceptible to idealistic ferment. It is the university's job to do the work of continuing reinterpretation, the work of intricate rearticulation of aspiration and materiality, that makes it possible to idealize the dominant traditions of the West.

Of all the speakers at the American Enterprise Institute it was Bennett who was most unyielding in applying these unstated aims to his critiques of university life. With his tendency to collapse differences and generalize on the basis of scattered anecdotes, his mask of avuncular intimidation did little to hide the fact that he is a genuine demagogue. Among his more frightening arguments was his assertion that black students should encounter nothing in their education that reminds them of their history of oppression and discrimination in America. The argument is supported by anecdotes of colleges, say, encouraging minority students to choose socially conscious majors rather than supposedly race-neutral areas like the hard sciences. Most of us, I think, would object to that sort of coercive advising. But Bennett expands on stories like this to argue that any curricular foregrounding of a history of slavery and racism inevitably humiliates minorities. In putting together a syllabus, then, we presumably must select poems about racial harmony and exclude the many powerful poems about lynchings in the South. All this Bennett couches in arguments about the need to fully abandon discriminatory practices and adopt a race-neutral form of education. In Bennett's model we abandon any reflection on how historical injustice bears on contemporary affairs.

This was the one place, however, where the panel's unanimity broke down for a moment. Bennett opened his presentation by remarking how balanced the panel was—a woman, a minority member, and a white male. He conceded that the white male was regrettably not dead, but reminded the audience that time would eventually take care of that. But the panel's gender and racial diversity— D'Souza came to the United States as an exchange student from India—also led to the one point of difference. It was quickly papered over, derailing the proceedings only for a minute or two, but it revealed a contradiction that may not open much chance for dialogue but does give us a place for productive counterarguments.

What happened was that Cheney felt it necessary to say that she had found it immensely helpful and liberating to read women writers while she was in college:

> I don't know if there's a difference here or not. At the same time that ideas do not have color or gender, let me suggest that experiences do. And I can remember as a graduate student coming across for the first time some writings of nineteenth-century women that I'd never heard of before who had remarkable things to say to me because their life as a woman had parallels to my own experience. A writer who had a life as

a man did not speak to me in quite the same way. It was a remarkable experience. It opened an avenue of intellectual exploration that I continue to pursue. In the same way I can well imagine that a person of color would feel the same kind of epiphany on first coming across— I've heard Skip Gates, Henry Louis Gates, talk about reading James Baldwin for the first time. You know here is a realm of experience that you hadn't heard reported on before. That is a wonderful thing. There is a great difference, though, between opening up the world so that people can explore all of these pathways and prescribing reading lists by quota. I do want to get the notion in here that, while ideas have no color or gender, experiences sometimes do, and I think this is a useful educational tool for all of us to use.

Ideas may have no gender or color, she emphasized twice, echoing statements by Bennett and D'Souza, but experience sometimes does. Bennett was speechless, having just declared that "when people are told that they must focus on that part of themselves which has to do with their ancestry, the color of their skin, they are of course insulted." But D'Souza hastened to add an observation that fractured the proceedings somewhat further:

> I think it was W. E. B. Du Bois who said that his experience as a writer was always to view the American experience through two different sets of eyes. He viewed it on the one hand as an American and, on the other hand, as a black American. And that these two perspectives are not the same. And it's certainly true that the experience of blacks in this country is distinctive. Many times they are lumped together with other immigrants. And of course they were not immigrants. They were brought here in chains. And so it is certainly the case that universities should encourage intelligent young black students to face these questions. To what degree is it possible to be patriotic or to embrace uninhibitedly the declaration or the constitution? But the problem is that they don't do that; universities don't engage on that kind of intellectual voyage, which I think would provide a true liberation.

Whether Cheney or D'Souza realized it or not, they had given away the game, opening the way to a curriculum self-conscious about race and gender and about the cultural and historical politics of knowledge. What kind of "liberation," one wonders, would D'Souza consider warranted by such an intellectual voyage? Does he realize that this "voyage" metaphor is itself the mirror image of the middle passage? It may be that both Cheney and D'Souza felt a moment of inner panic. Hence Cheney's irrelevant reference to quotas in reading lists and D'Souza's false assertion that universities don't encourage this sort of speculation. What Cheney's anecdote acknowledged, whether she realized it or not, is that there is a sound basis for something like an affirmative action curriculum, that one reason to add women and minority writers to the canon is that we have women and minority students who can use these works to confirm and articulate the validity and social basis of their own experience and as an especially relevant point of entrance to a still larger field of study. The same argument, indeed, would apply to the need to hire female and minority faculty members, who presumably could share some of their distinctive experiences with students. Since then D'Souza's position has hardened, as evidenced by his astonishingly reactionary *The End of Racism* (1995), but here he acknowledged that a history of oppression still has bearing on blacks' identities and on what the Right now falsely claims to be an equal opportunity society. Contrary to the argument implicit in Bennett's heavy-handed erasure of history, we are partly what our national history has made us be. One reason to open the canon is to recover the full textual evidence of that history. The canon we have now often succeeds in hiding it from view.

Although these three speakers wanted to include every critique of the canon under the umbrella of political correctness, there are many of us engaged in canon revision who have no interest in demands for political correctness from either the Right or the Left. I myself have no interest in joining the apoplectic cries to remove all dead white males from the curriculum. For one thing, there are too many dead white males on the Left now excluded from the curriculum because their politics were unacceptable. Part of my own project, as I explain in detail in the previous chapter and in chapter 8, is to recover and teach their work. But the most entrenched canonical works also continue to be read in ways that give them new and unexpected life. It is not the business of universities to curtail that rereading.

Does this mean that we have nothing to learn from critics of campus research and teaching? Quite the contrary. Bennett, Cheney, and D'Souza were all capable at moments of issuing challenges of real value, though they often used them to implicate people in positions they do not necessarily hold. At one point Bennett mentioned that there now exist in universities not only separate lunch tables for black and white students but also separate seating sections in football stadiums and libraries. "What's next?" he asked, "Wash rooms? Drinking Fountains?" The demagogic element in the question was his willingness to let audience members think universities had segregated these facilities, whereas these are instances of student self-segregation. That let him imply the problem could be solved by a bit of strong talk from university authorities, whereas the problem is embedded in (and partly inseparable from) race relations throughout the culture. Where Bennett *is* right, I believe, is in arguing that such practices are deeply troubling and in arguing that university faculty members and administrators should respond to these practices and encourage open debate about them. That will not guarantee ready solutions, but it will make the issue an appropriate ground for education. Where standards of political correctness stifle such debate they are doing universities no good. Interestingly enough, the expanded canon offers us considerable opportunity to encourage discussion of these matters. For in earlier periods both white and black authors were sometimes willing to take up issues of race in far more open and diverse ways than we are easily able to today. That is just one way that a recovered past can help us in the present.

But what is to help us in dealing with these attacks from the Right, attacks that are continuing in various forms in the late nineties? And why, finally, is the Right conducting them? It should be clear by now that silence from progressive college and university faculty will not suffice. Silence simply leaves the terrain of public common sense to the Right. And it is essential to realize that even wildly irresponsible and hyperbolic claims about the state of American campuses will seem plausible both to nonuniversity intellectuals and to the general public. If the Right is allowed to continue dominating media representations of campus politics, then we will eventually face a curtailment of academic freedom. That possibility is significantly enhanced now that the Supreme Court is well on its way to abandoning its role as a guarantor of civil rights and civil liberties while deploying notions of individual rights to undermine progressive social policy. Abortion is in this respect a pivotal issue in the effort to make some rights a matter of state-by-state debate and regulation. If academic freedom becomes substantially a matter of state law, with little practical grounding in national constitutional guarantees of free speech, its value will suffer everywhere, not just in those states most inclined to narrow its reach.

It is now widely recognized that the debates over political correctness have made cutting university budgets a great deal easier.[2] A delegitimated university is easier to defund. A delegitimated university is also easier for state governments to ignore when making basic policy decisions about higher education. Thus the California Board of Regents felt no need to consult the faculty when it decided in 1995 to end affirmative action admissions. The attacks on faculty political correctness strike at the heart of faculty members' social status by suggesting that we are incapable of independent thought or reason. Why would one consult political automatons when deciding whether to abolish tenure, end affirmative action, or shut down the philosophy department? The attacks on political correctness are thus nothing less than the leading edge of an effort to deny the faculty any powers of self-governance and any say over state higher education policy.

But the danger to campus life is no more important than the effects on the general culture. We tend too often in academia to mock our own potential for political impact; it thus seems hard to believe that an irrelevant and powerless institution like the university should be the focus of so much antagonistic energy. Yet we forget that universities are, if nothing else, a continuing source of arguments that are a genuine inconvenience to the far Right in its project of constructing a homogenous, dissent-free public culture. That role is even more important now that newspapers across the country are cutting back on their investment in serious investigative reporting. The Right realizes moreover, even if the Left does not, that at least in an extended crisis universities could again be sources of substantial dissent. As global power is realigned, opportunities for the exercise of American authority will arise. Not all these opportunities can be fulfilled in four-day wars. On the other hand, an increasingly impoverished and disenfranchised underclass in our own country provides other bases for discontent. These are just a few of the reasons why some on the Right want to take this opportunity to discredit every progressive impulse on campus.

No one strategy will suffice in this struggle. For this is not exclusively a debate by way of reasoned argument in classic academic fashion. It is a political struggle in which the Right has no intention of playing fair. While it is necessary to point out the inaccuracies and distortions in work like Roger Kimball's *Tenured Radicals* and D'Souza's *Illiberal Education*—the best efforts at that to date being Michael Bérubé's fine essay in the *Village Voice* and John Wilson's *The Myth of Political Correctness*—that kind of honorable counterargument will not suffice.[3] Careful refutations can, once placed on the public record, help prevent some people from being persuaded by the Right's lies. But it would be naive to imagine that people like Bennett and Cheney would be troubled by having inaccurate claims exposed. They will simply continue to lie as long as they feel their claims are getting more coverage. Certainly the Right feels free to repeat discredited stories in new arenas; when particular arguments or examples are effectively countered in a given discussion, they simply shift ground. These are not, therefore, people to engage in a dialogue with the hope of changing their minds. Public dialogue is only useful if it has the potential to reach other people.

One of the more notable efforts at an exchange between the Right and the Left on these issues was a two-hour "Firing Line Special Debate" held at the University of South Carolina and broadcast on many Public Television stations on 7 September 1991.[4] The topic of the debate was "Resolved: Freedom of

Thought is in Danger on American Campuses." Participants included William Buckley, Glenn Loury, Dinesh D'Souza, and John Silber on one side and Leon Botstein, Stanley Fish, Catharine Stimpson, and Ronald Walters on the other. The format, which restricted statements to ninety seconds, confirmed again that television's idea of in-depth coverage is to give us a full two hours of sound bites.

Neither side was altogether served well by the arrangements or the participants. Buckley, once someone to be reckoned with, a saboteur in the service of the far Right, has been effectively repositioned by history as a representative of the establishment. He is left with his cat's grin without his wit. Fish, often articulate, is not entirely dependable on these issues; with little previous interest in politics, he has, in effect, in this context been brought to prominence by social and political forces he does not understand. As a result, he meekly defends every politically correct position whether or not he believes in it. Thus he supports campus restrictions on speech because he thinks that is his duty, instead of demonstrating that the Left is by no means in agreement on such practices. Like many people engaged in canon revision, for example, I do *not*, as I show in the next chapter, support campus restrictions on speech. In this program Fish was also challenged to defend the new politically correct notion that blacks cannot be racist because they are oppressed. Instead of stating simply that there are different kinds of racism, that racism is not a uniform existential condition that one does or does not occupy—and that the racism of those in power is indeed different from the racism of the disempowered—Fish did his best to urge us to call the former racism and the latter prejudice. The one person who was impressive was Leon Botstein, president of Bard College, who refused all caricatured positions, mapping out his own thoughtful arguments on all issues, though Botstein has since been drawn increasingly toward the corporate model of ruthless governance at his own institution. Silber spent his time complaining about efforts to encourage nonsexist usage and assailing those who did not accept that it was no problem to transcend the perspectives of race and gender.[5] Buckley, increasingly muddled, treated us to the news that "McCarthyism is largely a historical fiction."

The program did not suggest that a real exchange of views on these matters has much future, at least for those whose careers or public image is tied up in the debate. It did, however, demonstrate that the stark presentation of the opposing sides is both powerful and risky, the risk being enhanced when the Left represents itself as being far more uniform than it actually is. The Right seems determined to try to present a unified front, which is exactly what the Left should not do, both because it isn't true and because it confirms the very charges of political correctness being leveled at us. Unlike the Right, moreover, the Left has no consensus about a common general cultural program in which this struggle plays a part. That is one of the reasons why efforts to sustain progressive counter-National Association of Scholars groups have partly failed. But the Left has no chance of winning this debate unless it at least positions its actions within a wider cultural context.

The current attack on universities is part of a struggle for power and influence in American culture. That partly explains why the Right amplified a few rather trivial incidents over political correctness into a national trend. (The real pressures on political expression are scattered throughout American culture—in religious institutions, in industry, and in numerous social and political groups on both the Left and the Right, including some on campus—and have no monolithic university incarnation.) The struggle for power and influence in American culture proceeds, like all hegemonic conflicts, by way of articulating diverse cultural forces, images, and discourses into new configurations that constitute possible ways of understanding our culture as a whole. Merely taking issue with local claims can have only limited use; we must also take on the larger cultural vision that is at stake when dealing with local issues. One of the things the program at the American Enterprise Institute suggested, however, is that the contradictions and competing interests in the Right's own high-profile constituency are one place to start. We need to seize opportunities to work on those contradictions whenever they arise, to expose the differences underlying the Right's surface unity. Beginning with the Reagan administration, the Right began to assemble its own multicultural, multiracial front. The April 1991 panel was another instance of that effort. But that sort of project covers over real differences and real competing interests. Now that the Right has taken that risk, we need to exploit it. Every such opportunity comes as a result of the necessarily continuing project of rearticulation by which political interests try to win popular consent. Every such missed opportunity signals more ground lost to the Right.

One opportunity has arisen as a result of the growth in campus-based conservative hate magazines on campuses across the country. Supported by a national network that supplies boilerplate conservative rhetoric and stories to be reprinted, as well as the names of "National Advisory Board" members like D'Souza and Pat Buchanan, these magazines are increasingly following the lead of the granddaddy of all such publications, the *Dartmouth Review*. Following that lead means adopting sexism, racism, and homophobia as standard positions. Like the current conservative effort in other cultural domains, it also means trying to get the last mileage out of the red baiting tradition. What is most troubling for many campuses, however, is the first local experience of the

Dartmouth Review's ruthless ad hominem attacks. Academics are far more accustomed to attacking positions than attacking people. The damage to the campus climate that can be done by hyperbolic, distorted attacks on individuals is difficult to overstate. Some campuses may find it necessary to mount counterefforts by detailing accurately the racist and sexist histories of those putting out such magazines. In other words, in order to move the debate back to issues, rather than individuals, it may be necessary to make individuals pay a price for their invective.

The genuine opportunity such magazines present, however, is the opportunity to expose the absurdity of national claims about political correctness and about attacks on Western culture. Based on distorted reports about a few scattered incidents on a few campuses, the Right has succeeded in creating a national moral panic that threatens to undermine progressive scholarship and teaching everywhere. When such magazines look for local evidence, however, it usually is not there and thus has to be blatantly manufactured. Even people within the university find it easy to believe there is a problem on other campuses. So the absurdity of local claims has real educational value when we draw attention to it.

At my own university, the University of Illinois, a somewhat clumsy local effort, *The Orange and Blue Observer,* published its inaugural issue in August of 1991. One of the cover headlines reads "Banned from Campus?" and prints pictures of John Locke and William Shakespeare, among others. On an inside page, I am featured as one of three faculty members on the "loony left," a phrase put in circulation by Margaret Thatcher:

> An instructor of modern poetry and poetry criticism, Professor Nelson epitomizes the "Tenured Radical." To Prof. Nelson, virtually no poetry of any worth exists before 1950 or after 1972. His mission as an instructor at the University is to forever annihilate the traditional literary canon (i.e., that body of dead, white European male authors such as Shakespeare, Milton, Keats, and Shelley who, solely because of racism and sexism, have regrettably emerged as "great").

There didn't seem to be much point in trying to tell these folks that I have been focusing for some years on poetry *before* 1950, let alone show them any of my relevant publications on canonical poets, since such defenders of the West are not known to be great readers, so instead I wrote a piece for the main campus newspaper pointing out that it wouldn't be easy to find an English professor here or anywhere else on the planet who wanted to ban Shakespeare.

On that point, it may be worth publishing a public conversation one of my colleagues had with a young woman recruit at the *Observer*'s booth on campus:

> *He:* It would be terrible if anyone was trying to ban Shakespeare.
> Who's trying to ban Shakespeare?
> *She:* Lots of people.
> *He:* Is there anyone here trying to ban Shakespeare?
> *She:* Oh, yeah. Lots of people.
> *He:* Who?
> *She:* Lots of English professors.
> *He:* Who?
> *She:* Well, Professor Cary Nelson hasn't had anything nice to say
> about Shakespeare.

The point, of course, is not only that a concern for accurate reporting is not exactly a hallmark of the Right, but also that credible local evidence supporting the moral panic about campus values is not easy to find. Nor is it as easy to reveal the comic implausibility of the Right's claims at the national level. John Wilson's definitive book *The Myth of Political Correctness* (1995), however, successfully discredits the stories the Right has publicized to date.

But new panics continue to be produced. My own entirely local Shakespeare story was supplemented by a brief media frenzy in the winter of 1995–96 when Cheney's National Alumni Forum managed to produce a Washington-based sensation over Georgetown University's English department deciding to drop its Shakespeare requirement. What the department actually had was a Shakespeare, Chaucer, or Milton requirement; it never needed a specific Shakespeare requirement because all its literature majors took Shakespeare anyway. So it dropped the requirement as irrelevant, with the expectation it could offer more Shakespeare courses that way. But when Cheney's new organization contacted the Washington media with this travesty, they lapped it up nonetheless.

The effort to demonize the project of opening up the canon, the only project with a chance of giving us the more diverse common culture we now need, is now—in the wake of the fall of communism across Eastern Europe and in the Soviet Union—being articulated to a more ambitious effort to discredit the whole American Left. What the Right is unable to recognize is that the common culture of a uniformly idealized American history and a narrow canon of idealized white male authors cannot survive the impact of the new social movements and new immigration of the past decades. The product of the Right's campaign can only be an America of antagonistic ethnic and racial groups looking for advantages over one another. As a result, the concept of democracy will gradually lose its progressive connotations and the United States will be an increasingly less admirable place to live. We cannot let that happen.

7

HATE SPEECH
AND POLITICAL CORRECTNESS

In a famous 1925 poem called "Incident," Countee Cullen described in only two stanzas something of the power that hate speech can have over those who are its victims:

> Now I was eight and very small,
> And he was no whit bigger,
> And so I smiled, but he poked out
> His tongue, and called me "Nigger."
>
> I saw the whole of Baltimore
> From May until December;

> Of all the things that happened there
> That's all that I remember.

It's not merely that the speaker here is a child, of course, but that he is attacked in a moment when he is offering friendship and thus likely to be especially vulnerable. He spent a full six months in the city, but that is the only event he recalls.

Hate speech has the power to effect lasting wounds; it can also channel and symbolize the much more pervasive and sometimes less easily isolatable structural forms of discrimination. And in some environments it may be especially potent. Hearing a racial epithet on Times Square in New York may not necessarily be especially wounding; one is after all more likely to be psychologically on guard in that setting. Hearing a racial epithet in a college dormitory might be another matter.

For many people a college campus is a place to insist on more humane and egalitarian behavior than one might expect in Bensonhurst. We cannot legislate a perfect world, we might argue, but we can regulate destructive and damaging speech in some specific social settings, and a college campus may be one such setting. Enforcing hate speech ordinances consistently in a large city might be impossible; enforcing them with some consistency on a college campus might be entirely possible. Changing the relatively self-contained campus setting could make a significant difference in the lives of the people who work there.

For these and other reasons a number of campuses in the 1990s have either passed or tried to pass regulations prohibiting hate speech and sanctioning penalties when it occurs.[1] Many such regulations will be struck down by the courts, but some campuses will work to draft regulations more narrowly as a result.[2] Thus we are likely to continue to see efforts to test the constitutionality of these ordinances in the courts.

I have opened my essay in this way because I want to argue the reverse case— that efforts to regulate hate speech are ultimately more dangerous than their benefits warrant—but I do not want to minimize the destructive effects hate speech can have. My position is obviously an awkward and impossible one where explicitly racist or sexist hate speech is at issue. A white male is not the most strategic spokesperson for First Amendment rights in this context. But racist hate speech in particular is the example we all must confront because it is so elaborately articulated to other forms of racism in America. And its history in our culture is so long and so deeply constitutive of our national identity. I want to lay out some of the problems with hate speech regulations, then, drawing on arguments that a number of other people have made in the last few years.

Perhaps the first point to make about hate speech is to clear the air about some activities that are already either fully or partially prohibited under other laws, laws, moreover, where the penalties are generally more severe than those in hate speech regulations. It may be useful to work with some familiar examples:

1. A student enters another student's college room in his or her absence and scrawls racist epithets across the walls. This act can involve breaking and entering and vandalism. It is covered by existing laws and regulations. Some instances might be prosecutable, and a college might well want to expel a student for this sort of behavior. We do not need to create hate speech regulations to punish perpetrators.
2. A group of white male fraternity members follows a black woman across campus at night making remarks that suggest a threat of physical or sexual assault. Once again, this kind of intimidation cannot be tolerated. Threats of bodily harm are not forms of protected speech. But we do not need new regulations to punish such acts.
3. A town or campus hate group burns a cross on the lawn of a black fraternity. Words are not involved, but the act is indeed communicative and certainly constitutes symbolic speech. Once again, existing laws against trespass or attempted arson may provide a sufficient basis for punishment.

Now I am not a lawyer and, even if I were, I doubt if I could claim expertise in state and municipal law across all the states in the country. So I am not offering to decide whether any given act is legal in a given locality. My point is rather that many serious actions that *include* hate speech are already sufficiently—and *narrowly*—regulated by existing law. Moreover, racist, sexist, or homophobic components to violations of existing law can justify both vigorous prosecution of such offenses and increased severity of sentencing for those found guilty. Vandalism at a church or synagogue can be punished more severely than vandalism at a bowling alley. The argument advanced by some—including some lawyers—that we are in danger from acts such as those I just described unless hate speech is regulated is often inaccurate.

It is certainly possible that the specificity of hate speech regulations gives them a more focused deterrence value. On the other hand, a stiff penalty for attempted arson for a cross burner has obvious deterrence potential as well. The one benefit one does lose is the educational benefit gained from debating hate speech ordinances or regulations. Awareness of the problem increases significantly when the issue is given wide discussion. Carefully chosen prosecutions under existing law could supply some—but certainly not all—of the same educational effect.

On the other hand, existing law will not prevent or punish the incident Countee Cullen describes, even if the perpetrator is older than eight. Cullen, of course, partly deals with it himself—by writing and publishing the poem. He thus employs the long-standing civil libertarian remedy for bad speech—more speech. Colleges are obviously uniquely empowered to adopt Cullen's remedy, not only by offering alternative speech but also by calling for more speech from racists on campus. As Leon Botstein argued recently, colleges have something to gain by urging people to express such views and then to debate them vigorously.[3]

That would have been my solution to the incident at Brown University in 1990—when a loutish, drunken student yelled racist and homophobic epithets at 2 A.M. I would not, however, insist on handling such students gently. If this clown persisted, I would not give him a moment's peace. I would encourage people to discuss and criticize his behavior in every class he attended. At the cafeteria, on the quad, I would encourage people to come up to him and let him know what effect he was having on people. Though I would not expel him for that one incident alone, neither did Brown; he was already on probation for earlier behavior. On the other hand, I certainly would not pretend, as Brown did, that he was expelled for conduct rather than speech, a distinction that Nan Hunter has shown to be impossible to maintain.[4]

There is some real value in involving people in more diverse and widespread efforts to challenge and eliminate hate speech. Adopting a regulation as a sufficient solution may seem satisfying, but it may also block recognition of how pervasive racism is in the culture. Other forms of discrimination require legal remedies. Hate speech may be more persuasively curtailed by more varied forms of social pressure. Once again, of course, there is a counterargument that such regulations do not claim to alter people's attitudes; they merely seek to alter behavior and eliminate its destructive effects. Even the effort to curtail these specific behaviors, however, might benefit from broad, continuing, and complex community involvement. Except for a long-term reporting and policing function, the only broad community involvement in hate speech ordinances comes in the initial period when the ordinance is being debated.

Yet the prospect of a campus environment free of racist speech is immensely appealing. Those who argue against hate speech regulations need to acknowledge that such regulations might well accomplish considerable good. The possibility that a strong university or municipal policy on hate speech could substantially reduce occurrences of hate speech in a town or on a campus offers a powerful inducement to support such policies. I share that desire and thus make a case against formal regulation only with difficulty.

In order to legislate all instances of the behavior Cullen describes—and to cover all such aggressions against women and minorities and various religious and ethnic groups and people of differing sexual orientations—it is necessary to write broad, vague regulations that make substantial inroads against our constitutional guarantees of free speech. In the end, as in the broad antipornography legislation championed by Catharine MacKinnon and others,[5] the evidence often becomes the effects testified to by victims of hate speech. It is not impossible that someone could claim to be deeply hurt by hearing me read Cullen's poem. And thus the text of a black poet speaking out against racism could be silenced as well. Again, I am not denying that I would rather have a campus free of racist epithets. I would. But I am not willing to stifle freedom of speech to achieve that end.

The effort to regulate hate speech has also helped support a related movement to regulate and, when advocates deem appropriate, penalize much less overtly offensive speech in the classroom. Here the challenge is to identify what speech constitutes a "hostile environment" detrimental to students' ability to learn. The American Association of University Professors recognizes that more, rather than less, freedom may be required in a classroom if its intellectual mission is to be realized—sometimes students need to be scandalized and offended, to be exposed to speech that is outrageous—but people concerned about students' feelings are sometimes inclined to argue the reverse, that a class is a captive audience that requires special protection. Particularly chilling is the tendency of some on campus, heavily influenced by MacKinnon, to consider the testimony of any student who feels offended to be decisive. Thus even if no one else in the class found it a hostile environment the student who did is definitive; that student's experience needs to be honored, even to the extent of punishing the offending faculty member. The result can be a grotesque mix of witch-hunt and kangaroo court that promotes an atmosphere of fear on campus and denies pedagogy its critical edge. All these restrictive practices, moreover, serve not only to undermine intellectual challenges on campus but also to train students to be intolerant of others' speech after they graduate.

Outside the classroom, on the other hand, it is clear that political life and public debate require some expressions of anger and perhaps something like hate. When I was part of a small group of college students thirty years ago who interrupted a Lyndon Johnson speech by chanting "LBJ LBJ, how many kids did you kill today?" I think I was partly engaged in hate speech. If I call David Duke racist and Pat Buchanan homophobic and Dan Quayle dumb as a brick I may, I suppose, hurt their feelings. Some audiences would take some versions of these remarks as fighting words. But I want the freedom to speak them anyway.

I use these examples because many Americans are likely to assume the freedom to criticize public figures could never be imperiled. But those are freedoms we are always in danger of losing. Let us not forget that people largely lost those freedoms in the decade and a half that followed the Second World War. That was a period when subversive public speech—like support for civil rights or support for democratic governments—was often punished by termination of employment. And criticism of public figures on those grounds was considered actionable in loyalty boards throughout the country.

In a country with little sense of history and even less sense of how current actions may impact our future, it is very easy to take advantage of immediate political opportunities and put hate speech regulations in place in those munici-palities or college campuses where sentiment seems to favor them. It is also tempting for victims of oppression to employ identity politics to demonize advocates of free speech and stifle debate on such issues. That could easily have happened at the University of Illinois conference where I presented an earlier version of this essay. I was, as it happened, the only speaker who spoke out against hate speech regulation; a number of the other speakers supported such regulations either in their formal papers or in comments during discussion. But everyone was cordial, and there was no effort to block debate. I agreed to speak in part in order to empower and create a credible space for audience members who reject both racism and speech regulation. I was not happy to be the only speaker taking that position, but I was not terrified either; at least for faculty members, there seems to me to be no excuse other than excessive personal cowardice to claim it is impossible to speak out against hate speech regulation at events dominated by Left-oriented audiences. Some students and faculty none-theless confided to me afterwards that they were still unwilling to speak publicly against hate speech regulations at a Left conference on race in America. That suggests that psychological restraints against taking politically incorrect positions are strong enough that we need to work harder at encouraging debate on difficult issues like this. At the very least one may point out that an atmosphere of political correctness that demonizes those on the Left who support free speech heralds the very dangers inherent in the future cultural work these regulations may do. In punishing racist speech in Minneapolis or Madison we give the radical Right the tools they can and will use to punish progressive speech everywhere else. Can and will. I emphasize that this is hardly a matter of speculation. For many of us, the Federal judiciary can now be counted on to suppress civil liberties for the rest of our lives. The press for years has been successfully terrorized and manipulated by the Right. If some of us on the Left now collaborate in the destruction of our basic and vulnerable freedoms we will pay a price in the end more terrible than the speaker does in Cullen's poem.

And we will end with a culture that continues to be deeply and institutionally racist. We will have accomplished nothing but our own destruction.

Why, in the light of this terrible risk, was a coalition of civil rights groups and unions—from the NAACP to the Anti-Defamation League of B'nai B'rith—willing to support a law so sweeping in its dangers as St. Paul City Ordinance 292.02, which criminalized any public speech or symbolism "which one knows or has reasonable grounds to know arouses anger, alarm, or resentment in others on the basis of race, color, creed, religion, or gender"? This wording on its own would have made a powerful repressive weapon available to reactionary forces. If it had been judged constitutional, it would have given license to restrictions on speech offensive to any group on any grounds. The only test would then have been the test of a group's political power. If you could get such a law passed, it would then have a good chance to be constitutional. Can it be that civil rights groups were so benighted as to be unaware that they are hardly the ones likely to be most able to employ legal weapons against speech in the decade to come? Unfortunately, some may be deluded about their relative influence in American culture. Others may have been assuming they would lose the Minnesota case and other similar cases and thus assuming the real function of such debates is educational. It is more likely, moreover, that many progressive groups, feeling cut out of the action for more than a decade of Reagan–Bush power, simply found it irresistible to go for this opportunity when they saw it. It is one of the few places where some seeming progress could be made by concentrating on local legislation. My argument is that hate speech regulation is exactly that—*seeming progress*—that will be turned against us and set the progressive agenda back decades. I urge people to think seriously about the past and the future and about the overall price that will be paid if future laws of this sort are found constitutional. On 22 June 1992, the Supreme Court found the Minnesota law unconstitutional.[6] But the issue is not likely be permanently settled. Proponents of hate speech regulation will no doubt try again. Other laws will follow.

But what about the conduct of the Right in the debate over hate speech regulations? Here I would like to deploy a little strategic paranoia. One of the things that worries me about the debate over hate speech is that the Right is playing as if it wants to lose the first round. They are treating what should be a major political battle as if it were merely a cultural struggle for our hearts and minds. In other words, in a serious political struggle you do not use cultural spokespeople—a bombastic, hyperbolic figure like William Bennett and a half-senile patrician like William Buckley—as your shock troops. These people are fine if what you want to do is keep the Left exercised but not if you want to send a strong political message to the Supreme Court. I am not suggesting that everyone on the Right has thought this issue through thoroughly enough to realize that they have much to gain by losing a case like this, though some may have. We can, however, be certain that if some college or municipality wins a similar case in the future—using a more narrowly drawn regulation or law—the Right will realize how to turn its supposed failure into a major victory.

I am not, I should emphasize, against legislative and regulative remedies. Mandated affirmative action, for example, has been and continues to be immensely helpful and necessary in college hiring. I continue to be in favor of forced desegregation in schooling. I would like to see universal health care mandated by law, and I would like to see the tax laws redistribute income more fully. I am merely against restricting and punishing speech. The solution to bad speech remains more speech, including speech that is politically incorrect. Of course this is a "solution" without guarantees; it is merely a practice, a means of making acts of witness and sustaining continuing struggle. That, I believe, is the best we can do. There are many rights and opportunities we can guarantee by law, but we cannot guarantee either ideal speech situations or social environments free of painful and destructive utterances. The effort to suture social life so that it excludes all unacceptable speech will always be frustrated. If that frustration is met by increasingly severe or more widely applied penalties it risks ending in tyranny.

After I presented this essay at the University of Illinois one of the other speakers—also a white male—came up to me to say that he wished people on the Left who held views like mine would remain silent. When I asked why he made two arguments: first, that at the present time alliances with minority members who favor hate speech regulation are more important than putting our own views forward; second, that the First Amendment has never been honored by the country in any case. All I can do in response is to repeat the arguments I made in the original paper.

Alliances based on suppressing our beliefs have increasingly less chance of succeeding. With the country's steadily more diverse range of minority, ethnic, and gender interests and disenfranchisements already in considerable competition with one another, alliances need to be based on careful and difficult negotiations over our similarities and differences. Less honest alliances can only work in moments of desperate crisis. Trying to enforce a single politically correct position on hate speech regulation will only fragment a Left that might reach effective consensus on other pressing political issues. I take Richard Perry and Patricia Williams's essay "Freedom of Hate Speech" to be moving, therefore, in the wrong direction, since they assume that anyone interested in multiculturalism will certainly be in favor of hate speech regulation. I am thereby left with no subject position in their politics, since I do multicultural research but am against hate speech ordinances. Perry and Williams also thereby reinforce the Right's image of the Left as monolithic, another cultural contribution that is less than beneficial.

Being against hate speech regulations does not, however, mean ignoring the often dismal record of the First Amendment's enforcement. Neither under slavery nor in the hundred years after its abolition did African Americans feel they had meaningful freedom of speech. No one who stood publicly against the First World War in America is likely to have felt sheltered by the First Amendment. Neither the Japanese Americans sent to prison camps during the Second World War nor the thousands of people who lost their jobs during the McCarthy era felt protected by the Bill of Rights. And any claim that Native Americans have been consistent beneficiaries of constitutional rights would be laughable. One could go on, looking at speech restrictions in institutions like public schools and industries. The only question is whether it would have been significantly *worse* without the Bill of Rights and subsequent amendments. I believe it would have been much worse indeed.

Critical legal studies has helped remind us that the law is subject to continual reinterpretation, that its enforcement is often a matter of social struggle and political expediency, that the meaning of a sentence in the Constitution is always open to change. That is not to say, however, that principles like those articulated in the Constitution are valueless. The First and other amendments to the Constitution are weapons to be used in the constant struggle to maintain a degree of freedom in public speech. Without those discursive resources to appeal to, the country would have been even more repressive than it has been.

Stanley Fish has spoken out in favor of hate speech regulation and buttressed his argument by claiming that there never has been and never will be any such thing as free speech. On the latter point, Fish is quite correct, though his model of communally arrived at consensual limits to what it is possible and reasonable to say is an excessively rational one. At least since Freud and Marx we have known that we cannot actually speak freely. Indeed, there are more powerful psychological and political constraints on speech than we are capable of realizing; most of what constrains our speech remains invisible to us. But within the boundaries we can recognize there are both degrees and instances of different kinds of freedom and repression; those are differences worth struggling over.

Fish concludes that, since it is all a matter of social competition, ideals like those embodied in the First Amendment have no value. This is typical of the kinds of errors critics make who were schooled in the apolitical atmosphere of American literary theory in the 1970s. Deciding that it is all a matter of politics throws Fish into a model of politics that is as hopelessly abstract and nonmaterial

HATE SPEECH AND POLITICAL CORRECTNESS

as textuality would have been a decade earlier. The point is that ideals and appeals to idealization are important components of political struggle—both for the Left and the Right. Appeals to the First Amendment are a significant part of Left political strategy. Pushed further, Fish's argument would lead to declaring the entire Constitution irrelevant. Does he really think he would be as free as he is to speak his views without it? This is not something that can be decided wholly in the abstract—by comparing arguments—as Fish believes it is. The issue requires careful study of both national and local material practices throughout American history.

If, as Fish claims, there is no such thing as free speech, it follows there is no such thing as freedom. Once again, all the modern philosophies of determination tell us history and culture radically constrain us and limit our freedom. We have choices to make, but we do not get to choose what range of choices is available to us. Despite this, freedom is not an empty term. Its relative degrees of realization make the difference between a life that is tolerable and one that is not. A freed slave may soon realize he or she is neither economically nor socially free, and that exercising speech rights has consequences, but that does not mean a former slave would prefer a return to slavery. The freedom of speech one does not have in the gulag differs from the freedom of speech one lacks in a university. One might imagine that this would be self-evident, but not apparently to a certain kind of dematerialized theorizing.

Of course a public confidence in "freedom" or "free speech" can be unjustified or self-deceiving, as it often has been in the United States. We can persuade ourselves that our speech is much freer than it is. But the solution is not to abandon the concept and opt instead for a social competition for the power to constrain and coerce. Consent to a national ideal of free speech helps preserve a greater degree of tolerance for speech. It also helps shape increased legal protection for speech. When a three-judge Federal panel declared portions of a law to restrict and penalize speech on the Internet unconstitutional in June of 1996, they invoked First Amendment speech rights. One judge referred to our constitutionally guaranteed "unfettered speech"; another acknowledged "our cherished freedom of speech does not cover as broad a spectrum as one may have gleaned from a simple reading of the Amendment." But all felt the issue had to be decided in dialogue with both legal precedent and the consensual idealization of free speech in the public sphere. Of course the consent has to be won anew at every turn of history. But the concept of free speech is a powerful tool nonetheless. Abandoning it or mocking it would make life worse, not better.

It is thus a considerable error for people on the Left to abandon the struggle to win support for their interpretations of constitutional law. It is also an error to cede popular interpretation of the First Amendment and other elements of the Constitution to the Right. The Right, of course, likes to treat the First Amendment as an untarnished ideal impeccably honored throughout our history; under pressure, a few will concede past errors but insist free speech *is* guaranteed now. Their aim is simple enough—to deflect attention from the real and continuing struggles over political freedom and material inequities. But there is no reason to credit the bombastic and disingenuous rhetoric that reactionary journalists, politicians, and members of the judiciary use to surround and muffle the First Amendment. The Left can foreground historical reality while still appealing to values that may be read into democratic ideals. Appealing to political reality does not mean abandoning the role of idealization in social life. Again, the proper tactic is more speech, not silence.

8

WHAT HAPPENS WHEN WE
PUT THE LEFT AT THE CENTER?

Some years ago, when I was beginning to teach from an expanded canon and working on the book on noncanonical modern American poetry described in chapters 3 and 5, I sent a draft of the manuscript to a senior faculty member who was a specialist in modern poetry. The book was an attempt to recover a large number of forgotten or devalued women, minority, and left-wing writers. My reader, wedded to the traditional canon of often politically conservative white males, had only one comment: "So you want us to read a lot of women, blacks, and Jews. What's the point?" At the time, I must admit the remark first left me pretty much speechless, though I was interested to note that my colleague was aware of the connection between the Left and Jewish culture, something I had not emphasized in the manuscript. In any case, my reader was not ready to hear the personal rejoinder the remark partly deserved; the problem, I might in other words have suggested, was not mine.

I offer this chapter, then, as a first gesture toward a belated response to that challenge of years ago. And I will begin by rephrasing the question in a more productive way: What happens when we put the Left at the center? At the center of our teaching. At the center of our research. At the center of the story or stories we tell about the American literary heritage. At the center of our notion of the culture's ideals. Does the Left belong in the last two of these places? Was it ever really there before?

Of course posing the question this way forces us to ask what it entails to assert that there is a center. Is there a core narrative or group of narratives about American history and culture in which the Left might play a significant role? How continuous or discontinuous is that narrative? What is excluded from it? Is the center unitary or multiple? If there is a center and a periphery, how do they relate to one another? Does the decision to foreground the dichotomy between centrality and marginality blind us to other social and political relationships, to more complex and compromised discursive positions?

At least since Saussure, we have potentially known that the center is necessarily relational, that it can neither establish nor sustain its identity and status independently. A center has no meaning apart from its dialogue with cast out and marginalized elements of a culture. Since Marx, we have known that the center wins its dominance and visibility through struggle; that is a message feminism, minority studies, and postcolonialism have specified and reinforced. Cultural studies has taught us that the struggle is continual, that centrality can only be sustained through constant work and rearticulation, and that the center, indeed, is never quite the same; its nature changes even when it claims to stay the same, when it claims such continuity as one of its virtues. Maintaining the configuration of centrality requires constant reconfiguration and adaptation. When new constituencies, issues, and images are drawn into the center—or into a dynamic relationship with it—then the nature of the center itself changes. Both cultural studies and poststructuralism, meanwhile, have reinforced our growing suspicion that the meaning of the objects at the center is constructed, not inherent, and that it is always open to renegotiation. Finally, multiculturalism has demonstrated that there are always more stories than the dominant culture chooses to tell.

Some people, moreover, establish the center of their lives elsewhere. They may win this distance from the dominant culture with great difficulty or it may be imposed upon them. Not all will even be conscious of it. To a given subculture this distance may seem unproblematic, even a fact of nature. In terms of their daily experience and their collective figuration of social space, the dominant (and usually metropolitan) center may appear irrelevant.

Indeed, because the differential relations between center and periphery are not only unequal and hierarchical but have historically also often been racist, sexist, and colonialist, some have suggested we should stop using the metaphor entirely. I would agree that the metaphor should be given no special priority in our efforts to characterize social life, and I would also argue that it needs to be flexible to have much interpretive purchase. Sometimes there are myriad centers; sometimes there are two centers in mortal conflict. The relations between center and periphery are also potentially reversible; sometimes they can be overthrown. Foregrounding the metaphor, indeed, can serve not to perpetuate given relationships but rather to provoke dissatisfaction with them and thus lead to change. It would be invidious, moreover, to assume such relations have to exist in any given social setting or historical moment. But the metaphor can help us understand the distribution of power, authority, and wealth in given contexts.

If you were a communist in the United States in 1952, you could, to say the least, fairly be credited with having put the Left at the center of your life; you also no doubt felt that you lived on the margins and you felt imperiled by the beliefs and powers lodged at the very center of the culture as a whole. When that center is after your head, you do not have the leisure to pretend it does not exist. The history of the brutal relations between centrality and marginality requires our continuing witness. Even in the American 1950s, however, even in that moment of nearly unchecked, ruthless power, the metaphors of center and periphery were more complicated than one might expect. Cast out of every central institution, the political Left was nonetheless at the very center of the political Right's anxieties and its opportunism, integral to the Right's self-definitions and to its metaphors for public life. Something similar could be said about many cultures' rejected others, which are often at the center of the dominant power's efforts to sustain its hegemony. From English efforts to promote their own cultural superiority by denigrating the Irish to Nazi Germany's absolute othering of the Jews, a rejected other is lodged paradoxically at the heart of the dominant culture's identity.

Two straightforward points are among the preliminary conclusions that can be drawn from this thumbnail sketch of how the metaphor of centrality has been complicated for us: first, that the metaphor has a significant history and considerable interpretive power; second, before discussing what we should or should not do, we need to admit that we now have at least some power to do as we choose. In other words, we can put the Left at the center of contemporary teaching and research if we choose to do so. We have the power to make that difference if we wish. We can choose to make our work answer to certain personal and political needs and desires. In the process, we can certainly alter the way we remember the past and thus the way we live in the present. Just what effect we can have on the future, as always, remains unclear. But it is perfectly clear that we live in a time when the traditional center no longer holds and that for some of us suggests an opportunity, not a reason for fear.

From the stories that have long been told in our schools, our textbooks, and our scholarly discourses, we might well have concluded that we would have to invent an American Left in order to put it at the center of our cultural memory. It is certainly easy enough, for example, to find narratives that either omit or marginalize the fact that there were several hundred socialist periodicals in the United States in the second decade of the century and that their combined audience may well have reached several million. In 1912, the peak year for the Socialist party, Eugene Debs received nearly a million votes for President. Norman Thomas came close to that in 1932. Just how many Americans felt significantly attracted to the culture of American communism in the 1930s we will never know; once again, however, the numbers were not insignificant. The Left's impact on the labor and civil rights movements and on poetry, fiction, drama, and the graphic arts has also been extensive. And many of its causes and arguments and public policy proposals have eventually found their way into mainstream law, though often only after being disarticulated from their origins.

The archive is thus not empty. We do not have to invent objects to study or people who contributed to or were influenced by Left culture.[1] We do not have to invent people who put the Left at the center of their lives. We do have to decide that these people and products matter: that they matter to us, first, that they mattered to themselves, second, and then perhaps that they mattered to the times in which they lived. We do have to invent and reinvent the narratives that include these people and the work they did. We have to decide what prominence to give the Left and what meaning it had in the past and might have in the present and future. As I argued in chapter 3, the meaning of history is always under revision, always being reestablished. At stake is the effort to gain some influence over what facts will count in that retelling and over who writes the new stories we will habitually tell.

It is at this point that the radical decentering of our myths of centrality comes helpfully into play. It helps us understand not only what opportunities are available to us but also the uncanny epistemology of our recovery projects. For although the archive is not without Left artifacts, there is another sense in which we have reason to doubt that they exist. To the extent that Left culture exists only so long as we continue to tell stories about it, to the extent that Left poetry and politics have meaning only when we speak of them, that otherwise Left culture falls silent, unable to be spoken of and unable to speak to us, to *that* extent, indeed, it will seem as though the left did not exist. There is a quite practical sense in which a forgotten culture seems never to have existed and in which the effort to recover it thus feels like phantasmatic invention. In failing to tell appropriate stories—both in academia and in our public culture—we have in a very real sense driven the Left out of existence. Reaching out to it from the vantage point of the dominant culture's coercive silence requires breaking through that aura of the improbable and the impossible. If the gods meant the Left to be at the center, the Right seems implicitly to argue, it would already be there. Once the barrier to speech is broken, however, everything changes; the objects and their meanings and the stories we can tell about them multiply. Suddenly what was not there goes on forever.

These generalizing abstractions, I should point out, grow out of the practical research and teaching my graduate students and I, along with many other people across the country, have done over the past decade. Sometimes that has meant doing resistance teaching amongst conservative students. Interested in the history of American anarchism and its impact on American poetry, Lee Furey began to seek out books, journals, and newspapers from the early part of the century. Expecting a small but notable body of work, she found that one recovered subculture led to another and another. Now, between anarchist and socialist poetry, a lifetime of rediscovery awaits her and her students, and our notions of what was radical about modernism need to be revised.[2] Mark Van Wienen noticed that a small body of antiwar poetry flourished in America before we entered the First World War and before some of the heaviest censorship in our history was installed and stifled most free expression. Journals led to archives, archives led to letters, and the small body of poetry became much larger; now the history of modernism and its engagement with public life looks very different to his students than it did before his work began.[3]

In my own research on and teaching of the 1920s and 1930s I concentrated on books, journals, and newspapers. That alone so multiplied the varieties of Left poetry that no single story could any longer account for it. Then I decided to follow up one poet, Edwin Rolfe (1909–1954), in detail. My collaborator Jefferson Hendricks and I contacted Rolfe's widow, still alive at eighty years of age in San Francisco, and arranged to see her husband's papers. A day into twenty-some boxes and it was clear there was a body of witty and anguished poetry about McCarthyism that had never been published. By the second giddy day, we had an unpublished poem by Langston Hughes, letters from Ernest Hemingway, and still more, all of it unpublished. Combined with the work Rolfe had published in books and journals, the unpublished poetry made it possible to say that he was the American poet who did the most sustained work about both the Spanish Civil War and McCarthyism. His *Collected Poems,* published in November of 1993, now makes that work available to everyone.[4] Here are some representative passages about American culture Rolfe wrote during the McCarthy period:

> The poisoned air befouled the whole decade,
> corrupting even those whose childhood vision
> contained no hint of bomb or nuclear fission . . . . (253)

> Knaves masqued like sovereigns decree
> what we shall say, listen to, see,
> The habit of slavery, long discarded,
> becomes our normal, comfortable suit. (216)

> What are we having for dinner tonight
> Whom are we having for dinner tonight?
>> Raw nerve ends on toast
>> Pickled cops' feet
>> Suckling pig with a gag in its mouth
>> And no talk—its ears are wired for sound. (259)

> Who used to lie with his love
>> In the glade, far from the battle-sector,
>> Now lies embraced with a lie-detector
> And can not, dare not, move. (259)

> This court, supreme in blindness and in hate,
> supremely flaunts its lickspittle estate;
> kills Jews today, as twenty-five years ago,
> it killed Italians. (259)

Considering that most scholars believe American poets retreated from political themes during the American inquisition in the early 1950s, Rolfe's work alone makes it necessary to begin rethinking the role poetry played in that period. Some of his work, of course, was unpublished, so it existed only in the most invisible and private way. When those trees fell in the forest, there was definitely no one there to hear them. Even Rolfe's unpublished work, however, requires us to reexamine our assumptions about what poets wrote (and found it possible to write) during the American inquisition.

But of course I began to wonder what other work might be out there. In the 1930s I was dealing with Left poetry that had been published but largely forgotten. After going through Rolfe's papers, I began asking what other poetry might have been written but proven unpublishable in a climate of intense repression. A year later I was on my way to visit the widow of one of the Hollywood Ten. Alvah Bessie had published a few poems in journals, but there was no evidence of them in his University of Wisconsin archive. Bessie's wife was convinced his remaining files contained only photocopies of the materials he had already donated, but I finally persuaded her to let me have a look. An hour's search seemed to prove her right. But then, a thick envelope emerged from the back of a file cabinet. In it was an unpublished book of political poems written while Bessie was in federal prison in 1951. As I left the house in the California hills, poems in hand, I drove past one building site after another. Everywhere the earth was being torn up, the past covered over with new construction. I asked a question we will no doubt never be able to answer: How many other repressed manuscripts of the Left have ended up in landfills? And one question we will have to answer if we are to put Left culture of the 1950s at the center: What does it mean to recover a past that might have had a public life but never did?

If left-wing work like Rolfe's or Bessie's is published and reaches an audience, if other scholars take it up and talk about it, then the landscape of the past will begin to look very different to us. Our understanding of politically conservative canonical work will have to make adjustments to account relationally for what other poets found it possible and necessary to write. History's dynamic will have new elements in play, new forces in contention, new options to offer to the present. Putting the Left at the center of our work, then, even by a deliberate act of will, an act provoked by a political commitment, can eventually force seismic shifts everywhere else in the cultural landscape. That has already happened dramatically with feminist and minority recovery projects and it will continue as a general recovery of Left history and culture makes it possible to see past filiations and alliances among constituencies that sometimes compete for exclusive priority in the contemporary scene.

For the effort to put the Left at the center is necessarily a project of rearticulation. The Left cannot exist at the center without a network of relationships—comparisons, similarities, differences, contrasts, allegiances, affiliations, disputations, contentions, representations, and misrepresentations—that enable it and keep it in place. To put the Left at the center, as I did in the course I describe in the opening chapter of this section of *Manifesto,* is to ask how everything else in the culture bears on the Left's values and actions. Putting the Left at the center thus means reevaluating the meaning of the alternative claims other political visions make on our past and future. It also means drawing different elements of other discourses into the foreground to mark their points of similarity and difference with the already varied and mutually contentious discourses of the Left. In the process a general realignment of our traditions and our understanding of them can begin to take place. In the end, if the project of putting the Left at the center succeeds, our past comes to speak differently to us; the inertial force of our central traditions makes different claims on our present aims.

Of course, while we are working to put the Left at the center, other people with very different conceptions of the American past and present will be carrying out their own raids on the same territory. That is the nature of cultural struggle. But if we leave the task of defining our national traditions and identities to the Right, then the Left will be visible as it would see itself neither at the center nor on the horizon. We do not have to know whether we can win this battle to benefit from the fight. This is a project that can begin in your research, your teaching, your daily life.

Indeed, the changes it first makes are local ones. Putting the Left at the center of your life changes your needs and desires, your work and its rewards, your relations and your conversations, your impact on your students and colleagues; it changes your understanding of the past and the processes that brought the present into being. And it multiplies possible futures that might otherwise seem culturally constrained.

Often, however, putting the Left at the center requires a certain bloody-mindedness, a willfulness about proceeding despite the incredulity of conservative colleagues. Putting the Left at the center means putting it where some people believe it does not belong. Indeed, my title is intended, whimsically, to suggest just that sort of unwarranted transposition, a violation of the logic of directionality. Putting the Left at the center often entails accepting that existing systems of meaning in academia will offer no context for semanticizing your work. It may, indeed, be easier to reward you for it than to comprehend it.

Putting the Left at the center also requires us to refuse to cash in all that project's relational consequences in advance. The scholar I mentioned at the outset, in effect, wanted all the implications spelled out before acceding to an expanded canon. But it is in the very nature of the recombinatory effects of a new relational landscape to be unpredictable. Putting the Left at the center sets off chain reactions here and elsewhere. Its broader cultural risks and benefits, the fruits of its foregrounding, the semiotic effects of its dissemination, all wait upon a future we cannot yet name. That is the nature of a revolution.

LESSONS FROM THE
JOB WARS

9

DICHOTOMY IS WHERE THE MONEY IS

ANTI-INTELLECTUALISM INSIDE AND OUTSIDE THE UNIVERSITY

As I have argued throughout this book, higher education in America faces a future that is far from uncertain. For if faculty members and administrators continue as they are, we can predict with unwelcome confidence the basic shape of the educational environment of the next millennium—increased class sizes, decreased academic freedom, fewer tenure-track faculty, more part-time teachers, a shakeout and reduction in the number of full-scale research universities, and little time for research anywhere except at a small handful of private institutions. And universities, meanwhile, will be increasingly exploitive employers.

In the fall of 1995, after I made similar gloomy predictions at one of our most distinguished universities, the campus's dean of liberal arts mounted the stage to say he thought the future fairly bright. There would be ups and downs, but he found strong, mostly unwavering support among his donors and alumni and thus good reason to believe we could proceed with confidence. We needed to make our case more strongly than ever, but, if we did so, results would reward our efforts. At a cocktail party later that day I told him I was surprised that he was so sanguine. "Oh," he replied, "I was talking about the four or five elite schools. The rest of you," he allowed, "are finished." So that is one blunt assessment of higher education's brutally hierarchical future. Chicago, Harvard, Hopkins, Princeton, Yale on one thin end of the spectrum, everybody else heaped together on the campus of McDonald's U.

Not, however, that the elite schools will be sites of uncompromised idealization. Yale, to take a surprising example, does roughly one-third of its undergraduate teaching with adjuncts, another third with graduate assistants. Its well-paid tenured faculty are responsible for a decreasing segment of the university's mission. Meanwhile, with its financial planners more uneasy than its faculty, the university has declared a financial crisis based on the difficulty it has *reinvesting* as large a portion of its endowment income as it would like. Nice work if you can get it. Yale's endowment has already grown astonishingly quickly over the last fifteen years. According to my New Haven informants, the local community has come improbably to the rescue, coughing up two or three hundred homeless people each year to do unskilled maintenance on campus. Yes, Yale now hires the homeless, not, you may be sure, out of compassion, but because they accept low wages and, needless to say, require no benefits. After all, they have no home addresses to which to send W-2 forms or medical insurance notices. At the other end of the spectrum, a community college in Florida recently raised its teaching load for full-time faculty to six courses per semester. This is, I would argue, all part of the same story, even though few faculty at either Yale or Dade County Community College have been in the habit of inventing narratives that encompass both sites.

The changes in employment policies being instituted by American educational institutions in response to both real and imagined financial pressures are making them less admirable institutions, less effective educationally, and more compromised ethically. Meanwhile, most faculty are far from articulate or thoughtful when confronting policy issues outside their disciplinary expertise. More than we would like to admit, there are problems—and frequent displays of ignorance—not only outside but also inside the university. As part of this effort to initiate an inquiry into how we got here (and what we can do about it) I would like to offer some observations about the relations between anti-intellectualism inside and outside the university. After demonstrating how academic life supports certain kinds of anti-intellectualism, I will conclude by identifying some areas where academic intellectual leadership is currently much needed. That will lead me from suggestions about the constraints of disciplinarity to an account of current struggles over graduate student unionization and eventually to public discussions of race and financial support for the humanities.

Let me say initially that contemporary academics come to this topic, anti-intellectualism, as products of a history that makes us singularly ill-suited to address it. Two things in particular leave us relatively incapacitated: first, the gradual collapse of the secondary school system over several decades in many places in the country has left Americans without any common foundation of historical knowledge and led many academics to conclude incorrectly that both their students and the general public are intellectually empty, that they know nothing; second, the extreme academic specialization of the second half of the century, combined with the relentless careerism of postwar university culture, has led academics to assume that the question of intellectualism—of what an intellectual actually is—is always already settled, settled permanently and institutionally, settled by someone other than themselves, settled most often by their disciplines, whereas in fact the nature and relevance of the intellectual life is historically variable and a continuing site of struggle and redefinition. Most academics have ignored that struggle and now possess no workable cultural notion of the intellectual life beyond their subdisciplinary research commitment. In other words, I am an intellectual because I study this or study that. No doubt those who haven't said anything new about what they "study" in a decade, along with those who are consistently wrong in what they say, would all consider themselves intellectuals if they gave it a thought. As for those who publish—whatever and whenever—well, they are *self-evidently* intellectuals.

The recent spate of media articles commodifying academics as public intellectuals—something the national media apparently believes academics can become by writing one book review for the *Nation,* the *New Republic,* or the *Village Voice,* without taking any ongoing, coherent, and strong stands on public issues—is evidence not of the vitality and relevance of university intellectual life but rather of its state of crisis. With no criteria for what an intellectual is—with no widespread, ongoing academic conversation about the nature of intellectual commitment and impact—we settle for sound bites or a de facto definition for a public intellectual: publishing outside the discipline. As a criterion for establishing significant intellectual impact it is as meaningless as the traditional imprimatur of disciplinarity. We need instead to recognize how difficult it is to specify what it means to be an intellectual—whether on campus, in business or politics, in ethnic or religious communities, or elsewhere. Such specific contexts—each both productive and constraining—suggest the impossibility of any universal model.

Is, for example, Newt Gingrich an intellectual or a demagogue? Assuming he was not aiming for ironic, self-critical synecdoche, I'm willing to say his insufficiently infamous prescription for the poor—let them eat laptops—amounted to demagoguery. Yet it is not easy to classify discourses that mix subtlety and simplification, let alone practices that opt only for the latter. On the other hand, I would argue that organic intellectuals who work in poorly educated communities and help them theorize their daily lives in terms they can understand merit the designation. Was Cesar Chavez an intellectual? Was Martin Luther King? Yes, in both cases, or so I would argue.

These are, of course, partly political judgments that I am making, an admission that does not trouble me, because I consider that inevitable. In any case, it is hardly necessary to declare oneself an intellectual in order to be one. In the wake of recent theory, you might reject the aura of unitary and self-sufficient identity the term suggests. On the other hand, you might be more focused on the aims and effects of your practices—the materiality of your work—than on savoring your own agency. You might also be a little leery of the honor, remembering that past intellectuals—from the Inquisition to Vietnam—have been ready to rationalize madness and murder. To the extent that anti-intellectualism means skepticism about (and wariness toward) intellectuals and others in power it is hardly a wholly unhealthy phenomenon.

But while we are making political judgments let us consider the case of a contemporary who tries to wear the mantle of intelligence, Lynne Cheney. Is Cheney an intellectual? Not by any criteria I can credit. Recently, in *Telling the Truth* and elsewhere, she has criticized the National History Standards for their avowed leftism. McCarthyism is mentioned over a dozen times, Teddy Roosevelt only a few. Repeatedly it has been pointed out to her that the multiple references to McCarthyism are clustered together in the brief section *on* McCarthyism, not scattered throughout the text so as to demonstrate an obsessive preoccupation, as her complaint is supposed to prove. She responds, as every right-wing public figure seems trained to do, by changing the subject and attacking from a different angle. If there is an appropriate contemporary ethic for intellectuals, perhaps it includes the traditional criterion of being willing to discuss objections seriously. Cheney, alas, repeats her discredited claim whenever she gets a chance. Unbeknownst to herself, a true postmodernist, she appears to believe there are no truths, that all representation is misrepresentation. I suppose we could ask her if she thinks she's an intellectual, though I wouldn't recommend taking her word for it. I'd call her an anti-intellectual ideologue.

Neither being placed inside the academy nor outside it, then, necessarily offers the best test of intellectual status. On the other hand, I take as refreshing evidence of a willingness to open the question of intellectual identity for academics, as recognition of its social and political constitution and contingency, the fine effort among graduate students at various campuses to seek recognition for themselves as employees and to win approval for bargaining agents for graduate teaching assistants. In choosing to think about and challenge preconceptions about professionalism, intellectualism, the nature of labor, the meaning of community, the appeal of alliances that cross class lines, and the ethics of existing campus power relations, such graduate student groups are taking leadership in doing what the academy has needed to do for two and a half decades. I applaud them, offer them my support, and urge all faculty members to do the same. The effort to win fair benefits and working conditions for some of higher education's lower-paid employees does not undermine higher education's core values; it enhances them. Part of what is remarkable about such groups, as I suggested in my introduction, is their diversity. At few other sites on contemporary campuses could one find young intellectuals of different gender, race, ethnicity, and economic background working and talking together in productive alliances. Both higher education and the country as a whole need such alliances now and in the future. We should foster them. Instead, most faculty members and administrators reject such efforts with anti-intellectual irrationality.

When I offered my support for the Yale graduate student union, GESO, at a conference held at Yale's humanities center in 1995, my disciplinary colleagues took it upon themselves to stand collectively against the tides of such unreason. David Bromwich, on stage with me when I made my comments in support of unionization, reacted in such a way as to look for all the world like a vampire bat suddenly exposed to a shaft of sunlight; he lurched forward, flung his arms out, then slumped forward, burying his head in his dark wings in resignation. At the time I thought his reaction extraordinary; as I was later to realize, its visceral, wounded character was emblematic of the deep revulsion Yale faculty would feel as the university's graduate student employees pressed their case more vigorously over the next year.

Bromwich himself was quite unable to speak at all when I came up to talk with him a few minutes later. His colleagues, however, soon spoke for him. The next day Yale English department faculty member Annabel Patterson rose to express her regret that the local media would no doubt cover my remarks about graduate student unionizing rather than the *important* issues addressed at the conference. In her own presentation Patterson went on to make the benighted suggestion that, instead of addressing academia's problems in contemporary contexts, we would be much better off reprinting earlier texts that express sympathetic enlightenment values. She particularly recommended John Adams, and quoted from him at length. Alas, only under pressure from the audience in the question period did she bother to admit that Adams later disavowed his progressive writings and became a reactionary. In fact he is one of Pound's sources in his overtly fascist phase. Bad choice, Professor Patterson. Finally, English department faculty member Paul Fry took the floor, sure that a bit of wit would slay the union dragon. "Students," he remarked, finding solace from the evident injustice of their cause in the polish of his rhetoric, "have cleverly decided to call themselves *workers,* which apparently explains the support they received here." His voice rose a good octave with the exclamation "workers," as if to extract every possible echo from such an absurdity.

What perhaps only one faculty member at Yale knew at the time was that the reprisals against GESO had already begun. Moreover, the shape of the administration's strategy had already been set by one of its senior members: single out GESO's leaders for individual punishment and seek to destroy their careers. The administrator in question was Richard Brodhead, A. Bartlett Giamatti Professor of English and Dean of Yale College. In July of 1995, long before the grade strike, he had written a letter of recommendation for the dossier of one of GESO's leaders. The last paragraph, one-third of the letter, was devoted to her union activities.

Brodhead opens his letter by praising the seminar papers she wrote for him, then begins his concluding paragraph by observing that both he and the student involved would agree that the union organizing effort has been a major focus of her graduate career. He makes it clear that he rejects GESO's goals but recognizes the goodwill of those involved. Then the axe falls. He reports that this particular student "is a poor listener on this issue" and "has on at least one occasion . . . shown poor judgment in the choice of means." He concludes the letter by once again praising her disciplinary work and by putting all readers on notice: she "will bring civic intelligence and concern about communal life to her future job."[1]

The picture created here is unambiguous; she is bright but ruthless, a rigid ideologue who will not listen to reason when her political beliefs and "concern about communal life" are at issue. This paints a rather different portrait from the witty, reflective person I have met, but perhaps Brodhead can no longer see her that way. A genial fellow who has functioned well within Yale's paternalistic hierarchy, his seminars are popular and he has helped many students with their dissertations over the years. But the combination of his deanship and the union's affront to Yale's pecking order have been too much for him. Just before his final sentence, he makes clear that the poor judgment at issue was her decision to write to one of Yale's major donors. The effect of Brodhead's letter, I believe, would be to eliminate her from consideration from almost any job for which she applied. I would remove any such letter from one of my student's dossiers. Did Brodhead have a right to say these things? Well, the AAUP guidelines prohibit mention of a student's political beliefs or activities, whether the writer is approving or disapproving of them. But equally problematic is the impression about the letter written to Perry Bass, one of Yale's donors.

The letter, sent from the GESO office, was signed by four people, among them the student at issue. It was part of a 1993–94 GESO campaign to arrange better compensation for and protect the quality of Yale's highest-level writing course, "Daily Themes," which reportedly includes Cole Porter and Bill Buckley among its graduates. The student, as it happens, did not even write the letter, though she did sign it. Moreover, GESO's entire organizing committee was fully involved, including at least one other student for whom Brodhead has written a letter of recommendation but without criticizing the student's union work. Some of this at least Brodhead knew, since the letter was copied to him; the rest of it he was responsible to find out before setting out to destroy a student's career. Brodhead refers to his claims as "allegations," which gives rhetorical indication of the significant weight he gives them. Meanwhile, one of his implicit allegations is that she made a willful, independent decision to contact Yale donors, when exactly the opposite is true.[2]

By the end of 1995 GESO's grade strike was under way, and other Yale humanities faculty had joined the attack on graduate students seeking fair treatment.[3] One reportedly responded to a teaching assistant's announcement that she was supporting the strike by standing up and announcing "You are hereby expelled from Yale University." "But professor," the student replied, "you do not have the power of summary expulsion." Instead the student was reported for disciplinary action. Sara Suleri, a brilliant postcolonial critic whose work I have taught in my own courses, urged disciplinary action against one of her teaching assistants who joined GESO's 1995 decision to withhold undergraduate grades until Yale's administration agreed to negotiate. Nancy Cott, a widely admired labor historian, spoke out against the union, and David Brion Davis, a distinguished historian of slavery, sought college guards to bar his union-identified teaching assistant from entering the room where undergraduate final exams would be given. Meanwhile, Annabel Patterson weighed in with more explicit anti-union sentiments, urging English department colleagues not to sign any petitions supporting the graduate student union, even petitions merely recommending against reprisals. After all, reprisals would be far more effective if the department faculty were united behind them.

Now what can we say about all of this? Patterson is quite right to argue that recovering and reviving forgotten texts can be an important contribution to contemporary debate. It's one of the things I do, so I'd hardly debunk it. But

DICHOTOMY IS WHERE THE MONEY IS

she serves no one well by trying to cover up the facts of her author's career. Nor is she helpful in intimating that it is unseemly for academics to engage directly in contemporary cultural and political struggles. That reluctance is part of what has brought us to the present crisis. Elevating our own preferences, practices, and anxieties to moral imperatives is a typically anti-intellectual move, both for academics and their countrymen, but it does not further the public scrutiny and self-scrutiny we need so badly. Bromwich, Cott, Davis, Patterson, Fry, and Suleri have all, notably, had some connections with Left theory, research, pedagogy, or politics. Bromwich is a contributor to *Dissent,* Patterson has made use of Marxist theory in her work. Cott, Davis, and Suleri are well-established progressive scholars. Some supported the long-running struggle of Yale's clerical workers to win bargaining rights. But graduate students were future professors! When it came to a challenge to their sense of professional hierarchies and identities these progressive scholars stood unthinkingly with their more conservative colleagues. Moreover, each seemed to take it as a personal betrayal for his or her teaching assistant to join the strike; so ingrained is the culture of paternalism that it is impossible for these faculty to think of their assistants as independent professionals with a right to define their own ethics and politics.

Davis's case is actually rather saddening. Yale's administration had written a letter to the faculty inviting them to turn in strike participants for individual disciplinary action. Davis decided to do so in a December 11, 1995, letter to Graduate School Dean Thomas Appelquist. Ironically, the course at issue was Davis's "The Origins, Significance, and Abolition of New World Slavery." If Brodhead's letter is in some ways the act of a scoundrel, Davis's letter is the testimony of a principled man who cannot imagine that GESO members have alternative principles of their own. He has two teaching assistants, one of whom—"my loyal Teaching Fellow"—turns in the final grades and one who participates in the strike despite his kindnesses to her. Having turned in his grades on time for forty-one years, he laments, now he is faced with the possibility of being late! Meanwhile, he cannot recognize that turning in a participant in a collective action for individual punishment raises its own ethical questions.

Despite warnings from reactionary journalists, many tenured radicals apparently present little challenge to the academy's dichotomous hierarchies. Many combine progressive scholarship with an unreflective, unyielding sense of professional identity and self-importance. Many are unable to recognize, let alone analyze, the contradiction between holding a progressive position in one area of their professional life and a repressive one in another. We need to give credit for this where credit is due. The contemporary university, combined with disciplinarity and its attendant professional organizations, is an interlocking late twentieth-century morphing technology: it turns dissenters into careerists, intellectuals into anti-intellectual professionals.

Let me make one final opening point about campus anti-intellectualism, illustrated with a minor local anecdote. Some years ago, one of my graduate students was walking down the hall carrying a large reference book he had borrowed from my office. One of my faculty colleagues noticed the book and asked to look at it. Leafing through the book, he remarked, "Wow! This looks really useful. I could use this book. But, say, tell me, how do you go about buying a book these days?" Flabbergasted, my student mentioned the location of a nearby bookstore and explained how to place an order for a book that might not be in stock. I take this story as concise evidence that not all members of the university community are fully devoted to the intellectual life, at least if we consider occasionally buying and reading books as one of its likely components for humanities professors.

It will not do, then, in speaking of anti-intellectualism in America to assume, speaking from any university, that anti-intellectualism is located decisively elsewhere. Indeed, anyone who has watched faculty members debate budgetary or curricular issues is unlikely to conclude that intellect and reason always prevail in higher education. Campus debates include demagoguery, misrepresentation, exaggeration, intimidation, self-delusion, and no lack of high and low theater. Scholarly writing, including my own, regularly entails polemicism with similar components. Contrary to the idealizing self-promotion universities sometimes engage in, the intellectual life on campus clearly exhibits some of the very flamboyant tactics of debate academics tend to deplore in the public sphere. Nor are universities necessarily good places for intellectual conversation and interaction. Many departments are notorious as places where faculty members never talk to one another and have no time for their students. Universities in larger urban centers are sometimes particularly fragmented; what intellectual life takes place is collective and collaborative only in the classroom; among the faculty themselves, at least those who are not running labs, intellectual work is often solitary.

That is not to say that I do not treasure my conversations with students and faculty or the time for intellectual reflection provided me by a university professorship. I do, but I also make choices about where I can give my time and often that means devoting less thought and care to interactions than I should. There is, in short, little to gain from imagining that we live in the New Jerusalem. We know that universities are places where faculty can babble green thoughts about the literary canon in the morning and harass their students in the afternoon. We know that institutions of higher education are compromised, imperfect sites that sometimes deploy disingenuous idealization to preserve campus inequities. Debates about student unionization are one of the places where idealization is deployed that way.

Nor, finally, can academics fairly deplore all dichotomous simplification and theatricalized rhetoric. There are moments in scholarly and public life when we need dichotomy and simplification. There are political occasions where the intellectual life must be compromised, both on campus and elsewhere. Thus in, say, thinking about the early 1940s, to take a stark example from modern history, I would not argue that a full understanding of the historical roots of fascism was essential at the time. It was not essential that the American public understand why the German people were drawn to Hitler. What mattered was how best to kill German soldiers, a challenge that was solved on the Eastern front. Positing democracy as a good and fascism as an evil, however simplifying, seems to me to have been a historical necessity. It would not, say, to pursue a purely hypothetical alternative, have been the most relevant moment to be preoccupied with our own national history of genocide.

Now, however, is a time when such a preoccupation—with our national history of both genocide and racism—is imperative and a necessary component of an American intellectual life. For we are likely to pay an increasing price for its legacy as the black urban poor are increasingly impoverished and criminalized. Some conservative commentators—notably William Bennett in a series of talks and television appearances—would have us stop focusing on this desperate history so that we can miraculously and instantly become color blind. To suggest, as the Right does, both in the television appearances I discussed in chapter 6 and elsewhere, that both the general public and the educational institutions that serve them should suppress or minimize the importance of the slave trade or the slaughter of Native Americans, is to adopt the anti-intellectualism of historical forgetfulness. On the other hand, it is equally unwise to assume, as the Left often does, *both* that what bearing these events have on the present is self-evident *and* that present-day persons can unproblematically or entirely embody this history. As I argued in chapter 3, the relation between our memory of the past and our present actions and responsibilities is open and unresolved. It is properly an area of discussion, reflection, debate, and action. Lack of knowledge undermines the potential for informed debate and impoverishes action in the present.

It is a colossal failure of our educational system that most Americans have little or nothing to say about the founding acts of genocide and racism that underlie and constitute our history. Yet neither the absolute positions of the Right or the Left—say nothing, say everything—present intelligible alternatives. We do not actually know how to do either. Between two impossible extremes—the Left's present wholly entailed by the past and the Right's present altogether unencumbered by it—lies the more uncertain and ambiguous present in which we live and in which university intellectuals must function.

What would it mean for us now to adjust our daily lives to acknowledge and fully account for the relentless slaughter of our continent's Native Americans? What would it mean for present-day Germany to be wholly entailed by memories of the Holocaust? What would it mean for no Germans to acknowledge any memory of it? How should American and German personal identity and national political life be encumbered by responsibility and memory? According to some conservatives we can jettison a dishonorable past in one fell swoop—just deny all special benefits to the poor and minorities. Self-reliance will take over, and we will enter the promised land chosen for all of us. Remarkably, I could wake up the next morning, drive through the South side of Chicago, and not notice that there are any black people there. The problem, of course, is not *whether* we should be entailed by our history, but how we are and should be.

Such messy and historically contingent conditions for advocacy and analysis, along with the material conditions of campus life, need to be confronted and reflected on if we are to revive some culturally significant role for campus intellectuals. Such a role, of course, would have to go beyond the media's current limited use of academics—as experts in narrow disciplinary areas—to encompass general social commentary and specific observations about the state of higher education. That we need to do so is clear, given conservative antagonism to any commitment to broad access to higher education.

At the same time we need to realize that there can be a high price paid in public debate for honesty and complication of the sort academics often prefer. It was decades ago that the novelist William Burroughs recognized that we had entered a playback public culture. The media brings a tape recorder to party A and says "What's the nastiest thing you can say about party B?" The recorded critique is next played back for party B, who is then given an opportunity for a rejoinder. And so forth. Such a system does not reward admissions of weakness and often refuses to play back complex or subtle arguments. In such a system differences become absolute, everything is precipitated into dichotomies.

Political life has to some degree been like that for much of American history, with no public space available outside opposing positions, though the most readily available discourse exemplifying positions has surely become more and more compact in recent decades. Academics often assume they can articulate positions independent of the opposing sides in a controversy, that such independence is the hallmark of the intellectual life. Yet it is more often the case that there is neither meaningful outlet nor audience for discourse not committed to one side or the other. In other words, to have an impact on his or her contemporaries an intellectual may have to identify explicitly with one side of a

DICHOTOMY IS WHERE THE MONEY IS

cultural or political controversy. For some that may seem partly anti-intellectual, but it is often the only alternative to irrelevance.

Where there may be space for change, however, is in the structure and disposition of arguments supporting a particular position. Thus the ongoing meaning and impact of an apparently fixed stance may be subject to significant revision. Some arguments and meanings can be discredited, others brought newly into play and given prominence. The ongoing work of rearticulating and transforming a position is work available to intellectuals in the public sphere if they choose to take it up. But this often entails stark political commitments of a sort many academics find unsettling or unpalatable.

There is also space for articulating and disarticulating issues to and from broad political positions. And my ethic for intellectuals of both the Right and the Left includes a responsibility to resist multiple pressures for ideological conformity. Over the long run both the Right and the Left lose by assembling a laundry list of issues and demanding allegiance to a fixed position on all of them. Certainly on campus, pressures for conformity sometimes slide into genuine intimidation. The recent term for this long-standing anti-intellectual phenomenon is political correctness, a practice having no inherent politics. For a taste of it try arguing for abortion rights, gay rights, or the rights of welfare recipients at a campus Young Republicans meeting. Try arguing against hazing at fraternities that practice it. I don't know that we can create campus environments that preclude intimidation — either from the Right or the Left — but I do believe intellectuals can identify it forthrightly when it occurs. That can go a long way toward defusing it.

On the practice of disarticulation and rearticulation — terms taken from the British cultural studies tradition discussed in chapter 4 — let me give one important example of a site where academics need to work. What broad public support for higher education still exists in America is linked to education's credentialing function and to its potential to increase graduates' status and income. Affirmative action, diversity, and multiculturalism on campus are concepts now linked not to these values but rather to rhetoric about special interests, to efforts to remedy past injustice, and to complaints about political correctness. What academics who support these efforts now need to do is, for example, to *dis*articulate diversity from arguments about injustice and *re*articulate it to arguments about economic gain. In other words, we need to convince people that education that puts students into contact with diverse populations best prepares them for the contemporary workplace and maximizes their income-earning potential. In other words, employment and population trends suggest that students who do not become knowledgeable about (and learn to work with) different ethnic and racial groups will have less successful careers.

The same thing applies to efforts to open up the literary canon, which the Right has articulated to special interests and political correctness, rather than to concepts of democracy, historical accuracy, and adaptability to a changing cultural and economic landscape. Here a multiple project of rearticulation is necessary, one that not only enables progressive scholars to win back control of popular notions of democracy and historical accuracy but also disarticulates historical recovery projects from special interest pleading and rearticulates them at once to practical self-interest and objectivity.

These changes involve both reasoned analysis and competitive advocacy, but like it or not, there are many public and campus occasions when nondichotomous dialogue is of no use, when stark oppositional conflict is the only game in town. When the opponents in a debate are interested in victory and not mutual enlightenment, an academic intellectual may have to play by their rules. Failure to do so means losing the game.

The continuing debate over defunding NEH and NEA exemplifies the failure of academics to accept these realities. If Congress severely cuts or eventually eliminates funding for the National Endowment for the Humanities, the endowment's academic supporters will be partly to blame. Throughout the Reagan and Bush presidencies the endowment's heads—William Bennett and Lynne Cheney—consistently politicized the granting process and undermined the agency's reputation for fairness and impartiality. Bennett, so NEH staffers privately report, kept a blacklist of progressive scholars whose applications he routinely rejected. Cheney instead packed review panels with political conservatives to assure the results she wanted. Her impact on awards for individual fellowships, where staffers could often ignore recommendations for evaluators, was inconsistent but on larger institutional projects it was substantial.

While there were occasional news stories about the conservative politics of the endowment, neither the higher education community as a whole nor its key disciplinary organizations pressed for congressional inquiry into these unethical practices. Only by placing lower-level NEH staffers under oath could Bennett's and Cheney's politicization of the endowment have been fully exposed.

As a whole, the scholarly community instead opted for passivity, friendly discussion, and a policy of cooperation—partly out of naive faith that a scholarly agency would automatically retain scholarly rather than political values, partly out of fear of reprisals, partly out of greed (the desire to continue receiving as many grants as possible), and partly because academics assumed reasoned dialogue was the proper intellectual behavior. As a result, Bennett and Cheney and their conservative allies have remained credible national commentators on the NEH and the general state of the humanities; Bennett indeed now reigns as a kind of public prince of virtue. They should long have been discredited or at least more successfully marked as controversial figures. If they had been discredited NEH and NEA would now have a better chance of surviving. Bennett and Cheney were not interested in conversation; they were interested in winning. And winning is what they appear to be doing.

As it happens, I approached both the president and the executive secretary of the Modern Language Association several years ago to suggest that the organization speak out against NEH policies. The executive secretary said we had more to gain from cooperation than conflict. MLA's president told me—to my astonishment—that Lynne Cheney was actually a very reasonable person with whom we could work. In short, I believe this particular cultural and political struggle required more combative and antagonistic participation by university intellectuals. It required taking sides forcefully; it required harsh criticism of individuals and their practices. It required translating university research into accessible language for broad public consumption so that it could not be so easily discredited by conservative commentators. Some academic intellectuals are actually taking up tasks like these, even though what they say and write may not resemble what they might publish in a scholarly journal.

In the struggle over NEH we may see the future of support for humanities research at public universities writ small. For in 1995 a new argument surfaced in Bennett's and Cheney's congressional testimony. Previously, their purported concern was over funding the wrong kind of humanities research; now they've gone on to argue the endowment should be defunded because the humanities as a whole have so deteriorated that they no longer merit public support. The issue for them, of course, was not quality but politics. Politicized under the Republicans, NEH under the Democrats is now giving out awards in a reasonably even-handed fashion. But Bennett and Cheney do not want such results, for that gives too much support to progressive research. With conservative think tanks funding the only cultural commentary they think it essential to see published, it makes sense to cut their losses and defund all university-based humanities scholarship. Where Congress has not feared to tread, state legislatures may follow.

Elite private institutions with large endowments may be able to sustain the status quo indefinitely, though even they appear to be increasing the percentage of their enterprise dependent on exploited labor. Public higher education, however, is in political and financial danger. If it is true, as I believe it is, that America needs all its research universities as sources of alternative social critique, historical reflection, and basic research, then significant numbers of academics need to devote part of their time to either multidisciplinary or more public intellectual activity.

Multidisciplinary research and writing, one of the categories in which *Manifesto* itself falls, is designed to reach academics in a variety of disciplines. It is designed to encourage reflection, build common knowledge, and work toward consensus *within* academia, an activity that is absolutely necessary if academics are to begin identifying anew with the general enterprise of education and begin speaking for it effectively in public. It is also an activity that recognizes academia itself as an important segment of public life, something faculty members are often inclined to deny.

Increasing attention to the public sphere does not, however, mean that we should speak with one voice, as University of Virginia English professor Patricia Meyer Spacks has argued in public talks in 1996. She has identified me as one of the "critics of the university" whose remarks may further undermine public confidence in education. That confidence can only be restored by cleaning up our own house, a metaphor that embraces the need to eliminate the limited amount of waste in university budgets and the need to treat our employees fairly. Only the proper internal conversation, then, can lead us to the public sphere effectively. That conversation must include principled internal criticism, not only because it can help rebuild public trust but also because an ongoing campus conversation would be a sham without it. The corporate mentality of enforcing uniformity on all issues is inappropriate for higher education; it undercuts both our self-understanding and what others admire in us. Of course there are some issues, like academic freedom, where a united front in academia is appropriate, but we can hardly speak out for academic freedom while trying to stifle internal debate and criticism. As a graduate student at Yale remarked during the Local 34 strike in February of 1996, "We have an obligation to ask for more of this university than prestige and resources. We have a right to ask for this university to be the thing that we believe it should be." A commitment to community and collective morality is a prerequisite to restoring the university's public image.

As I implied at the outset, that next step also means learning to respect the alternative knowledges that students and the public possess. Like other academics, I despair when my students clearly do not know the things I think they should know, including much of anything about history. But I also realize they are not empty; they know other things—not only those things they need to know to survive but also, often, their special areas of interest and passion. Some of us at least need to speak to such audiences outside academia. That will not always be easy, and it cannot be done without pain. There are genuine rewards in making our work more accessible, but there are also losses. For some of our ideas need not only to be simplified for public consumption but also abandoned.

And sometimes the process feels like self-betrayal, like willing self-extinction. Cultural struggles are often compromising. But now the only alternative is the end of higher education as we know it.

In any case the present configuration of academic identities is untenable. The simple, unexamined assumption that scholarly publication automatically certifies intellectual authenticity and confers and constitutes an intellectual identity can no longer be sustained. Does a book read, say, by less than a score of people matter? Such books are published all the time. What about an essay read by no one? We have assumed for decades that disciplinarity inherently confers worth, a comforting fiction that economic forces are rendering increasingly hollow. But if we abandon publication within a discipline as an unreflective, virtually sacralized source of meaning and value, what do we put in its place? It is an astonishing and immensely revealing fact that most academics have absolutely no answer to such a question. That points to a certain further anti-intellectualism in academia, an anti-intellectualism more problematic and pervasive, more disabling even, than the type exemplified by my colleague who had forgotten how to buy a book. For it points to a community of people who read and write without having any deep sense of why they do so. In a broad cultural sense, their disciplinary identity has protected them from the necessity of thinking. Whatever it means to be an intellectual, that surely cannot be it.

10

LATE CAPITALISM ARRIVES ON CAMPUS

THE CORPORATE UNIVERSITY'S EXPENDABLE EMPLOYEES

As any faculty cocktail party conversation from Maine to California will reveal, wishful thinking about the job market is alive and well in academia. I sometimes think wishful thinking is academia's major contribution to the public sphere. But every colder gaze cast on our economic future suggests that things will not get better either now or later. The job market—especially in the humanities, but also in the social sciences and the theoretical sciences—may remain depressed throughout the decade and beyond. And if all of us in higher education remain disengaged—indifferent to our public image, to the network of institutions and values that define our options, and to the competition for limited resources—the job drought may outlast us. The kinds of professional identities many of us take for granted now may no longer be available to us in a decade. The life of a college professor will almost certainly no longer resemble what it does now. Already, the once transitory identity of job seeker has become semipermanent for many. As for those of us who train Ph.D.s, if we were really training people for jobs as professors, we might only supervise two dissertations in the course of our careers.

The capricious and often brutal job market in academia is unfortunately part of a general transformation in the nature of American employment. Over the next decade we are likely to see a gradual increase in the percentage of part-time and fixed-term college teachers, a decrease in the percentage of tenured and tenure-track employees, increased teaching loads, and a notable drop in salaries for beginning faculty in some markets. With book publication increasingly threatened in the humanities it may become difficult to justify hiring research faculty. With many college teachers looking more and more like migrant factory labor—lacking health benefits, job security, retirement funds, and any influence over either their employment conditions or the goals of the institutions they work for—the ideology of professionalism seems increasingly ludicrous. Once an accoutrement of privilege, it is rapidly becoming an impediment at once to self-understanding and effective action. Certainly few part-time or term-contract faculty would readily identify themselves with Yeshiva University's faculty, who were judged ineligible for unionization because they had managerial responsibilities. While many faculty have not yet acknowledged the changes under way, college teachers are nonetheless in the process of joining late capitalism's transitory and disempowered work force.

That is not to suggest, however, that large-scale economic changes leave the education sector powerless or that its own actions are irrelevant. Modern Language Association president Sandra Gilbert suggested in a 1996 *MLA Newsletter* column that academia's job crisis was part of a national pattern we could do nothing to resist. And she suggested as well that by counseling resistance I was proving myself "disaffected." Yet when resources are scarce and public support undependable, the obvious need is to enter the competition, not remain on the sidelines. Indeed, the first thing we need to do is to recognize how we have abetted the crisis. The overproduction of Ph.D.s, for example, which is one of our own contributions to the crisis, has helped make academia economically and politically vulnerable. Obviously if the new humanities Ph.D. were a relatively scarce commodity, it would be far more difficult to treat Ph.D.s like unskilled workers. Similarly, academia's opportunistic (and wholly unreflective) acceptance of government predictions about the 1990s job market helped turn that market into a disaster. The U.S. Labor Department looked at anticipated retirements, matched them with expected numbers of high school graduates, and estimated how many new faculty positions would open up, nowhere asking whether the social will to *authorize* those positions would materialize, nowhere asking whether other social needs might be given higher priorities both by state legislators and by the nation's citizenry. Academia's own inclination to see itself as immune to other sectors of the economy was thus reinforced by Labor Department statisticians' inclination to ignore all determinants they could not quantify. Meanwhile, two academic studies coauthored by William Bowen, based partly on benighted predictions of faculty shortages growing out of the time it takes graduate students to complete their doctoral training, have also helped justify large graduate programs.

Of course there have been signals both academics and government planners might have read differently. In the twenty years between the abolition of free tuition at the City University of New York and the massive budget cuts proposed for the State University of New York by the new Republican governor in 1995–96, signals abound. We might, for example, have asked how the International Monetary Fund's austerity policies for developing countries helped establish a cultural environment relevant to education's future in America. We might have asked whether Margaret Thatcher's effort to abolish tenure in British universities and turn higher education over to technological rationality reflected not only local politics but also widespread cultural tendencies in the postindustrial world. We might have wondered whether the increasing ethnic and racial diversity of California's postsecondary student population was linked in any way to the public's decreasing willingness to fund higher education out of tax revenues. We might have wondered whether persistently (and scandalously) unequal funding in elementary and secondary education, with poor communities relegated to substandard facilities, might herald similar disparities in higher education. We might have worried that the loss of any powerful notion of the common good in the public sphere in America might threaten the relatively recent commitment to broad access to higher education. We might have asked whether increasing reliance on industry to fund research in the sciences might have implications for the humanities. We might have wondered what the policy implications might be of the New Right's cultural attacks on higher education since the 1980s. We might have questioned whether the decertification and disempowerment of unions that began with Reagan's handling of the air controller strike would prove prophetic for the rights of non-unionized employees in other sectors. In other words, people concerned about higher education might have been interrogating its structural and semiotic relations with other cultural domains and economic and political forces. We might, in short, have been involved in an ongoing cultural analysis of education and in taking actions that analysis suggested. Like many academics, I have waited too long to make some of these issues central to my life. Meanwhile, events we could not have anticipated—like the end of the cold war and the end of the post–Sputnik era's paranoid commitment to education—added other problematic elements to the mix. Yet nothing about higher education—neither its disciplinary divisions nor its ruling illusions—made active engagement with such matters likely. So instead, academics wait passively and hope for better times.

Not surprisingly, hand-in-hand with passivity and wishful thinking goes increasing anxiety about a future we can almost glimpse but dare not name. For there is widespread fear that large-scale higher education in the liberal arts has lost its public mandate. Not only is it added to a list of items seen not as rights but as privileges, but also any sense of the general societal benefits derived from broad access to anything beyond technical training is being largely eroded. Lack of public support and overproduction of Ph.D.s thus combine to make higher education one of late capitalism's notably vulnerable industries. As students and faculty in the humanities begin to reflect on the possible long-term collapse of the job market and what it entails, there is a wide range of issues—many rarely addressed—that we should begin to discuss and debate. Had higher education collectively taken up the problems raised in the previous paragraphs we might not be facing quite this crisis today. But we are, and I would like to concentrate first on its human consequences. I will raise a few such issues—growing out of the job crisis—in the form of a short list of lessons learned over the last several years. When appropriate, I will offer relevant anecdotes to lend my arguments experiential weight. These are paradoxical lessons, however, lessons taken from a site of impossible contradiction, lessons that need to be both learned and unlearned.

I am writing, I should emphasize, out of more than a decade's empathy with students struggling to find employment. Despite hundreds of hours of advocacy and advice, I am haunted by the knowledge that all I can do at the moment to help them collectively is write yet one more book, adding, at the ironic minimum, yet one more line to my own vita. Reaching out to a powerless constituency is not, of course, likely to do anything notable for my career. Still, I feel I owe the unemployed two promises before I begin: I will pull no punches and tell no lies. I will speak the truth as I see it. Here are the paradoxical, double-edged lessons I have learned so far:

1. YOU NEED A BOOK TO GET A JOB. This is the commonsense anecdotal wisdom offered repeatedly these days as a way of imposing at least a cruel reason on the uncertainty of the market. Yet it is far from obvious or straightforward. As the competition for jobs continues to implode on itself, expectations inevitably not only escalate but also become increasingly contradictory. You need not only to be a dedicated teacher and a fine scholar but also to project both these capacities as mutually exclusive and wholly consuming attributes. Thus demonstrable success at publication—often as much a requirement as an expectation—makes you look like someone who doesn't care about teaching. Especially at schools where the rest of the faculty have never published, that may be the easiest way to deal with superior accomplishments while reinforcing your own self-image. Intelligence is at once commodified and treated as a potential character flaw. Meanwhile, completing a book—before you get a permanent job—while teaching five courses part-time at two schools at opposite sides of Los Angeles—is neither easy nor conducive to psychic health. And there is the risk that a book completed before you are hired won't "count" for tenure. Some schools refuse to give tenure credit for work completed before you arrive on campus, a particularly brutal standard for those who have produced major scholarship despite teaching at several institutions for poverty-level wages.

Meanwhile, a book can remove a certain element of humility from a candidate's persona. Widely published young scholars are less likely to request mentoring, less likely to defer to senior scholars. They may not know their place or act the way untenured faculty are supposed to act. After all, some senior faculty will think, perhaps unconsciously, what's the point of hiring assistant professors if you can't lord it over them? Certainly I know of cases where departments passed over more accomplished young candidates because they didn't have the nervous eagerness of the candidate with, say, only one or two articles or with no publications at all.

In one of the notably schizophrenic ironies of the current market, some now not only tailor their vita and letter of application to meet each job's specific requirements—a sensible practice—but also "ration" their accomplishments according to what they think a particular school may want and tolerate. In order not to frighten off a department whose faculty doesn't publish, some candidates will omit publications or conference presentations, simplify descriptions of projects, and omit mention of intellectually challenging or politically controversial commitments. I have not yet met anyone who has taken a book off a vita, a gesture equivalent to a kind of suicide, but certainly many are aware that a book may rule them out of consideration in a department militantly opposed to research. So with publication comes the added anxiety about whether one can publish enough to become attractive to a research university or only enough to be rejected at lesser schools.

But for candidates who have been on the market for several years—increasingly the case for many people—a book seems the only way to break a pattern of failure. It is no guarantee, especially with large numbers of people on the market with books of their own, but it gives you perhaps an extra fistful of lottery tickets you would not have otherwise. Worst of all, however, is the fact that the very book that might get you tenure at, say, Cornell University, could easily keep you from being hired there. The sort of work expected of a *colleague* is often quite different from the sort of work desired of a fantasy object—Professor Clark Gable or Professor Marilyn Monroe. On the job market, publication can be psychodynamically contraindicated.

The problem here is that assistant professor hires are occasions for rampant libidinizing by search committees. They may seek, usually unknowingly, to hire themselves or to avoid doing so. And they will entertain all sorts of speculative fantasies, some semiconscious and others openly acknowledged and debated. The ship of hope can easily run aground on a good book. Why? Because once a book is there you have become less a subject of speculation than a reality. Unlike a manuscript, a publication is already all that it can ever be.

In the sciences, one fantasy predominates—the potential successful candidate is almost always a potential Nobel Prize winner. In the humanities, it's often a name that signals a fantasy identity. In early 1970, when I was hired at Illinois, or so I learned later, I was touted in Urbana as "the next Northrop Frye." It wasn't, I should emphasize, that my future colleagues so much admired Frye, but rather that his was the only theorist's name they could come up with at the time. One of my colleagues, hired around the same time, was proclaimed "the next Marjorie Hope Nicholson." Obviously, these fantasies are historically specific, since neither Frye's nor Nicholson's name would, as it were, whet anyone's appetite in the market of the nineties. Well, my colleague didn't become the next Marjorie Hope Nicholson—notwithstanding the rumors that she attended her funeral hoping like a future bride to catch the funeral wreath when it was flung toward the grave—and I didn't become the next Northrop Frye. Perhaps in partial compensation Frye did give me a blurb for my first book; my department, therefore, had to settle for seeing Frye's name half an inch from mine in a *PMLA* ad. The likelihood of a red diaper baby—and a Jew to boot—becoming the next Northrop Frye was never overwhelming, but then fantasies don't have to be intricately tested against reality. Meanwhile, I hadn't actually published anything and, happily, no writing sample was requested of me, so Illinois—which might not have liked what it read but didn't read anything—was free to imagine anything about me it wanted.

A job opening is a field of dreams. If you build one, Roland Barthes will come. And imminent Ph.D.s are the best objects for this sort of dreaming. But an author of a book? Well, once you can read a candidate's book, fantasies of becoming turn into accomplishments of an always lesser order. It's one of the reasons senior hires can be so contentious. The unpublished Ph.D. is an untested politician who can promise you anything. Or one—more accurately—that you can use to make any imaginable promise to yourself. A published scholar is a mere mortal like the rest of us, tethered to intractable material facts and far less pliable psychodynamically.

If there is a real lesson in increasing expectations about publication, then, it's this—every publication before you are hired is a double-edged sword. It's at least as likely to damage your candidacy as to enhance it. Does that news imply any advice, or merely intensify the madness? Well, it does suggest that you be aware of these paradoxes. Ask yourself what dreams *others* can dream in the presence of your work. Your own dreams, for the time being, may be less pertinent.

2. NO ONE WANTS TO HIRE DAMAGED GOODS. Five years of itinerant teaching (if you are lucky), six years of assembling dossiers and asking for revised and updated letters of recommendation, seven years of revising your dissertation description, eight jobless years of knowing you are more accomplished than any number of tenured faculty, nine years of borrowing money from your family or your bank at a time when you thought you might be giving some back, ten years of grading freshman composition papers every other week, eleven years of paying annual conference registration fees for the sole purpose of winning access to a reduced-price hotel room, twelve years sardined into elevators wondering if the anguished faces around you resemble your own; thirteen years of watching the superstars of the profession strut and preen while you wonder if you can sustain any piece of your own intellectual life—all this and more may exact a price from you. And that price may suddenly increase for no clear reason—psychic inflation being predictably irregular.

I have seen candidates—in interviews—lose control and lapse into bitterness about their circumstances or, alternatively, make brittle efforts to demonstrate how character enhancing all these "opportunities" have proven. In recent years, when I talk with interviewees one-on-one they always break down and plead for the job. In the eighties I never encountered one that did. For years the anxiety built into the job search has been intense. We all know—though few of us admit it—how fragile and circumstantial is the difference between a successful career and no future we can readily imagine for ourselves. The difference is one job offer; that's all I had, though when I went on the market, it never occurred to me to worry about it. Women, of course, had reason to worry in the job market of the 1960s because many hiring committees discriminated against them, but at least the number of jobs matched or exceeded the number of new Ph.D.s. Now no one does much else *but* worry.

In my own case—going out on the market in 1969 with a dissertation fully drafted and scheduled to be defended the following spring—I caught the declining wake of the sixties boom and got a job at the University of Illinois. As

I arrived on campus in the fall of 1970, the market collapsed almost entirely; that year there were virtually no jobs to be had. If I had spent one more year earning my Ph.D. I probably wouldn't be writing this essay. I'd most likely be a forgotten instance of its subject matter, an unemployed Ph.D. I keep my own history in mind when dealing with today's graduate students; it's a practice I recommend to others as well. For those of us with tenure, it's not a time to naturalize our identity and status but rather to recall their historical contingency. These contingencies are, of course, not only personal but also social and institutional. Put simply, we will not be able to adapt to new social and political pressures if we cannot reflect on our own individual and institutional histories.

As time goes on for the typical long-term candidate of today, of course, the strain accompanying that individual history is more difficult to disguise or displace. The risk increases that you will appear irretrievably wounded—that you will already seem a casualty of the market long before you have given up marketing yourself. It's what I am calling the "damaged goods" phenomenon, and it's one of the costs of the current market we never seem to address.

In fact, since the job crisis in various forms has now gone on for a quarter of a century, some people have been long-term candidates for twenty years or more, piecing together a course here or there, sometimes a visiting appointment, while they publish books and essays and reapply for tenure-track jobs year after year. At some point, part-time work combined with futile annual job searches clearly defines the shape of a person's entire career. One department head who hires a number of such people feels free to call them the profession's "discards." Damaged goods indeed, but sometimes accomplished scholars and teachers as well.

Despite such realities, the acceptable self-presentation and identity for job candidates has always been clear: I'm available but sought after. I'm interested but not anxious. There are other schools interested in me, but you have a chance if you act quickly. I'm eager but not needy. And above all, I am psychically unencumbered: cheerful, seasoned, but not bitter. Damaged goods? That's the person in the hallway waiting for the *next* interview.

But increasingly many long-term candidates *are* damaged goods, and there is an often unconscious reluctance to bet on their chances for recovery. The implicit pressure on candidates to hide or misrepresent their emotional condition could hardly be more intense. No one wants to hire an unheroic, unheralded victim, however much sympathy we might be able to muster. For the long-term candidate, then, the unreality of the identity they must put forward in interviews may be intensely alienating.

For hiring committees to become conscious of this problem is hardly to guarantee any benefit to the long-term candidate. So, once again, is there any advice to offer about the psychology of extended candidacy? Or only another cost to be acknowledged—a cost of overproducing and cheapening the commodity of the new Ph.D.? Well, I can only say that those who go through repeated job searches without suffering disabling consequences are to some degree living their lives elsewhere. Though they do everything they need to do, the job search is not the emotional center of every fall and every spring. They break through into a kind of calm, occupying themselves more with their work, their friends, their family, whatever identity matters to them. The sooner you get there the better off you'll be.

3. S/M DAYS—OR—THEY CAN'T DO ANYTHING TO YOU THAT THEY HAVEN'T ALREADY THOUGHT OF DOING. Scant reassurance, you may say, and that is my point. We are looking at a future in higher education that will feature a new wave of abuses—petty and not so petty—invented in response to a long-term buyers' market.

In 1994, one of Illinois' best students was called for an on-campus interview at a small Midwestern school. For years, bottom-feeding departments have proposed on-campus interviews either with no reimbursement of travel expenses or with reimbursement conditional on accepting a job if it's offered. In other words, in the latter case a candidate who is rejected by them gets reimbursed but a candidate who rejects them doesn't. The school in question dangled package No. 2. As I always do, I recommended that the graduate student wish them well, decline to make the trip, and break off negotiations. But no one takes this advice anymore. As it happened, the candidate made the visit and was met not by a department member but by the dean. The English department consisted of three full-time faculty; under the circumstances the dean took charge of all new appointments. After a fairly conventional day the dean took the candidate out for a one-on-one dinner. Drinks and appetizers were encouraged and indulged in, and the dean did his or her best to sell the school. By the end of the dinner it was clear an offer was on its way. With another campus visit a few days off, the candidate deferred a decision. Within a week, however, she called to decline the job, realizing that meant no travel reimbursement. But that was not the end of the matter.

As it happened, the dean had paid for the candidate's hotel room (one night) with his or her own credit card. A note arrived a few days later asking the candidate to reimburse the dean for the night's lodging. Apparently the dean could hardly sign his or her own reimbursement form. Catch-22. But there was another surprise in the envelope—a demand to pay for the dinner as well—and not just for the candidate herself. The dean also wanted his or her own dinner to be paid for; after all, the dean presumably reasoned, if it were not for the need to entertain the candidate, the dean could have eaten more cheaply at home. Seeking only her own counsel, our graduate student wrote to say she'd pay for the hotel as soon as she got her next paycheck, which she did. But the dean wasn't letting her off so easily on the meal. Over a fortnight a series of dunning phone calls were placed demanding payment for dinner for both of them. Our student's resolve began to falter, and she asked for our advice. Don't pay for *either* meal, we all urged. And I added a special caveat. I wanted to be able to tell the story—with the student's permission—and she would come off better at the end if she stood her ground and refused to pay for the meal. And so she did refuse. A small victory in the job wars, but one that pleases me nonetheless. For the request to pay for dinner is highly unusual, but the request to pay for your own travel is not. An MLA official told me in 1995 he doubted such practices ever occur. I have encountered them so often I can only wonder what world he's living in. Several job candidates have written to me to suggest the refusal to pay travel may reflect the fact the department already knows whom it wants to hire and doesn't want to waste money on fake visitors. Their institution, on the other hand, may require multiple campus visits. In any case, institutional claims about poverty are really claims about priorities and about power. They will meet the expenses they feel they have to meet. Moreover, if professional associations penalize this kind of activity it will largely cease.

Finally, the story about the dinner—exquisitely petty to be sure—is instructive nonetheless, for it lets me modify the lesson: *they will sure as hell do things to you that YOU haven't thought of.* The advice: despite all efforts to undermine it, your dignity is worth preserving, at least on those strategic occasions when you can identify the possibility. As to the dean, whether he or she borrowed money to pay the dinner bill, charged it to an expense account, robbed a bank, worked overtime, or tightened his or her belt and chalked it all up to the perils of life at the top, I do not know.

But I take this story—and others like it—as warrant to ask that all professional organizations establish commissions to investigate abusive search practices. I recommend public censure of departments that, for example, can be proven to have conducted fake job searches. And I recommend that offending departments be barred for a specified time from access to a profession's job market infrastructure—job lists, convention hotel rates, and so forth. Professional organizations are very reluctant to police either members or member departments. Even those that have accepted such responsibilities—like the American Medical Association—do not have a very impressive record of results. But only disciplinary organizations can set appropriate job search practices. In the current climate, unenforced standards are often meaningless, for the buyers' market is guaranteed to multiply abuses.

Of course many abuses are difficult to prove. And certainly some who think they have been mistreated have simply succumbed to the paranoia attending an abusive market. But investigative procedures and modest (but public) sanctions would be a deterrent. Simply having discipline-based committees that could talk to departments about unprofessional practices would be a great help. Who else is to do it now? Job applicants? Members of the offending department? Neither is well positioned. The most one could commonly expect from these people is to report abuses. As the American Association of University Professors has found, schools would rather stay off a censure list. That's one of the reasons the AAUP's censure list has a preponderance of less distinguished institutions. Quality schools would rather not join that group.

I suspect that a whole range of practices we have traditionally deplored and some not yet invented are going to become commonplace in academia. We cannot drastically overproduce Ph.D.s for years without transforming the market and, sooner or later, the nature of academic employment. At some colleges and universities, such transformation has been occurring for years—the practice of farming out courses once taught by full-time tenure-track faculty to part-time instructors who work on a kind of piecework arrangement with neither future guarantees nor current benefits; recent studies suggest that perhaps 45 percent of all faculty in higher educational institutions are now part-timers, compared with 34 percent in 1980 and 22 percent in 1970.[1] And though academic life at many institutions has managed to sustain its traditional perquisites, it does so largely by inertial force. Sooner or later the people who balance the books will recognize openings and opportunities and seize them, especially since many other industries have already undergone similar changes. Faculty members in higher education must assert their difference from other industries.

Imagine the following conversation between the president of a state university, a member of the state legislature, and the state's governor. The president: "I know you feel we should improve the student/faculty ratio and offer more small courses, but we can't afford to do so with our current budget." The legislator: "How much do you pay new faculty members in, say, English or history?" "Well, we pay them $35,000 to $38,000 a year. Of course we could advertise new assistant professorships for $20,000 and easily fill them—in fact, we could probably hire twice as many faculty for the same amount of money—but that wouldn't be fair. We'd make a lot of students, parents, and voters happy as a result, but it wouldn't be right, don't you agree?" The legislator: "You mean the people of this state are paying twice as much for college professors as they have to?" The governor: "Hell, I can cut salaries for new faculty in half and proclaim myself 'the Education Governor' on the same day."

If all this seems unnecessarily paranoid, remember that there are already here and there across the country full-time faculty earning $25,000 a year to teach four or five courses a semester. One American university greeted 1995 by advertising a new kind of position—a tenure-track lecturer in English, not eligible for promotion. In other words, after the probationary period, tenure could be granted but not promotion. The position was as a lifetime lecturer. No accomplishments could make the person eligible for promotion. The teaching load would be set at four courses per semester; salary is negotiable, but I was told by the chair of the search committee it would probably be in the mid-20s. Finally, to avoid embarrassing tenured faculty of higher rank, occupants of lifetime lectureships would be actively discouraged from publishing in areas other than pedagogy. I did not ask whether lecturers would have to wear a scarlet "L" on their jackets. Nor did I ask whether these positions were devised in dungeons replete with instruments of torture. To that question I already knew the answer: the jobs were crafted in the bright light of the university's new identity as corporate boardroom.

And while we are speculating about the future we might contemplate faculty salaries or teaching loads—or perhaps the abolition of tenure—as an initiative on the November ballot in one state or another. While that may not be likely to happen soon, contemplating the possibility makes for an instructive exercise in gauging the degree and nature of our public support. In fact in 1995 and 1996 the University of Minnesota began discussing the possibility of decoupling tenure from salary—you would have lifetime employment but not a guaranteed salary. One proposal was to link a portion of a faculty member's salary to tenure, say 50 percent, and have the balance subject to reduction for reasons of funding or job performance.

What we know *now* is that we have drastically overproduced new Ph.D.s in the humanities. (I propose a program to combat this oversupply in the next chapter.) Despite most tenured faculty not wanting to confront the consequences, we are beginning to see what the human cost of this programmatic self-indulgence has been. What we don't yet know—but can begin to learn from the example of other industries—is what the structural and institutional cost will be. Meanwhile, we are burdened with what may become the academic equivalent of the passenger pigeon, a species driven to extinction—two full generations of faculty members brainwashed into believing they are above politics and economics, that the public sphere is a soiled space they are metaphysically empowered to transcend. That distaste for the public sphere cuts many ways. It leads faculty members to distrust young scholars who have had to work outside academia for a few years. And it leads many of us to claim powerlessness before the legislature and the public. That is a powerlessness we have eagerly embraced for decades, trading safety from public scrutiny and rage for any chance of influence. We have embraced political impotence as part of our identity as professors for so long we have come to believe it is inevitable.

It is hardly surprising in this context that disciplinary organizations like the Modern Language Association opt to fiddle while Rome is ready to burn. I choose this cliché advisedly, for if humanities disciplinary organizations insist largely on celebrating their traditional cultural commitments while social support for higher education is crumbling, if they disdain the public sphere and avoid challenging their members, then fiddling while Rome burns is an apt metaphor. Indeed, one member of the MLA staff privately insists there *is* no job crisis. And as for the Association of Departments of English (ADE), it preoccupies itself with *defending* English departments and handing out soap and towels at summer camp institutes for department heads. I believe the organization's response to the anguish of hundreds of young scholars has been wholly inadequate. For twenty-five years it has been part of the problem, not part of the solution, denying or minimizing the crisis, collecting statistics so as to minimize the problem, and carrying on with business as usual. Both these organizations risk becoming corrupted by the unjust economic and social relations in which they are embedded and which they help to sustain. I recommend that the ADE find a new national director willing to take on these issues aggressively. I place special pressure on the MLA and the ADE here because they are the professional organizations I know best and have some direct responsibility to change, but the patterns in other disciplines are no better and often worse. In many respects, alas, the MLA is the most progressive disciplinary organization. Moreover, its national leaders inevitably feel considerable need to balance various constituencies against one another.

Thus real change, if it is to come, may also require mass action from below. Given the low priority most tenured faculty give to addressing our economic problems or confronting graduate student exploitation, it would be a mistake to rely on them. It is one thing to educate tenured faculty and put pressure on them, quite another to depend on them for either solutions or action. Thus I believe it is imperative for the unemployed to rise up and either transform the existing structures of professional disciplinary organizations or pull them down. Building strong organizations for job seekers, planning street theater and perhaps civil disobedience at annual meetings, might be places to start. Even if the more disruptive of these actions are not taken—since few people on the market, understandably enough, wish to risk their chance for a job by disrupting an annual convention—there is real educational value in debating the advisability of these sorts of direct actions. The threat to intervene in talks and cocktail parties could win concessions and help awaken faculty to conditions they now choose to ignore. (Similarly, serious efforts to unionize graduate students on a campus can win improved working conditions long before the unions themselves are formally recognized.) In any case, a sympathetic MLA or AHA (American Historical Association) or APA (American Psychological Association) president might well, for example, be happy to grant time for a brief but effective symbolic intervention at a public event, such as a presidential address. Such a project might more easily gain faculty support. If we do not begin discussing such options, we will never know what they are. Meanwhile, those who no longer have anything to lose might ask how they can work together to awaken the organizations that have abandoned them.

I have encountered annoyance at these suggestions from all quarters. Let me answer the one reaction I take seriously—anger from the unemployed that I ask them (rather than tenured faculty) to take the lead in promoting change. Obviously some tenured faculty will speak out on these issues as I have, among them my colleague Michael Bérubé, Stephen Watt at Indiana, and Robert Holub at Berkeley. But too many tenured faculty respond to the job crisis by wondering whether they can get through their careers without having to deal with it. Of course everyone concerned should press their tenured colleagues to act, but I would not count on them to do so. In any case, it is probably naive to imagine that a mass movement for change will come from above rather than below.

At the very least it is time for job seekers to work together to explore what collective power they might have; choosing whether to exercise it is a separate issue. At present, disciplinary organizations apparently consider job seekers a powerless, temporary, and generally irrelevant constituency. They will either win jobs and acquire different interests, or they will give up and disappear. National officers consider it counterproductive to risk alienating permanent members who pay full dues. Moral suasion alone apparently will not drive these organizations to do anything to inconvenience or discomfort permanent members. These seem the only explanations for the extraordinary and consistent resistance disciplinary organizations display toward even the most modest changes in their practices—such as refusing to permit member departments to require writing samples and dossiers with initial applications, until now a common and expensive practice burdening job applicants. The perceived power relations have to be altered. Job seekers have to become a constituency to be reckoned with, a constituency dangerous to ignore. There is no other option.

I am glad there was a session or two at the MLA's 1995 and 1996 annual convention and an issue of MLA's annual journal *Profession* devoted to the job crisis, especially since the 1994 issue of *Profession* includes several good essays, but there wasn't much evidence of official interest in these topics in the organization before then. Meanwhile, these business-as-usual responses look more like structures for representation and containment than responses to a crisis. To get some sense of what a professional organization *can* produce, compare the thorough and realistic social, political, and economic assessments in AAUP publications like *Academe* and *Footnotes* with the sometimes self-satisfied, patrician, condescending remarks in recent issues of the *MLA Newsletter.* Here is Patricia Meyer Spacks, in a fall 1994 "President's Column," commenting on the series of letters she received in response to her remarks in the previous issue:

> Graduate students . . . preoccupied with their fear of unemployment . . . recorded personal horror stories, and they frequently communicated their rage—often rage directed at the MLA. . . . I felt grateful for all these letters and gratified by them, even the angry ones, because they implied willingness and effort to participate in a large conversation. . . . I will now bring to my own involvement in the discussion of academic unemployment and its consequences a consciousness informed by all the reactions, all the suggestions, I have encountered. Those who responded to my column will have at least indirect voices in determining the future course of the MLA.

So glad you have packaged your pain and sent it to me in letters, MLA's president seems to say, I hope you are uplifted by this epistolary audience. How pleased we should all be that my consciousness is enhanced. Let us have a conversation about a profession that eats its young. The real problem, of course, is neither with a few leaders nor with the MLA, both of whom mirror their tenured constituencies. But we need MLA and other disciplinary organizations to lead not follow, to challenge their membership not pander to their most reactionary elements. Not quite ready to sing "Happy Days Are Here Again," the MLA's national staff contents itself with offstage renditions of "Keep Your Sunny Side Up."

Yet if I did not think there were a good chance of shifting some of the organization's resources and priorities away from traditional publication and toward political and social engagement with the practical issues confronting higher education, I would not be ending this essay as I am. And the MLA already does more than many other academic groups in terms of offering advice and gathering data, even if its data can be misleading. A job in Afro-American literature, offered every year for a decade without being filled, looks to a reader of the MLA's reports like ten tenure-track jobs. Despite *two decades* of wondering how many people are actually on the market, we still have no mechanism for answering this question, though we know that less than half of new Ph.D.s have found tenure-track jobs in most of the last twenty-five years and though a national survey of MLA members and job candidates could be attempted. Other disciplines need to do the same thing. A questionnaire at the front of the annual job list would be a start; designed to be returned by applicants and to elicit their personal histories, it would enable us to see for the first time how many people are actually on the market and how long they have been actively seeking a job. Dealing with these and other challenges means devoting money to them and not to other things. If people attending annual professional conventions only to be interviewed are to be excused from paying a registration fee, the rest of us will have to pay more; so be it. These are some of the things we must demand. For the gap between our disciplinary organizations' present commitments and the social reality we face is wide and unacceptable.

We can begin to glimpse what is at stake by looking at the political economy of graduate training and instruction. The economic facts—for large-scale public universities—are astonishing. Consider just my own department, the English department at the University of Illinois, one of the campus units that makes heavy use of graduate students as instructors. In the 1994–95 academic year my department paid graduate students to teach about five hundred courses.[2] Their starting salary was $2,500 per course; the average graduate student salary was $2,642 per course. A starting salary for a faculty member in English is about $9,250 per course; the average departmental faculty salary is $11,875 per course. Most graduate students and faculty have the same teaching load, two courses per semester or four courses per year. Ignoring the significant differential in benefit costs (graduate students receive none) and using the starting salaries for comparison, we can make a simple calculation.[3] How much *more* would it cost to hire assistant professors to teach those five hundred courses? The answer: almost three and a half *million* dollars, which happens almost exactly to match the department's existing budget for instructional personnel.[4] So we would nearly need to double our annual personnel budget in order to transfer these courses to faculty members. If we base the same calculation on average graduate student and faculty wages, which provides a more realistic estimate of expenses over time, the annual cost difference comes to $4,616,500. Of course we could increase the teaching loads of the existing faculty—say to six courses a year— but that would give us the highest teaching load among peer institutions and still leave us with four hundred courses to staff. The conclusion is unambiguous: my department is completely dependent on cheap graduate student labor.

Now, is there any way to consider this a fair arrangement? Well, after three years of teaching, graduate students become rather experienced in the classroom, often more experienced than the young faculty we hire. New faculty of course have completed their dissertations, whereas advanced graduate students have merely *almost* completed their dissertations, a difference often more symbolic than real. All in all, only academic politics and an entirely artificial hierarchy justifies the huge salary differential. Needless to say, the state of Illinois is not about to give us the extra four million dollars to hire more English professors. What underwrites the fragile ethics of this whole enterprise is the logic of apprenticeship—graduate students are in training to become higher-paid professors. But if there are no jobs the whole logic of apprenticeship collapses and graduate student teachers become exploited labor. As for the ethics of hiring part-time faculty? There the ruling concepts are market opportunity and fiscal expediency. Meanwhile, the injustices generate rage and self-loathing, contained by the ideology of professionalism.[5] At stake in any effort to change this system is the entire complex of economic, social, and political forces operating on higher education.

Understanding that social reality, once again, will require a major education effort, for faculty members must be encouraged to look beyond their disciplines to recognize the broader forces shaping their future. Educating their membership is another key role for disciplinary organizations. For the emergent work patterns in academia replicate those in the culture at large. The simultaneous increase in unemployment and underemployment (part-time positions) characterizes many American industries. Increasing class size or teaching loads represent much the same sort of speedup and productivity pressure we see on assembly lines and among office workers. Shifting from tenure-track employees to disposable term-contract or part-time teachers saves paying benefits in academia in quite the same way as it does in a factory. Meanwhile, special benefits for corporate executives look much like the high salaries and postretirement deals worked out for college administrators.

While for industry generally this partly represents a return to working conditions that preceded unionization, for academia it is a real change. While hardly utopian working environments, modern universities have never in the past depended so heavily on disposable employees for their teaching staffs. Even clerical workers in some departments have long been considered employees to be nurtured—their skills to be developed, their performance to be rewarded over time—rather than temporary employees to be discarded the moment they would become eligible for benefits and long-term employment. But universities are now moving toward the broader pattern of work in America—the disposable employee with no security and no voice. The exploitation of many graduate teaching assistants—given less than 30 percent of the pay of a full-time faculty member for teaching the same number of courses, in a fake apprenticeship that no longer leads to a permanent job—is only one of the more obvious consequences.[6] While it is unlikely either factory workers or university teachers will soon see common cause in their situations, it is time at least that those of us in academia recognize the parallels and act accordingly.

What the MLA and other professional organizations *should* do is admit the nature and scale of the problem instead of relentlessly trying to put the best possible face on it, and call a moratorium on business as usual for a year. Stop devoting so much of the organization's financial resources and staff time to its book publishing program for a year; if the books are viable, they should be issued by university presses. Cancel all annual conference sessions on literature, language, and theory for a year, and devote the conference instead to examining the state of the profession, the crisis in the job market, and the future of higher education in America. Consider this a call for just that action. Perhaps it would be the only annual MLA meeting in a decade the *New York Times* would not ridicule.

Of course, such a conference would require different organizing strategies, and it might take special effort to get people to attend it, though many tenured faculty have stopped attending their discipline's annual conference anyway. My point is that the kind of debate that needs to take place cannot take place in the shadow of business as usual. If that means that the Edgar Allan Poe Sniffing Society and the Sons of Sir Walter Scott cannot hold their annual brunch and keepsake exchange at the convention, so be it. Again, I write on behalf of every job candidate to tell you the academic profession is sick and broken and in need of change. In the meantime, take Mao's advice: dig tunnels deep, store grain everywhere.

11

WHAT IS
TO BE DONE?

A TWELVE-STEP PROGRAM
FOR ACADEMIA

L et me begin with a riddle for higher education in the 1990s: In three
letters, what is the name of a lengthy and expensive cultural enhancement
program for term employees in the academy—employees, in other words, who
have been hired for a fixed term and no longer? Stumped? Perhaps, like many
Americans, just bored? Or, like most of the higher education community, eager
to change the subject? The key part of the riddle again: *a cultural enhancement
program for term employees.* The answer: the Ph.D.

It is true that a few of these term employees will be selected for permanent
academic jobs. Not necessarily the best and the brightest of them either, though
some of the most talented will succeed. But for the most part, a patchwork of
local cultural and political forces will operate—with a logic that no outsider

could possibly grasp—to select candidates for tenure-track jobs. The academic job market is, in a sense, like a lottery, though one whose rules grow out of the dynamics of local power and folly.[1] Nothing, for example, in the self-image of academia would suggest that departments should avoid hiring the most intellectually innovative candidates from a field of applicants, but they often do, sometimes because they are threatened by them, sometimes because no one on the search committee is well enough informed to have a clue about the quality of the candidates.

Wait a minute, cry the self-appointed angels of the faculty, momentarily distracted from reciting a litany of eternal cultural truths, those aren't term employees; those are graduate students. We are off to a bad start. We are trying to pose this riddle to a faculty audience already offended at the idea that graduate education is professional training, rather than an initiation into transcendent mysteries. Graduate education, they might argue, is the means by which our most sacred secular knowledge passes from one generation to the next. After all, as the up and coming president of a major national disciplinary organization declared at a dinner party recently, "We're not running dental schools!" Indeed not. Young dentists-to-be might be a lot harder than graduate students to deceive, intimidate, and exploit.

Is this what higher education has come to? Unfortunately, the answer is yes. Before most of our graduate students were born, back in the 1960s, you never thought about future employment in the midst of graduate school. Back then, in a seller's market that will never return (except for groups or specializations that are in short supply), department heads sometimes traveled around the country seeking out job candidates. Back then, all the petty abuses of graduate study receded into memory as a new job and a different status loomed. A distinguished scholar who received his degree even earlier, in the late 1950s, told me he remembered everyone getting a job, including those he was convinced weren't very good. Now, some believe the best students succeed, but that is not always the case. For the large number of academics who believe we can ignore present conditions until better times return, it is past time to state the obvious: the good times are over.

As I argued in the last chapter, the problem with graduate study now—in a long-term environment where jobs for new Ph.D.s are the exception rather than the rule—is that apprenticeship has turned into exploitation. Let me expand the claim here: when apprenticeship leads to no future it becomes not only unethical but also pathological. Apprenticeship with no future is servitude. For then the abuses of hierarchy and status have no compensatory and canceling structure. Without a viable job market, Ph.D. programs have only one economic rationale—they are a source of cheap instructional labor for universities.

In my own department, "teaching assistants" for the most part design their own syllabi, conduct all classes, and grade all assignments. Many of them, moreover, do absolutely splendid work—dedicated, impassioned, innovative work. They often deliver much better teaching than permanent faculty would in beginning courses, especially courses like composition and beginning language instruction that have notoriously high burnout rates.

To think of replacing such a labor pool is unpleasant, perhaps impossible, and certainly pedagogically ill-advised. The alternative most appealing to some politicians would be to assign the courses to existing faculty, who would then teach *six* courses per semester, approximately the pattern in high school teaching. Responsibilities for those courses would include grading roughly 1,200 composition papers a year. At that point there would be no time for faculty to read enough to keep up with their field, let alone do any research of their own. Of course many cultural conservatives would rather the humanities had no field to keep up with; the humanities, they feel, should serve an unchanging, unquestioned heritage that is simply transmitted from generation to generation. In any case, these "solutions" hold little appeal for universities.

The alternative most often chosen is the part-time employee. They can, true enough, often be paid even less than graduate students for the teaching they do. Community members can sometimes be paid half as much or less per course, but they often have less institutional loyalty, and less current knowledge of the discipline. Graduate students, on the other hand, are likely to be up-to-date and likely to believe they have something to lose from a bad job performance. They provide a cheap, dedicated, relatively stable labor pool with enough turnover to assure that their work is of high quality. Moreover, the logic of apprenticeship, however flawed and self-deceiving, is ready-to-hand to convince faculty members they are not exploiting these "trainees"; it is a lot harder to convince yourself you are not exploiting part-timers who may have the same advanced degree and qualifications that you do. Indeed some faculty members avoid meeting the part-timers they employ; they live their professional lives as if their part-time colleagues did not exist. Graduate students, on the other hand, are one's intellectual progeny; thus they are to some degree to be cherished, not avoided.

Thus, when they were more or less assured of becoming faculty members, graduate teaching assistants' low pay as apprentices seemed unimportant. Student loans, while burdensome, could be paid off in time on a faculty member's salary. Now our humanities graduate students—many with an accumulated debt of $25,000 or more—talk about celebrating their Ph.D. by declaring bankruptcy.[2]

Meanwhile, the discrepancy between faculty members' high cultural murmurings and the reality of looming unemployment on the street makes graduate study increasingly embittered for graduate students and increasingly conflicted for all involved. Those who complete the Ph.D. enter into a job search that is brutal and demeaning for all except a few. And it may go on forever. For those who do not simply give up, five or six years of post-Ph.D. job searching is commonplace. Still longer searches are not unusual. One long-term job candidate, now a tenured colleague at another school in Illinois, became a faculty member eighteen years after receiving his Ph.D. Few of us could search that long without going mad. Most just give up. One of our recent Ph.D.s lived with his wife for a year in a tin cow shed on the Texas border. Unemployed, they lived off the land. Though they still have dreams, their main ambition was for running water.

LEPERS IN THE ACROPOLIS

Neither those who persist and persist and eventually succeed, nor those who persist and fail, persist and fail, persist and fail again, leave the experience unchanged. Yet no professional organization I know of cares to find out the human consequences of a half decade or more of such professional hazing. The long-term job seekers of the academy are like lepers in the acropolis—a distraction, a betrayal, a burden, a mirror that offers us an image of ourselves we do not want to see. One speaks of them to cast them out of mind. How many of them, we need to ask, think of themselves in the same way, speak of themselves for the same reason, to relieve themselves of self-awareness?

Meanwhile, all who teach undergraduates with passion and intelligence are, almost inescapably, recruiters for the discipline. To teach with affection for one's subject matter, to praise students for doing good work, is potentially to draw students into graduate study in the field. And all of us who teach at institutions with large graduate programs benefit from having someone else teach less attractive introductory courses. With the institutional dependence on cheap labor now a structural necessity and the personal gain for faculty members from this structure unavoidable, complicity with the system is universal. There is one nasty solution to this problem—to give up mass higher education for the poor and the middle classes and make it instead an option only for children of wealthy parents. Some conservatives find that alternative attractive; it would return higher education to the race and class it originally served.

Yet without graduate students there would be no teachers of future generations and no young faculty to carry on research traditions. Of course, if we are only giving a full-scale post-secondary education (as opposed to instrumental job training) to a small subset of those generations, then we do not need so many future faculty members. As for research, no doubt some believe industry could fund the only research that matters, applied technological research with an immediate commercial payoff. Many of us realize how short-sighted that is, but much of the public does not. The humanities in particular has done little to help the public understand the need for continuing research. It is thus especially vulnerable—first to arguments that teaching should replace released (or assigned) time for research, and, second, to arguments that technological innovation can make teachers of an immutable tradition obsolete. Indeed, as CD-ROM and other computer technologies improve over the next years and more complex prepackaged courses gradually become available, technology will begin to place even more downward pressure on the depressed academic job market. CD-ROMs may actually be the first technology to hold real promise of eliminating teaching jobs.

This inherently unstable system survives at present because undergraduates continue to apply to many graduate programs in large numbers, despite the depressed job market and despite journalistic attacks on some disciplines. Yet many people, we need to realize, enter graduate school without clear career goals. They come to study literature, music, art, history, physics, philosophy, mathematics, or anthropology because they like doing so and because they cannot yet see themselves in a full-time job outside academia. Many never actually envision themselves at the front of a classroom until their departments put them there. But both those graduate students who only do research and those who also devote substantial time to teaching acquire serious career aspirations in the course of their doctoral studies. In fact they acquire an identity they did not have at the outset. These commitments can become very deep. We are, after all, talking about six to eight years of teaching and research while working for the Ph.D. For many, temporary jobs after the Ph.D. add more years to the pre–tenure-track full-time teaching and research; the total time can be twelve years or more. At that point, or earlier, some lose even their part-time or temporary jobs; then those unemployed academics feel less like trainees who haven't made the grade than like seasoned professionals arbitrarily fired in mid-career. Indeed, some have publications and teaching awards to prove they *have* made the grade. Then suddenly, in their thirties, they are cut off from a field they have inhabited for a decade or more. And they have to invent an alternative future they have not even imagined, let alone one for which they have trained. For faculty members denied tenure there may at least be some rational explanation for the shock. For the failed job candidate, especially those whose achievements are real and whose further promise and potential are confirmed by faculty advisers and journal editors, no reasonable explanation comes to mind. Their life suddenly becomes incomprehensible.

The appallingly insensitive response some senior faculty members have made to this crisis is, unfortunately, well exemplified by the public statements some leaders of disciplinary organizations have recently seen fit to make. In "The Job Market and Survival," a brief comment that Modern Language Association president Sander Gilman published in the newsletter issued by the organization's graduate student caucus, the self-congratulatory focus is on telling everyone what a wonderful organization the MLA is. Its "big umbrella . . . welcomes" everyone; graduate students are "simply younger colleagues." Consolation for unsettled tenured faculty, on the other hand, was the apparent focus of a presentation Sandra Gilbert, then soon to be president of the MLA, made at Iowa City, at an Association of Departments of English conference in June of 1995. The problem, she suggested, is not with the job market but with graduate student and faculty attitudes. Studying a discipline intensively animates your soul; you should be grateful for the opportunity. As for the chance to teach rhetoric for a few years, she argued, graduate teaching assistants should think of it like a stint in the Peace Corps: it makes the world a better place; do not expect it to lead to a permanent job; feel fulfilled by the experience and then get on with the rest of your life. Of course teaching assistants are not bringing an unfamiliar skill to a foreign country. They are sparing Sandra Gilbert and other tenured faculty from a teaching responsibility that would otherwise fall to them. What *life* is it that—shall we call them Gilbert's "Composition Corps" volunteers—are supposed to return to after twelve years in the field? Gilbert's ideology would seem more fitting were it embodied by the archetypal dead white male of the canon debates, rather than by one of our leading feminist critics. Gilman, notably, has often been cast of late as a defender of the oppressed, but apparently underpaid graduate students or adjunct teachers with no future are either not oppressed or inequities are easy to overlook or under-value when you are complicit in them.

Having been treated to reactionary humanism (in the person of Sandra Gilbert) chastising graduate students to improve their souls, we now have the benighted Left (in the persons of Jim Neilson and Gregory Meyerson) urging them to improve their politics. "A graduate education in the humanities may equally be a political education," they write, "a means by which students learn to read the historical, social, and economic truths hidden and distorted by capitalist culture" (271). So what are these Ph.D.s without academic employment to do? Humanists want to maintain large graduate programs to keep heaven peopled with sensitive souls, while some Leftists apparently imagine that corporate America will be staffed with the newly minted untenurable radicals who cannot get faculty jobs. That's all well and good, but I don't encounter any unemployed Ph.D.s savoring their very personal lesson about capitalism—their entry into the jobless future. The self-satisfied promotion by academics of a long-term research degree as a preparation for writing ad copy or working in K-

Mart is at best cruel and unusual punishment for its victims. About a politically and culturally consciousness-raising master's degree I have no problem; as I will argue, it's a place for warranted expansion. Doctoral programs are not. I say that with no little sense of loss, since I am deeply invested in working with doctoral students, but I also know the present system is brutal and unacceptable. One can imagine, say, a two-year M.A. in "rhetoric and cultural politics" combined with training in being a union organizer; a graduate of such a program might feel culturally enriched and empowered. A Ph.D. who has to give up both teaching and research will not.

But such are the contradictions of subjectivity when people feel their privileges threatened. Such too are the perils of an academic star system that has rewarded careerism as though it were a selfless intellectual quest; we will encounter this sort of disjunction repeatedly in years to come, as we turn to our supposed academic leaders in a time of crisis and discover they have little sense of solidarity with the profession as a whole. As with the progressive scholars at Yale who had no patience with graduate students asserting their rights, the values faculty members promote in their research may have no bearing on their daily lives. Meanwhile, one may contemplate the result Gilbert's claims would have were they more honestly translated into the language of a recruitment brochure: "Come and teach marginally literate business majors how to write! Help students increase their earning power! Loans available to help cover your expenses! Good job performance ratings will have no effect on plans to terminate your employment!"

As for real recruitment brochures, suffice it to say that it is disingenuous and dishonorable to claim that warnings to prospective graduate students about the job market are sufficient, that such warnings take faculty and institutions morally off the hook. The undergraduate senior can easily dismiss warnings about a career to which he or she is still quite uncommitted. The commitment comes later, the career seduction comes later, identity formation comes later. It is with a certain corrupt relief that faculty and administrators note they can post job warnings and still lure applicants into the labor pool. That they can do so is hardly surprising, since applicants are focused on studying subject matter, not planning careers. Meanwhile, the income from graduate teaching seems to an undergraduate like enough to get by on. The package is appealing, its eventual psychological cost often at once large and unimaginable. Nonetheless, the pool of applicants will eventually decline once those who teach undergraduates really hear the job market's blunt message: there is no future in the Ph.D. The message will not in any way mean what it means to graduate students whose careers are cut off in mid-stream—the reality for new Ph.D.s with six or more years of teaching experience. To undergraduates the message will instead be partly symbolic, vaguely invoking disaster or impossibility, and partly incomprehensible. But the symbolism will be negative and it will be decisive for some.

Meanwhile the contradictions in the present system, with its high ideals and brutal consequences, make life structurally schizophrenic for some. Consider, for example, the strains and rewards of directing a graduate program. Ecstatic at bringing brilliant students into the program and seeing them develop into fine scholars and teachers, graduate program directors then face a sense of guilt and despair when those same students fail to get jobs. Imagine, furthermore, what it feels like to see some of your faculty colleagues write brief, lazy, and indifferent letters of recommendation in this context. It is hard to imagine that this system can sustain itself indefinitely.

Some parents of undergraduates, on the other hand, especially those who resent having their children taught by teaching assistants, might welcome the widespread collapse of graduate programs. After all, they think they are paying for professorial teaching. And the crude, widespread reputation of teaching assistants—again fueled by the media—is of people who do not care and who do not speak English. That is certainly not the world I know—the world of teaching assistants in fields like history, philosophy, and English—where dedicated young professionals deliver the best possible teaching at the lowest possible cost. In many cases senior faculty would deliver an inferior product. Although, for example, I have taught composition and enjoyed it, I would now find it demoralizing and intolerable to have to grade hundreds of composition papers each semester. There is no way I could do it as carefully and thoroughly as my graduate students do. So what is to be done?

Well, one valid argument is that there is no oversupply of new Ph.D.s. What the country lacks is the will to pay their salaries. As the need for a more highly skilled work force increases, while secondary education in many cities remains in a state of near collapse, further education for high school graduates is an increasingly urgent social need. We are simply less willing to pay for it, less willing, more broadly, to see collective goals and values like mass higher education as meaningful. For too long we have assumed such values were immutable laws of nature, rather than vulnerable and contingent functions of changing cultural relations. Now, in the wake of our laziness and naiveté, as Ernst Benjamin and my colleague Michael Bérubé and I have pointed out, other social needs have higher priority.[3] So the argument that we actually *need* all these new Ph.D.s is politically and economically irrelevant. So what, again, is to be done?

One modest alternative to overproducing Ph.D.s is to expand specialized terminal M.A. programs that are designed to lead to alternative careers. Students in those programs could do some of the teaching that we cannot afford to hire faculty to do. But effective career-oriented master's programs will take time and ingenuity to devise, and the number of students who can benefit from them may be limited. Not all schools, moreover, will be equally well situated to make the cooperative arrangements with potential employers that could help make such programs successful. Broad solutions to the problems we face, then, will require more varied remedies.

A TWELVE-STEP PROGRAM FOR ACADEMIA

The first thing faculty members must do is admit their responsibility and recognize their potential to address the problem. In a 1994 presidential column in the *MLA Newsletter,* Patricia Meyer Spacks confidently declared that faculty members could have no influence on public policy toward higher education. Sandra Gilbert took much the same line two years later. But as Linda Pratt recently argued in her essay in *Higher Education under Fire,* that is simply not the case. It may be comforting for Spacks and Gilbert to confess impotence, since that relieves them of responsibility for doing anything, but citizens who are willing to organize and act can influence budgets and policy. Certainly those faculty members who have their own lobbyist in a state capital will be surprised to learn that faculty members are powerless. Second, we need to recognize that the job crisis is a complex problem that needs to be addressed on many fronts. No single "solution" will suffice, nor will all faculty be equal to all the tasks involved. I am writing a book about the problem because that is something I have learned to do. I am not certain, however, that I am the best person to talk with parents or legislators. So people need to be connected with the tasks they are best suited to perform. With all these warnings in mind, then, let me make a series of recommendations about what can be done:

1. WRITE A BILL OF RIGHTS FOR GRADUATE STUDENTS, TEACHING ASSISTANTS, AND PART-TIME OR ADJUNCT FACULTY. If we admit that teaching assistants are not apprentices but rather term employees simultaneously undertaking a rigorous discipline of cultural enrichment, their rights, their rewards, and the expectations we have of them will change. Assuming the job market may remain depressed for years, it is time for a national conversation about the meaning of graduate study under these conditions. Such a conversation might result in something like suggested guidelines for a campus bill of rights for all groups who teach on campus.

For some time permanent faculty have hesitated to press for firm rules and better working conditions for adjunct and part-time faculty for fear that regularizing their status would increase the permanence of these categories of teachers. The hope has always been that these positions were temporary and would eventually be filled by tenure-track faculty. But decades have passed in which that strategy hasn't worked. So it is now time instead to work to upgrade their salaries and guarantee them grievance procedures and appropriate benefits. If the gap is closed between adjunct and permanent faculty salaries, so the argument goes, we may make adjuncts and part-timers a less appealing hiring category for university administrators. Frankly, I think the end result will most likely be a reduction in starting salaries for all beginning positions, but the abuse of temporary and semipermanent employees has to end. Tenured faculty need to stop ignoring these people and become responsible for all workers on campus. We need a national debate among all in higher education about the ethics and instructional consequences of current and emerging employment practices.

For many reasons disciplinary organizations are unlikely to initiate such a debate. Many of their members would not welcome discussion of these issues, and the organizations themselves seek to please and balance all constituencies. Moreover, the existence of something like a graduate student bill of rights opens the question of how to deal with departments that refuse to honor it. Most disciplinary organizations are more inclined to rationalize and justify department practices rather than police or criticize them. Departments want advocacy, not scrutiny, from their national organization, and faculty members may see the organization's primary role as producing field bibliographies, awards, and providing them with career opportunities, not ethical challenges.

For all these reasons, the best places for honest debates about the future of graduate study may be both individual campuses and multidisciplinary organizations. Small group discussions on campus can take place outside the surveillance of budget-minded administrators. At almost every other level in academia honest discussion risks penalties. At the national level debate needs to take place among people not invested in avoiding the truth. The membership of multidisciplinary organizations is often better informed about the public standing and financial status of higher education than is the membership of most disciplinary organizations.

2. TEACHING ASSISTANTS AND ADJUNCT OR PART-TIME FACULTY SHOULD UNIONIZE. Whatever credibility a national bill of rights for these groups might have, it will never be fully realized on individual campuses until they exercise the power they now hold only in potential. Withholding their teaching services represents a genuine threat to the capacity of many schools to sustain business as usual. Yet even on large campuses heavily dependent on part-time or graduate student teachers, this power will vary. For some schools historically invested in their national prestige, the power to embarrass faculty, administrators, parents, and alumni by protests, work stoppages, and strikes may be significant. Yet administrators at some elite schools, like Yale, seem to take a certain pride in bad publicity. In any case, withholding instruction alone will not win recognition at most institutions. And it will exert surprisingly little pressure on politicians; for them it is more an opportunity for demagoguery than a political risk. Again, with higher education partially delegitimated in the public sphere, graduate students will be easier to represent as privileged rather than exploited. On some campuses, especially those in small towns and cities where the campus is a major employer, the real power is economic. Effective union organizing on a campus requires a careful analysis of the economic impact of the campus and a major effort to educate and build alliances with all potential allies.

Wielding economic power from a small community, moreover, requires solidarity from faculty and staff. Other unions would need to honor picket lines and refuse campus deliveries, and all employees would need to work together to provoke an economic crisis in the relevant political and geographical area. Interestingly, this can sometimes be done *without* everyone going on strike—by scheduling an economic action immediately after a monthly pay check is received and then withdrawing all savings from state banks and credit unions, refusing to make all mortgage or rent and utility payments, canceling all nonessential services and repairs, and making no purchases from merchants in the state. One might organize group shopping trips to other states for all purchases. In this way certain campuses can potentially get the business community to pressure boards of trustees and legislators to make concessions to a union. So a teaching assistant union that strikes can produce all the beneficial effects of a campus-wide strike *without,* say, faculty and clerical staff striking *if* those other groups are willing to take the economic actions outlined above. Many businesses, financial institutions, and public utilities in smaller communities—including banks, water, gas, electric, and phone companies—maintain surprisingly low cash reserves and are quite dependent on a monthly influx of university income. A properly run strike in such a community simultaneously denies them that income and drains cash reserves. This strategy would not work in New York City but it could work in many college towns. It could work in New Haven or Urbana if the faculty, students, and staff were united. It is certainly past time for faculty to begin thinking about the character of employment throughout the campus community; the front lines for the defense of tenure may, surprisingly enough, prove in retrospect to have been the cafeteria and the electrical shop, not the faculty senate.

In an April 1996 article in *Lingua Franca, New Yorker* staff writer Emily Eakin responded to an earlier version of this plan by remarking "here was revolution matter-of-factly laid out in an easy-to-follow, twelve step formula." My "program for improving graduate student life," she allowed, "made the grade strike at Yale look like kid stuff" (p. 56). While I am amused to be characterized as the Bakunin of Urbana, it is also instructively depressing to see a *New Yorker* writer placing these ideas—drawn from the long history of union activism—on the extreme Left of American politics. It gives us a good indication of how much education needs to take place before academia's exploited employees can win public support for the actions they must take to win their rights.

Indeed, just organizing the relevant employees and then winning support from other campus constituencies can present major challenges. Both aims require careful strategic choices. Because graduate student salaries vary so widely from discipline to discipline, it is often best to organize around a set of more universal issues like health insurance, child care, tuition waivers, employment status, retirement credit, and working conditions. Special care also needs to be taken to reach out to undergraduates and win their support. Unfortunately, sympathy for their instructors has not been high among students of the eighties · or nineties. So a strike needs to connect with their self-interest. Those undergraduates who understand that they themselves will soon be graduate students may be amenable to becoming better informed about equity issues for T.A.s Others may be reached by making class size a bargaining point. Smaller classes mean more individual attention to students and perhaps a real benefit in terms of the quality and marketability of their education.

Whatever problems tenure-track faculty unionization presents to differential reward systems based on individual merit—especially at research institutions—there are few comparable problems with teaching assistant, adjunct, or part-time faculty unions. In fact I believe graduate students or adjuncts who unionize have much to gain and little to lose but their illusions, their false consciousness, and the myths of professionalism that can make them complicit in their own exploitation. Unionize. To expose the ideology that blocks understanding of the present reality, it is worth repeating a slogan that too many of us find antediluvian and melodramatic: You have nothing to lose but your chains.

3. MAKE TEACHING ASSISTANTS EMPLOYEES. This is the crucial perceptual and legal issue, one often only achievable through group action and unionization. If graduate students are primarily acolytes learning a spiritual discipline, they may have few rights. On the other hand, if they are primarily there to perform an instructional service for which they are paid, then they are primarily employees. If neither identity takes precedence, they still have reason to seek fair recompense and working conditions. Employees may be eligible for retirement benefits, unemployment compensation, and better formal agreements on working conditions. In any case it is time for a clear-headed discussion of this issue, combined with an effort to grant graduate students the best of both worlds.

4. A YEAR'S WORK FOR A YEAR'S WAGE. In my own department most graduate students teach the same load as faculty—four courses a year—but unlike faculty they do not earn enough to live on for twelve months. Many must get second jobs or take out loans to get through the summer. *A Year's Pay for a Year's Work* seems like a good first principle and a good rallying cry for teaching assistants, and part-time or adjunct faculty. Recognizing that graduate student teachers *are* employees being paid for their work makes it more difficult to reject this principle for all these groups.

5. CHALLENGE THE PRIORITY GIVEN TO FACULTY SALARIES. The last thing faculty members want to admit is that they are in competition with graduate students and part-timers for limited resources. I believe it would be better to get this usually hidden conflict out in the open rather than deny its existence, since teaching assistant or adjunct salaries will otherwise always have the lowest priority. A possible moral and political challenge to faculty might be organized with a question something like this: Are you willing to give up all or part of next year's raise to fund a 20 percent salary increase for all teaching assistants earning less than $14,000 a year?

On my own campus I was recently a member of a college-level financial planning committee that recommended using some vacated faculty salaries to increase the size and number of graduate student fellowships. Many of my English department colleagues felt betrayed by this decision and called a meeting to protest it (and other elements of the committee's report); some criticized my role in the process. Most regained their composure after some discussion, but both the level of their anger and its unreflective character surprised me. Few seemed embarrassed at arguing that increased graduate student support was a bad use of limited resources. Thinking back over the years, however, I recall that an incompetent tenured faculty member was usually considered a tragic figure to be tolerated and nurtured. A teaching assistant with problems is often someone to be fired.

6. URGE COMMUNITY COLLEGES TO HIRE PH.D.S. The claim that new Ph.D.s are only interested in research and not interested in teaching is both false and malicious. For many new Ph.D.s the dissertation represents at once the first and the last major long-term research project they will undertake. In fact, even at research universities many new Ph.D.s are primarily invested in being teachers. Some even gain community college teaching experience while on the market seeking a tenure-track job at a four-year college or university. Since many community colleges are either reluctant or flatly unwilling to hire Ph.D.s for full-time jobs, a valuable human resource that could benefit both community colleges and

Ph.D.-granting institutions is being wasted. The disciplinary immersion and commitment and intellectual focus built into the Ph.D. has pedagogical value at all instructional levels. If universities built working relationships with junior colleges—relationships that should include teaching internships and should honor the pedagogical and political expertise of existing junior college faculty—it should eventually be possible to increase the percentage of Ph.D.s on their faculties. Of course significant numbers of tenure-track junior college appointments will not open up unless those institutions decrease their reliance on part-time faculty. Thus this is obviously not a short-term solution, but the job crisis is not about to disappear. Despite the problems with this scenario, it is worth investigating. It could be one part of a multiple-front strategy for dealing with the job crisis.

7. EXCHANGE POSTDOCTORAL TEACHERS. One of the dangers of the current market is the temptation to establish a permanent class of underpaid and overworked faculty. Solutions that open a new phase of temporary employment—salaried at at least $25,000 per year for postdoctoral teaching fellows—are risky but preferable to some of the alternatives in place. Moreover, teaching after earning the Ph.D. does somewhat increase marketability. Formal exchange programs—either between two universities or among larger groups of schools—would take some of the anguish and uncertainty out of the current yearly search for a temporary position. Three-year postdocs would give people a somewhat secure base from which to apply for permanent jobs. Although I believe administrators should work hard to create such programs as soon as possible, it is also necessary that such programs, as I shall argue more fully in the next chapter, be strictly limited to schools that have their own doctoral programs in the field and that have significantly reduced those programs in size.

8. CHALLENGE DISCIPLINARY ORGANIZATIONS. As Steven Watt recently pointed out to me, academic disciplinary organizations were eager to be creative and innovative in responding to a Ph.D. shortage in the 1960s. They adjusted requirements and streamlined programs, all to produce more Ph.D.s more quickly. They have been singularly inchoate in the present crisis of oversupply. These organizations often see justifying disciplinary turf and practices as their central mission. Graduate students and part-timers are not their primary constituencies. The logic of the bureaucracies that run the larger organizations is obvious: never offend the membership. Lest anyone have any doubts, remember that the members who count are the permanent faculty. Once again, graduate students, adjuncts, and their precious few allies among the tenured faculty must exert maximum pressure on their disciplines; to be effective, all those deeply concerned about the job crisis must not only act individually but must also gather together to act collectively. Disciplinary organizations must be compelled to direct more of their resources toward examining and intervening in higher education's crisis and less of it toward enhancing their members' careers.

9. FIGHT FALSE CONSCIOUSNESS / EDUCATE THE EDUCATORS. Many AAUP members realize that faculty members can affect both public perceptions and state budgets, but the AAUP does not have enough members, a fact that says less about the AAUP than it does about the benighted social consciousness of most American faculty. Too many faculty members believe members of their discipline are their only relevant professional community. How many of these people can be reeducated I do not know. But I do know we need to intervene in the process that brainwashes each new generation of faculty. Graduate students need to be socialized into a much broader conception of academic citizenship; they need to be trained to take on a wider set of social and political responsibilities. Course segments on the cultural politics of education, for example, need to be part of every graduate curriculum. At key points in every class I teach I now ask students how the general public might respond to the kind of arguments the class is making. How, I add, might those arguments be reformulated to win greater public approval. The time when faculty could ignore the public is over, but we can only train effective academic citizens if reflections on the meaning of citizenship are embedded in a wide spectrum of courses. We face a long-term crisis and new generations of faculty must realize they have a role in the definition and struggle over the country's priorities.

10. CLOSE MARGINAL DOCTORAL PROGRAMS / PREVENT NEW ONES FROM BEING CREATED. The current oversupply of new Ph.D.s cheapens the degree and guarantees that administrators and legislators will undercut salaries and increase work loads. No one who has seen clearly the misery of long-term unsuccessful job candidates would argue that the current system is grounded in decency, professionalism, or sound social policy. The collapse of the job market has made higher education pervasively corrupt. The display of our intellectual commitments lures students to the partial ruin of their lives. Then we tell them professionalism and maturity dictate they should internalize all their anger and anguish.

Although some graduate programs should be smaller, reducing the size of programs across the board until they all become nonfunctional is hardly the best solution. In the end, some ineffective, underutilized, and marginal degree programs should be closed. (Some on the Left, including Jim Neilson and Gregory Meyerson, have argued that this is an elitist and undemocratic suggestion, because it limits "access" to doctoral programs. Broad access is, I believe, a terribly important issue for the undergraduate degree, as is class, race, and gender diversity in doctoral programs. But simply maintaining huge Ph.D. programs so that thousands of students can feel betrayed when their training comes to nothing is irrational.)[4] Not every Ph.D. needs, for example, to be granted at every institution in a given state. Moreover, nearby schools might think seriously about offering joint degrees, thereby reducing the need for all subspecializations to be represented in every department. Such joint doctoral programs would also offer professional fulfillment to faculty in areas of declining enrollment, including a number of once-popular foreign languages.

Perhaps worst of all, however, are the continuing efforts to open new doctoral programs in fields already oversupplied with unemployed Ph.D.s. It is hard to believe that such efforts continue in the present crisis, but they do, and both faculty and administrators must be firm in rejecting them. It is important to realize, however, that the cynical constituency for creating new, unneeded, and widely destructive new doctoral programs is more varied than one might think. Sometimes the impulse arises out of the unprincipled greed of departmental faculty. But it is equally likely to come from upper-level administrators who see doctoral programs as a source simultaneously of prestige and cheap labor. In this context I found it quite difficult to recommend active resistance from an assistant professor at another school who asked me how she could discourage her colleagues from starting a Ph.D. in English. The leadership has to come from elsewhere. As a first step, disciplinary organizations in fields oversupplied with Ph.D.s should issue strong statements arguing against the creation of new programs and should distribute those statements to everyone in the higher education community. Such statements would not be binding, but they would sometimes be effective.

The head of a disciplinary organization came running up to me at a 1994 convention yelling that legislators and administrators were using my publications to argue that programs should be closed. So let me state my position clearly. Legislators rarely have the knowledge to judge either a program's quality or its synergistic and service role on a campus. But faculty members do have that knowledge, and some poor-quality and underutilized degree programs, they must realize, deserve to be closed. At some point, across-the-board budget cuts stop making sense. It is time for faculties to take the lead in program evaluation and termination. And it is time for national disciplinary organizations to develop broad and discipline-specific criteria for judging program effectiveness.

11. ENCOURAGE BOTH INEFFECTIVE AND EFFECTIVE FACULTY TO RETIRE AND REHIRE EFFECTIVE ONES PART-TIME. This is the most risky recommendation I am making, because it is readily subject to the sort of abuse the AAUP has long worked to guard against—politically motivated attacks on tenured faculty. Yet the contrast between some dysfunctional tenured faculty and many multifunctional young Ph.D.s is especially stark and painful in the present crisis. Of course there are not enough incompetent or marginal faculty of retirement age to provide jobs for all unemployed Ph.D.s, but there are enough in some departments—5 to 10 percent—to have some real impact on the crisis.

Both the degree and nature of faculty problems vary considerably. We all know tenured faculty at our own or other institutions who skip a third or more of their classes, continually abuse their students intellectually or sexually, or teach the discipline as it existed twenty years ago because they have not kept up with their fields. Some simply have lost interest in their jobs and now put their energies into other activities. I know a faculty member who was simultaneously a full-time minister for a congregation in a nearby city, another who simultaneously worked forty hours a week in a sales job in a clothing store, a third who seemed to devote all his time to his dog-breeding business. But these are not the very worst stories. Indeed, in some cases higher education takes significant risks to its public image, financial support, and the tenure system in keeping dysfunctional faculty members on staff.

Interestingly enough, many such faculty members are willing, even eager, to retire. Yet one result of long-term bad teaching and intellectual stagnation may be a salary so low that retirement is financially impossible. So colleges and universities need to offer individually designed financial packages that respond to different problems and make retirement feasible. Perhaps one principle colleges and universities could adopt is this: no faculty member with thirty years of service should have to retire on less income than a new assistant professor in the arts or humanities would receive. That states the problem both baldly and realistically, and sets an individual retirement package goal that few are likely to regard as a reward for incompetence. It also acknowledges the real financial risk some underpaid faculty members face at retirement time, while asserting that universities have no business trying to sustain higher disciplinary salaries after retirement for those faculty who have not performed competently. There is no reason why a retired marginal commerce professor should earn more than a retired marginal philosopher. At the same time, national organizations may need to concern themselves with formulating more general principles for individual retirement packages to avoid political abuse of the option.

All that is being offered in most of these packages, it should be clear, is an opportunity to retire at a somewhat higher salary than the faculty member would otherwise be able to achieve. Nonetheless, many faculty will need considerable unpressured time—certainly a number of months—to think through the implications and make a decision. Those whose teaching is adequate should be offered

WHAT IS TO BE DONE?

the opportunity to accept a term contract to teach one course per year after retirement. Of course the combined impact of increased budgetary restraint and the collapsed job market may also lead colleges to confront serious long-term personnel problems they have unprofessionally avoided, like people repeatedly charged with sexual harassment, and in those cases retirement packages should be promoted more aggressively.

At the other end of the spectrum—our most talented faculty who are of retirement age—we need a very different sort of approach: an extensive program to encourage well-qualified faculty to retire but continue teaching and doing research and administration.

All across the country there are distinguished well-paid faculty members who could retire at 70 percent or more of their current take-home pay. At some universities, including Yale, there are faculty who could nearly *double* their income by retiring. Such people have typically participated in more than one retirement plan and have reached an age when actuarial tables grant them a high payout rate. They stay on salary because there is no other way to continue doing the work they love to do. Indeed, in many cases the people most eligible for well-paid retirement are the very people universities do not want to lose. Not only are they valued teachers and scholars; often their long experience in university governance and well-established disciplinary leadership makes them irreplaceable. Many have no wish to retire. Yet at the same time their salaries could be almost entirely shifted to retirement programs. In a surprising number of cases, universities are paying high salaries to people when there is absolutely no reason to do so.

Of course retirement usually carries with it not only a sense of emotional loss and exile but also a loss of prestige, research resources, responsibility, and contact with students and colleagues. We therefore need to create a new category—call it "senior scholar"—for selected faculty who effectively retire on paper only, because they would be rehired soon thereafter and retain all their prior authority. They would continue to teach—most likely on partially or substantially reduced loads according to mutual agreement. Moreover, they would retain all the rights and privileges and most of the responsibilities of full-paid faculty. They would serve on hiring committees, vote on tenure and promotion decisions, direct dissertations, and remain eligible to serve as department heads, deans, and higher administrators. They would have full access to travel and research support. On the other hand, no senior scholar would be required to accept any committee or administrative assignment he or she did not wish to take. They would be paid perhaps 10 to 30 percent of their before-"retirement" income to supplement their retirement benefits.

Some restrictions often apply, but few are insurmountable. Faculty members generally need to terminate employment before drawing on their annuities. Most faculty on these plans could not retire before age 59½ because of the IRS penalty that would apply, but very few have accumulated enough resources to retire before then anyway. Once rehired, they would either cease making retirement contributions or do so under an entirely new agreement. At my own institution, which participates in a state retirement plan, faculty members can be rehired so long as their combined retirement annuity and postretirement income do not exceed preretirement pay. However, if they are employed at a nonparticipating institution after retirement, there is no restriction on their income. Some institutions require a time period—sometimes as short as two months—to elapse between retirement and rehiring.

To take a hypothetical case, a faculty member at the University of Illinois who retired at age 65 with thirty-five years of service and a salary of $75,000 would receive an annual retirement income of about $52,000. If the university rehired that faculty member for, say, $18,000, even for half-time teaching, it would be able to hire a full-time junior faculty member with the money saved and have significantly more benefit from the resources allocated to both people, along with money left over. On this basis, for every two senior scholars retired and rehired, one could hire *three* new faculty members in the arts, humanities, or social sciences.

Because the people targeted for such an agreement would include some of our most highly paid and accomplished faculty, the financial benefit from each person converted to a senior scholar could be substantial. In fact there are significant numbers of such potentially convertible appointments where colleges and universities could save as much as $50,000 per faculty member. In some cases—where people of retirement age are paid $150,000 or more—the savings would be much greater.

In order for senior scholars to retain their existing power, influence, prestige, and responsibilities, some institutions would have to make basic changes in their governing statutes or charters. But sometimes much less effort would be required. At the University of Illinois, for example, departments could extend voting rights to emeritus faculty who are still employed as teachers simply by changing their departmental bylaws, a process that would often take only a few months. Other institutions would have to adjust the program to match retirement rules or change the rules themselves. Is it worth the effort? Well, there are institutions that could reap an immediate benefit of several million dollars for new faculty appointments. Moreover, unlike most other proposals for dealing with the fiscal crisis, everyone involved would benefit from this program. There are no victims and no losers.

If what I have just said is to be true, however, it is important that senior scholar appointments be available to faculty in all disciplines. I have in mind that these positions would be selective, that they would be offered to high-quality teachers and scholars, not to every retiring faculty member. My aim is not to create a universal benefit but rather to offer productive faculty a way of retiring before they otherwise would, while continuing to serve their own or other institutions. But it would be educationally indefensible and morally reprehensible to offer such appointments only to income-producing disciplines, whether those with access to outside grants or those with wealthy alumni. The arts, humanities, and interpretive social sciences must be eligible for an equal share of these positions.

But what does such a senior scholar gain? Some would have reduced teaching loads and more time for research. All would gain greater flexibility in accepting or refusing assignments. All should be free to take unpaid leave whenever they wish. Some senior scholar appointments could be permanent; others could be for terms of five or ten years.

The only thing senior scholars would lose is their annual salary increase. But in fact some academics are already at a tax bracket where salary increases carry no significant material benefit. At best symbolic, at worst some salary increases satisfy greed and ego alone. In declaring themselves beyond such concerns, senior scholars would gain a certain respect and a certain ethical authority. No longer significantly dependent on their institutions for their income, they would be partly beyond temptation or coercion. Far from being marginalized, they might be uniquely valued sources of disinterested advice and service.

At its crudest level, this is a proposal for creative cost-shifting—effectively moving salaries from annual budgets to retirement accounts. But it would make it possible to increase the size of the faculty in the best possible way—by retaining the most experienced people while also reinvigorating the professoriate from below.

Institutions have from time to time made ad hoc arrangements to keep individuals on after retirement, but usually not without retirement's attendant stigma and generally not without substantial loss of professorial function. Most faculty members, moreover, continue to be offered only the two mutually exclusive alternatives: continue working full-time on the university budget or quit. A formal program like the one I am proposing could reduce all those problems and make a significant contribution toward alleviating the job crisis. All it would take for this to become a widely available option is for a few of our better institutions to adopt it. Those institutions would find it easier to recruit and retain senior faculty. Other schools would soon copy them. Once this option were widely available and widely present as a budget item, visiting senior scholar appointments and senior scholar exchanges would be easy to arrange. That would benefit both faculty interested in experiencing new environments and institutions barred from rehiring their own faculty. In the meantime, the absence of any widespread program of this sort often means that departments negotiating with individual faculty have no financial resources to draw on and either cannot rehire faculty at all or can do so only at excessively low salary rates. Negotiations in that context are often doubly humiliating: the stigma of reduced authority is combined with a humiliating salary. We have allowed the present retirement system to persist out of inertia and thoughtlessness. It is time to overhaul it and make new options available that can benefit higher education generally.

To do so, however, does require highly selective programs. The universal retirement offers promoted in California did little good and much damage, sometimes nearly incapacitating individual departments. One protection against the dangers of this and other retirement programs would be universal adoption of a new principle—that no faculty member should retire without receiving a legally binding agreement from a dean stating that he or she will be replaced with a tenure-track faculty member within two years. National organizations should develop such contracts and distribute them widely.

12. POPULARIZE THE ACHIEVEMENTS OF THE ACADEMY. In its desire to curtail diversity, enhance privilege, and compete for power and authority, the New Right has successfully trivialized or scandalized the most innovative social science and humanities research of the last twenty years. Journalists willing to cash in on American anti-intellectualism have helped the Right at every step. Disdaining the public sphere, most faculty have foolishly let this happen without effective counteraction. Now there is no chance that higher education can compete for funds successfully unless we can reverse this process, rearticulate our achievements, and recreate popular common sense about our research and social aims.

In my own field, literary studies, the twenty-year effort to open the canon and recover a fuller sense of our literary heritage should be widely viewed as a triumph of democracy. Yet it has been successfully demonized and represented as a loss of standards and value. What should in a democracy have been a public relations triumph has been disseminated as a disaster. The route from a public loss of faith to a cut in public funding may not seem direct, but it is direct enough. Perhaps no more instructive evidence for the complex, multifaceted nature of the present crisis exists than this. Indeed we cannot address the crisis without taking up all such cultural relations. Those who doubt these connections exist should remember, as I pointed out in chapter 9, that two former heads of the National Endowment for the Humanities testified before Congress in the spring of 1995 that the Endowment should be cut because the intellectual decay of the humanities meant they were no longer worth funding.

No one person could possibly work on all twelve of these recommendations. Some of the points above, therefore, speak to particular constituencies and particular individual strengths. The range of social, political, and professional fronts requiring action may also seem rather daunting. Yet this list of suggestions—a list that needs to be debated and amended—also demonstrates that we are not powerless, that there are things to be done. Those faculty members who care deeply about the crisis—and there are many who do, even if they do not represent a majority—should be encouraged that a coherent plan of action is possible.

If, moreover, we look back over the last twenty-five years, it is apparent that the job crisis has been with us in varying degrees all that time. Even the brief upturn in the 1980s was not enough to bring employment to those new Ph.D.s who failed to get jobs in the market collapse of the 1970s. Not, of course, that we have any idea what these numbers are, since most disciplinary organizations prefer not to collect data that make them look bad. Indeed, one head of a disciplinary organization recently criticized me in conversation for spreading news about the profession that might discourage people from enrolling in the undergraduate major. The three clearly expendable constituencies in all this are graduate students, adjuncts, and part-time faculty. They pay the highest cost for the inequities of the present system, and almost everyone else involved wants to keep things as they are.

One way to create an appropriate context in which to address the problem is to ask what would be the most ethically sound response to the crisis. One answer would be to close *all* admissions to doctoral programs in fields oversupplied with Ph.D.s for a fixed period of time, say five or six years, so that institutions would be forced to hire from the existing pool of candidates until the backlog of long-term candidates was substantially reduced. Most teaching assistants would then for a time be candidates for the M.A., a shorter degree program with fewer economic inequities—less debt accumulation, less reason for vestment in a retirement program, and substantially less discrepancy between salary and experience—and much less psychological cost. There are many reasons why that solution would create problems of its own, but at least the proposal highlights the seriousness of the crisis.

A surprisingly accurate 1994 article by Tony Horwitz in the *Wall Street Journal* took the rather clever route of comparing two recent generations of faculty members—their salaries, teaching loads, job security, and sense of professional satisfaction—and found many young faculty leading very different lives from their parents in academia. Of course many would simply reply that at least these young faculty have jobs. And that comment would be entirely to the point. For the job crisis and the oversupply of Ph.D.s color everything we do. Indeed, the market will almost certainly lead many campuses to reintroduce all the injustices the AAUP has fought against for decades. More than just a risk to salaries, the job crisis is a risk to the tenure system and a risk to free speech. When Mary Burgan remarked recently that "tenure is the equivalent of welfare in the public mind," she offered a succinct figure for the challenges we face.[5]

One potentially positive outcome of this multilevel crisis would be a renewed recognition that all of us professionally involved in education are to some extent in one boat that rises or falls with the economy and public faith in our enterprise. The interests of junior colleges, small liberal arts colleges, and full-scale research universities will never wholly converge, but they now have points of convergence that merit strategic alliances. The job crisis highlights some of those common interests, since new Ph.D.s from the elite schools have for years had to take jobs—when they could find them at all—at all sorts of institutions. Thus the most prestigious schools now have reason to be concerned about academic freedom, tenure, and the general quality of life everywhere in higher education. More than vigilance will be needed to preserve the values in which we believe. We need to marshal our resources for a major struggle of some duration. We are already past the best time to begin.

WHAT IS TO BE DONE?

REACTION AND RESISTANCE
AT YALE AND THE MLA

UNION ORGANIZING
AND THE JOB MARKET

I t was late in the 1995 Christmas season. In the general culture the parties
were over until New Years. But at the annual meeting of the Modern
Language Association job candidates had nonetheless to be feted. So in a
cramped room high in some forgettable hotel, Cactus State University was
offering boxed wine, pretzels, and chips to people being interviewed for a job in
critical theory. *Boxed wine?* Yes, indeed. Years ago at my home university
distinguished French theoretician Henri Lefebvre had delivered what proved to
be my single favorite line from a conference on the current state of Marxism: "I
cannot believe what cheap wine these American Marxists drink!" But that was
1983, and we were at least talking about bottles with corks. Now it was to be
boxed wine. Could the wine be sending a message? Either universities had fallen

on even harder times than I had thought or the sponsors of this party knew it did not matter.

In a rare moment of solidarity among the candidates for the job, they decided the second explanation might be more to the point. These cocktail parties for job candidates are one of the more notable hazing rituals of the job wars. All the candidates being interviewed are invited to mingle with all the department faculty members attending the annual convention. Not certain how much is at stake, some candidates work hard to make an impression on key faculty. Others give up, unwilling to risk the mixture of alcohol and anxious ambition, and actually talk with the competition (one another). At this party there wasn't much choice. Either very few faculty members had left the high desert for the windy city of Chicago, or very few bothered to show up around the groaning board. The candidates meanwhile began to trade stories. Some found the interviewing committee strangely uninformed about their dissertations and vitas. It seemed at moments as if no one had actually read their materials. And certainly the party seemed ill designed to impress anyone or woo them to the school. A rumor began to circulate: an inside candidate had the inside track. Some, though not all, of the candidates felt their interviews were at best half-interested, at worst a sham. As it happened, the inside candidate pursued another option, and one of the other candidates was hired, so the folks at Cactus State behaved honorably after all. But we can be sure that somewhere that season someone did not. Fake job searches where the candidate of choice is known beforehand do occur, and they need to be stopped.

Among the folks who do not deserve academy awards for this year's job market performance (and among those who do not merit the disguise I provided for Cactus State) are the faculty members who ran a 1995–96 search at the University of California at Santa Cruz. Late this year an Ivy League graduate student received a phone call from California instructing her to express mail a writing sample to the Santa Cruz committee immediately. The student promptly complied. Such requests, which generally follow a review of job candidates' vitas and letters of application, often show one has made the first cut. Although most writing sample requests nonetheless come to nothing, they are the first actual feedback you get from search committees and thus a meaningful signal of approval for your work. Needing confirmation, the student called California in a few days to make sure the shipment had arrived. The secretary answered, telling her there were *hundreds* of writing sample packages piled up in the office, many of them sent by express mail or FedEx. They were running late on the search, there being many worthy cultural distractions on the coast and among the redwoods spilling down across the campus, and they realized they hadn't gotten around to requesting writing samples from candidates. Instead of reviewing the applications and making a first cut, eliminating at least those wholly inappropriate for the job, they began to send notes requesting a writing sample to every applicant, but as the deadline approached and applications continued to arrive, phone calls and express mail requests became necessary. It cost UC-Santa Cruz $100 in postage, perhaps more than that in phone bills, but you've got to give your all. Meanwhile, as much as several thousands of dollars in photocopying and mailing fees were spent making up for Santa Cruz's sloppy work. As for the student's package? Well, there was no way the secretary was going to sort through them all, but it was probably safe to assume her package was there. Less safe, perhaps, to assume it would be read carefully.

Departments at some other California schools, like a number of departments in the country, in fact demand that all candidates send full dossiers and writing samples from the outset, a practice that produces vast mounds of material that no individual search committee member can hope to read. The alternative, having everyone send a three-page single-spaced book or dissertation description, not only saves candidates money but also gives people on the search committee a chance to review all the applicants' work. That method, however, requires search committee members to move efficiently to make a first cut, eliminating perhaps 75 percent of the applicants, and asking for dossiers and writing samples from the remaining 25 percent. A far more humane process and one that produces immensely well-informed committees, it nonetheless requires more rapid coordinated effort, an effort some schools are unwilling to make. Instead, some claim to read a thousand writing samples and dossiers carefully, a claim one may reasonably dispute.[1] In the spring of 1996, one graduating senior from a California school, an applicant to our graduate program, assured us she knew the fate of most job searches by new Ph.Ds: she had been hired to shred candidates' writing samples before they were sent to the landfill. This is but one of many cases where academia might well clean up its act in anticipation of eventual media attention.

For as far as the media are concerned, the discipline of English, and especially its professional organization the MLA, have for decades had only one story (with short legs) worth reporting: *the professor has no clothes.* But as this and other anecdotes will suggest, times change insofar as the professoriate continues to find new ways of displaying its nakedness. Of equal importance, however, is the fact that there is new evidence of some resistance to academia's increasingly exploitive working conditions. My aim here is to report on both trends.

While MLA interviews were in progress, and while cocktail parties were under way at the annual meeting, down the street, in a larger room, the MLA's delegate assembly was in session and running late as usual. Peter Brooks, distinguished professor of English and Comparative Literature at Yale, was rising from the floor to read a Yale faculty resolution repudiating a job action organized by the emerging student employees union (GESO) and to challenge the assembly's right to consider an emergency resolution submitted by New Haven graduate students facing administration reprisals. A hurried consultation had taken place with his colleagues Margaret Homans and William Jewett, both in attendance to support Brooks's position, and a new nonsubstantive strategy came to mind. A number of the delegates had left the hall after four hours in session without a break, and Brooks doubted there was still a quorum remaining. It was a tacky way to block discussion of a serious issue, but anything goes when you have God on your side. Of that, the Yale faculty have a long tradition of being persuaded. In any case, Brooks's maneuver failed; after a delay for a head count, discussion proceeded, and MLA's delegate assembly voted to submit a motion censuring Yale to the entire membership for a vote.

Among the documents the delegates had in hand was a concise and pointed resolution adopted unanimously by the American Association of University Professor's Collective Bargaining Congress earlier that month:

> We believe that all academic teaching staff, including graduate teaching assistants, have the right to collective bargaining, and we urge the members of the Yale University administration to honor this right. As members of a faculty union, we know that it is sometimes necessary to engage in job actions in order to achieve the goals of educational quality and workplace fairness. Those who participate in such efforts— whether a teaching strike, grading strike, or other academic job actions—do so not out of disrespect for education, but its opposite: out of a commitment to the value of teaching. We hope that such efforts will be respected, and in no case should they be the subject of academic reprisals. We urge our Yale colleagues to uphold these standards in the current unionization drive of Yale graduate teachers.[2]

Like the owners of steel and textile mills decades earlier, Yale's faculty knew better. But for MLA's delegates the AAUP statement helped remind them that job actions are a tradition with a long history, a history with its own ethic and notions of responsibility. Yale's Nancy Cott, herself a progressive labor historian, like Brooks apparently felt those traditions had no bearing on the present crisis. That same month she got up before the American Historical Association to give her version of Brooks's anti-union speech. Put yourself in our place, she argued to the historians, imagine how you would feel if *your* graduate students were withholding grades. It was to be another failed strategy, another institutionalized incapacity to see oneself through others' eyes, for with that argument the assembled historians could not contain a response. They did what Cott asked, put themselves in Yale's place, and realized they would, unlike Yale's faculty, support similar efforts on the part of their own students. Laughter broke out, and soon their own resolution of censure was passed.

Brooks himself, as it happens, had risen before to speak on this topic. At a meeting of the Yale faculty earlier that December he had stated with some conviction that graduate students were not in fact being economically well treated in New Haven.[3] Over two decades their salaries had steadily fallen to a smaller and smaller percentage of what a new assistant professor would be paid. There were thus matters of equity that Yale should attend to and correct. It was a somewhat rambling and disjointed talk, but eventually the other shoe emerged from the fog to fall. Despite believing in the necessity to address salary disparities, Brooks went on to argue that GESO, the graduate student union, had no legitimacy. It should be resisted forcefully; striking students should be severely punished. As if angry that his marvelous condescension toward student needs was not met with appropriate gratitude and affection, he proposed that a resolution offering faculty support for the administration's hard-line position be reworded to be more emphatic; it should declare, he argued, that we are "at one with the administration." Whether the new rhetoric more satisfied faculty needs to feel conjugal or theological is unclear, but it was enthusiastically adopted. Meanwhile, Brooks himself still felt the need to find metaphors simultaneously evoking marriage and ordination; the following month he told a *New York Times* reporter that graduate students "really are among the blessed of the earth . . . so I sometimes feel annoyed at them seeing themselves as exploited." Those of us working at more decisively secular institutions find it hard to deploy phrases like these, but their use has certainly been among the marvels of the Yale labor dispute.

Since December, Brooks has also developed a more effective argument—that present inequities suggest graduate studies need to be rethought from top to bottom and that a union contract would only harden the present structure and keep it in place. Union rules, in effect, would inhibit creative thinking and block structural innovation. Of course this is much the same Reaganite argument forwarded by George Guilder, Dick Armey, Jack Kemp, and every Republican economic libertarian; what follows is claims for deregulation, elimination of wage guarantees, elimination of union influence. A number of things are notable about this strategy. First, as with some of the Republicans who make this argument, it makes Brooks's position seem that of a concerned, progressive player open to real change; second, it helps redirect faculty anger now uneasily pointed toward their students instead toward those more anonymous working-class institutions that so many Yale faculty can more wholeheartedly despise;

third, it disguises interested investments in long-term negotiations over relative power as a thoughtful concern about the viability of the negotiations themselves. The real issue is who has the power to *shape* the present and the future. Many Yale faculty do not want to share that power with organized graduate student representation. Yet any planning for the future would be helped by significant improvements in graduate assistant wages and benefits, changes that can only be won by collective bargaining. Far from constraining future options, better working conditions would open options and make them fairer.

Now since GESO is devoted specifically to improving graduate student working conditions, it may seem that Brooks's position is more than a little contradictory. And indeed it is. But it is not without logic, for Brooks's implication is that graduate students should properly receive whatever benefits and salary Yale's managers deem appropriate. It is up to those in power to decide what Yale's workers receive, not the workers themselves, especially when those workers are supposedly faculty in training. For faculty members, or so most at Yale believe, properly negotiate such matters, if they are unseemly enough to negotiate them at all, entirely *as individuals.* Since graduate student salaries may vary from discipline to discipline and according to their stage in the program, but otherwise have no individual variation, and since faculty-to-be should properly accept their identity as individuals-in-waiting, graduate students should properly shut up and cheerfully accept whatever Yale gives them. Unions, in other words, are an affront to the psychology of paternalism. That seemed to be one of the motives behind Yale historian David Brion Davis's decision to turn his "bad" GESO teaching assistant in to the disciplinary board: she had betrayed his personal trust and sponsorship.

Other Yale faculty were more succinct. Some, echoing poorly remembered lines from John Wayne movies, put in circulation phrases suggesting GESO had put the faculty's "back to the wall." "They're holding us hostage" and "We've got to draw a line in the sand," volunteered other professors eager to deploy cliches in times of crisis. John Hollander, dreaming an alternative dream of hierarchy, suggested dumping ungrateful graduate assistants and returning to those halcyon days when assistant professors did a lot more teaching than they do now. Michael Denning and Hazel Carby, along with David Montgomery among the very few faculty at Yale capable of applying political and economic knowledge to the university workplace, stood up to defend the union and recommend against reprisals for the students withholding grades, but they were effectively ignored. Too courteous to shout them down, unable to engage substantively with their arguments, other faculty went on as if they had not spoken. Carby would later challenge her colleagues by asking if they wanted the union leaders' heads on pikes ringing the campus. If we are talking about desire, about the punishment fitting the crime of academic treason, the proper violence with which to meet heresy, the answer might actually be yes. Yale's faculty and administration—God's chorus—were indeed overall of one mind and one voice: these are students, not employees.

Just how everyone at Yale knows this is hard to say. Apparently, participants in one institution cannot be two things in different contexts. Graduate students of course have long recognized a certain contradictory doubleness in their identities. They are clearly students when they are sitting in a seminar taught by a senior faculty member. When they are in front of a class giving a lecture or leading a discussion, when they are grading papers and exams from that class, on the other hand, they feel rather like teachers. When they receive a modest salary check from Yale in payment for performing those duties, with deductions noted, they feel very much like employees. That was the unruffled perspective adopted in recent judicial rulings in Kansas and San Diego: graduate students are employees in one capacity, students in another. There is no reason to place them in only one mutually exclusive category. But perhaps Yale has been keeping a telling secret all year. A missing GESO representative was actually killed by a hit-and-run driver. His organs are spread out on the autopsy table set up in the faculty lounge for this purpose. The proof is there for all to see: this is a student, not an employee.

Interestingly enough, a significant number of Yale faculty supported the clerical workers in their long-running strike of recent years. The administration stonewalled, resisting all efforts to recognize or negotiate with the union, and they remain today determined to break Locals No. 34 and 35 despite their formal recognition as bargaining agents. Now, once again Yale seems hell-bent to teach academia how not to handle a labor dispute. And this time the faculty is mostly solidly behind the administration. In real terms the amount at stake financially is modest to say the least. Symbolically, the partial transfer of power and authority is apparently substantial. And faculty who merely deliver a weekly performance in a large lecture course obviously do not like learning that they do not know their undergraduates' names and do not decide their grades, that their courses—contrary to the illusions that sustain their self-images—are hardly *their* courses at all.

In actuality, full-time tenured faculty at Yale teach only a third of the under-graduate courses and often teach them at an impersonal distance, delivering their wisdom like pigeons roosting high above in the ivy. Given that graduate students and adjunct faculty deliver two-thirds of the teaching, it behooves Yale to speak well of them. Graduate students at many schools receive a good deal of supervision and pedagogical instruction in their first year of teaching. After that, they are largely on their own, often not only teaching but designing courses. At many large universities graduate students teach three or four courses a year for seven years or more. Only an idiot would imagine that someone who has taught ten or more courses is still a nestling, in training, unable to fly on his or her own. Obviously most of these "teaching assistants" become experienced teachers after a few years, and some of them become genuinely talented. When parents complain about how much teaching is done by graduate students, schools might well consider responding by telling the truth: by showing that these young scholars are in fact seasoned and experienced professionals. That is the only sensible defense of pedagogical practice at large institutions.

Unfortunately, Yale sometimes reacts by distorting the truth, crediting courses jointly taught by faculty and students entirely to the faculty. Typically, faculty members provide the weekly entertainment in a lecture and teaching assistants lead discussions and do all the grading. Whatever the appropriate calculation for representing the division of labor in such courses should be, it surely is not faculty 100 percent, graduate students *nada,* a fiction that helps enable Yale to claim graduate students do only 3 percent of their teaching. Worse still is Yale's response to the current crisis, insisting that teaching assistants are not salaried professionals but trainees who cannot and should not be trusted with (or paid for) independent teaching. At this point Yale can be credited with fouling everyone's nest, not just its own. For the widespread reliance on graduate students for independent teaching throughout American universities requires us not only to admit but also to celebrate their competence. If they are just nestlings, unable to feed themselves or others, then the whole aviary may come tumbling down.

There are, in short, two mutually exclusive arguments to make. Either these folks do good work and should be paid accordingly or they do marginal work for marginal pay. Set on making the second argument, Yale's disingenuous arrogance imperils everyone. Nor is GESO the last we shall hear from graduate student unions. As the long-term job crisis empties out the logic of apprenticeship, graduate students will increasingly demand fair compensation for their work. Trainees at McDonalds now have better opportunities for advancement than many graduate students. The pressure toward unionization will only increase. Graduate studies that have no future require a better present.

Yet faculty members continue to opt instead for symbolically infantalizing graduate student teachers as a way to rationalize and justify the system's inequities. This strategy was recently brought full circle by a remarkable proposal from MLA's 1995 president, Sander Gilman. Writing in his presidential address in the May 1996 issue of *PMLA,* Gilman seemingly quite reasonably recommended increasing the number of postdoctoral teaching appointments available to new Ph.Ds. who cannot find jobs. Many schools are already initiating or enlarging such programs for their own graduates, but it is fine to have MLA's encouragement on record. Then Gilman went on, incomprehensibly, to explain how this would save money because postdocs, unlike teaching assistants, would not receive tuition wavers. But of course tuition wavers in the humanities generally involve no transfer of funds; they are *waivers,* just like the term implies. So there is no money to be saved; in fact, if postdocs receive higher salaries than graduate assistants—as they surely should—then they will be more expensive.

Gilman knows, however, that postdocs are not likely to receive a good deal, so he once again deploys the logic of infantalization to justify a new system of inequities. He proposes that all postdocs be assigned a faculty mentor. Of course not all faculty members would be eager to make a major emotional and professional investment in a short-term employee, but the failed human logic is not the worst part of Gilman's proposal. What is worst is the real reason for infantalizing new Ph.Ds by suggesting they need mentors—to justify their low salaries. As I think of two of my former students who were on the job market in 1995, both in their fifth attempt to find a job—one with a book in press at Cambridge, another with a book in press at Illinois, both with teaching experience at several schools—it does not take much reflection to realize they need a job, not a mentor. What advice they do need they get from their peers and the people who have worked with them for a decade. They do not need Gilman's marvelous condescension.

What is significantly new in Gilman's essay is his proposal for an organized national program of postdoctoral teaching fellowships. I believe Gilman's national clearinghouse for "mentored" postdoctoral fellows is one of the most ill-considered and dangerous plans ever to receive the MLA's imprimatur. One might have titled his address "How to End Tenure," because that is the result it would help to produce. There are any number of administrators who would love to turn a significant amount of their lower-level undergraduate courses over to postdocs costing 50 to 60 percent as much as faculty members. Gilman even throws in the added plus of "limited benefits." We all know what that means: no health care for the kids, no vestment in a retirement program.

Of course any national program would instantly run into the wide discrepancies in the salaries, teaching loads, and benefits offered postdocs. Some English departments presently assign two courses per semester, while others demand three or four. Some offer full family health care, others only coverage for the faculty member. Some prohibit participation in retirement programs; a few offer TIAA/CREF. And access to travel money and other support varies widely, as does the per course salary rate. Putting all these differences on the table where they can be compared might shame some programs into treating their postdocs and adjuncts better, but we need to remember that much of corporate higher education is now without shame. What is really needed are national disciplinary standards for fair treatment, something Gilman never mentions.

Any doubts about whether departments would take opportunistic and cynical advantage of his proposal may be put to rest by one anecdote: Gilman first advanced his plan in a presidential column in the fall 1995 issue of the *MLA Newsletter*. Within weeks, one English department head in a department without a Ph.D. program cheerfully distributed a memo advocating replacing their adjuncts with a postdoc program. Of course such a change would merely rename part-time labor so as to make it appear nonexploitive. What the hell, the memo implied, if it takes mentoring to make this look ethical, we'll mentor. Meanwhile cheap labor would still be substituting for tenure-track faculty.

Gilman proudly announces that his postdoc program would emulate how things work in the sciences. Did the man talk to any scientists about their own employment crisis and how their long tradition of postdocs is playing into the depressed job market? I have. The science postdoc that used to lead to a tenure-track job is now becoming an end in itself, producing a permanent class of second-class scientists who take postdoc after postdoc in search of a faculty position that never materializes. Meanwhile, their benefits are indeed "limited," their prospects, retirement plans, and job security nonexistent.

I am all in favor of postdocs if they are created as temporary measures under very specific and limited conditions. After no little prodding from me, my own department offers three-year postdocs to its own new Ph.Ds. They have worked well for those people who have used the time to improve their marketability; some have ended up with tenure-track jobs who might otherwise have washed out of the profession.

I am also in favor of postdoc exchanges, since they would give people teaching experience in different settings. But real dangers mount at that point. There need to be strict guidelines: first, no department without a Ph.D. program should be permitted to participate in a postdoctoral consortium or exchange program; second, no department should be allowed into a consortium unless it can prove that it has reduced the size of its own doctoral program over the last twenty years. The point is that funds to employ postdocs must come from vacated teaching assistantships, not from decommissioned faculty lines. Liberal arts colleges and universities without doctoral programs in a given area would be barred from participation.

Even with these safeguards, a formal, well-publicized interinstitutional post-doc program would encourage many schools to shift a portion of their personnel budget from tenure-track faculty lines to postdocs. This would accelerate already existing trends in higher education—away from permanent, full-time tenured faculty toward adjuncts, part-timers, and now postdocs. Such people have little control over a school's policies and curriculum, fewer free speech guarantees, less support for research and independent intellectual inquiry, and a good deal less job satisfaction. Gilman may be gleeful at the prospects, but someone at MLA headquarters ought to have urged him to think through the implications of his plan more carefully.

It is important to realize, moreover, that postdocs—whom fate has arranged to pay $10,000 to $20,000 less than their identically qualified classmates who happened to get jobs—are not always the happiest employees. Indeed, those postdocs who *never* get permanent jobs may end up spending ten or twelve or more years before an abrupt and premature career termination. That may leave them even more wounded and rudderless than new Ph.Ds who fail to find employment. Such human consequences merit more reflection than Gilman's self-congratulatory proposal appears to manifest.

Condescension and an unreflective sense of privilege and power are at the core of both sets of stories here—misconduct by potential academic employers on the job market and bad faith by academics toward their current low-paid employees. All this comes together in a stunning remark from the chair of the Yale English department. Contemplating the necessity of refusing to rehire teaching assistants who joined GESO's December 1995 job action of withholding grades, Linda Peterson analyzed the situation as clearly as she could: "How can we hire people . . . who have publicly stated they're willing to strike?"[4] But what about prospective employees who haven't taken a public position on strikes? Should they be asked to sign a loyalty oath? Or should Yale, preferring decorous and deniable litmus tests, follow Bush administration practice for extracting anti-abortion pledges from prospective judges and administer the oath *sotto voce?* No harm in Yale learning from its graduates. Meanwhile, if it works for graduate students, why not faculty? Surely Peterson would feel the same about hiring a faculty member who would support a teaching assistant's right to strike. Determining all this in advance and with a sufficient degree of certainty of course puts us back either on my mythical autopsy table or back in the decades of employer surveillance and infiltration of industrial unions. No wonder Yale is angry. Not only do they have to budget to hire scabs; they've got to start looking for spies and informers. Ah well, perhaps some of the present faculty will inform for free. Should they do so, no doubt they'll feel empowered by what they imagine to be the eternal values of higher education. Actually, they are merely instruments of post-PATCO employment ideology in the U.S. Like other corporations, the university is determined to reduce the percentage of its employees with any powers of free speech in the workplace and any say in their own working conditions.

The analogy with unionization efforts outside academia is particularly telling, because it puts Yale's high-minded righteousness in its proper context. Efforts to force private universities to recognize faculty unions have been largely decimated by the court ruling that identified Yeshiva University's faculty as having managerial responsibilities. Just how the National Labor Relations Board would now deal with graduate student unionization at private institutions remains to be seen, despite a negative 1972 ruling, but Yale would surely face some difficulty proving that its fledgling teachers are full-scale managers. What is most telling, however, are the parallels between union-busting activities in industry and academia. Threats, intimidation, reprisals: all these and more Yale's faculty have applied enthusiastically without realizing not only the moral repugnance many in the world feel toward union busting but also the flat illegality these actions would have in many industries. At present, Yale's faculty and administration are proudly contemplating actions that would be illegal in an industry across the street. Somewhere down the line someone is going to point out that goons in academic robes are still goons after all.

At that point not only the economics of the university will be at stake but rather its entire still somewhat idealized social status. Higher education's autonomy, never more than relative, is still subject to further erosion. If universities can be shown to be run at best by categorically self-deceived people and at worst by self-interested liars, their position in the public sphere will suffer considerably. Disingenuous claims about teaching assistants not being employees is a good example of bad-faith public relations that may backfire. In my own department, our downsized graduate program can no longer provide enough teaching assistants to staff our composition classes. So we hire more than 30 percent of our rhetoric instructors from other departments. The upper administration at the University of Illinois persists in claiming that all these folks are in training for their future careers.[5] But what about the thirty-three graduate students from the College of Law we hired in 1996–97 to teach rhetoric? I suppose in some alternative universe the administration could float a news story headlined "Law Students Learn Courtroom Advocacy By Grading Composition Papers." In this universe, however, it appears that these folks are hired to do a job. So our own fledgling graduate student union will no doubt have to argue in court, since the administration is determined to see the union as a threat. It is not just the lives of our current colleagues that are at stake in these struggles, I would argue; it is the whole future of these institutions.

But are there solutions to these problems short of academic armageddon? Actually, there are. Let's take Cactus State's dilemma first. They've had a visiting faculty member there for a year; they like him, and students are happy with his courses. So long as the department has a recent history of good hires—of hiring faculty who improve the quality of the department—administrators should allow them to make the visitor an offer of a permanent appointment without conducting a search. If they have *not* been making good appointments, then they should not be allowed to make *any* appointments; making them go through a search procedure will not improve matters. Most faculty appointments need to be made through openly advertized searches, but we also need flexibility to make occasional targeted appointments, and the range of categories that warrant setting aside affirmative action rules—from appointing academic partners or spouses to making visiting appointments permanent—needs to be somewhat flexible. In no case should a department be compelled to go through a sham search; it corrupts department personnel and brutally exploits unsuspecting applicants. Professional associations that determine a department has conducted a fake search (that includes interviews), so as to provide paper justification for hiring someone it had chosen beforehand, should subject that department to severe financial penalties. There is perhaps one form of fake search that is halfway tolerable: a job is advertised with requirements so specific that only one person can meet them, and no other candidates are interviewed. We should all get beyond the necessity of such games, but at least this one does no damage.

Suppose, on the other hand, a department felt its visitor or inside candidate had the inside track but still wanted to check the competition to make certain it was making the right choice. In that case a more constrained search could be conducted. Only after screening applications carefully should a limited number of dossiers and writing samples be requested. If the inside candidate is still in the lead, but the department is still somewhat uncertain, the remaining pool of applicants could then be narrowed further by phone interviews. Finally, if there is a small group of genuinely competitive finalists, they could be brought to campus at the institution's expense. Variations of this procedure are perfectly plausible, so long as no one is made to travel to an interview under false pretenses.

What about Yale's problem? Well, though Yale's faculty would have little more chance of understanding what I am about to say than they would have of understanding the language of extraplanetary visitors, the fact is that the crisis in New Haven is the product of something akin to mass psychosis among faculty and administrators. If GESO is recognized as a bargaining agent, Yale's massive $4 billion endowment will *grow* at a somewhat slower rate, and graduate student teachers will receive somewhat better salaries and benefits. Nothing else will change. That is the risk, if it can be called that. The faculty member who asked "How will I be able to continue teaching my seminars once my students are union members?" will find his seminars running just as they did before. Yet Yale has responded with misrepresentation, hyperbole, hysteria, vindictiveness, and intimidation. Because what is threatened is an illusory and increasingly unsustainable self-image. An ideology is under siege, and Yale is more than happy to defend it by sacrificing people's careers. They may succeed for a time, but then the administrators of this failed policy will receive their golden parachutes. In the meantime, those who can see this madness for what it is must call it by its true name.

Early in 1996 GESO's grade strike collapsed, in part because Yale was set to fire all strike participants, and the lack of a substantial strike fund gave GESO members no alternative, in part because faculty cooperated with the administration in reassigning classes, crossing picket lines, and bringing charges against striking students. If the faculty had stood with the students, the administration would have been isolated. Yet if Yale's graduate student labor problems appear to have quieted down by the time this essay is published, it will be partly because GESO has returned to organize its base and because the public focus has shifted for now to other New Haven unions. Yale's administrators could decide to avoid more conflict and public embarrassment and cut their losses by negotiating. But nothing, unfortunately, could be less likely. Some administrators, especially those less ideologically trapped by faculty notions of prestige and privilege, oppose unions out of a simple power calculation. If organized employees have more power, I will have less; surely that is bad for Yale (or wherever), since I know what is best for the institution. The one thing labor peace at Yale will *not* mean, I am sorry to have to predict, is that Yale's faculty will have come to their senses. The idiot savant culture that faculty members are bred in—narrow subdisciplinary expertise and broad cultural ignorance—does not equip faculty members to see themselves in any alternative social context. Of course faculty fantasies of omnipotence look comically illusory from most nonacademic perspectives, but there are a few areas—including the capacity to expel students or put them on probation—where that power is real. In exercising it, Yale's faculty feel a whole worldview confirmed. The satisfaction they feel in contemplating reprisals is only enhanced by the refining element of regret. It is such a mix of emotions that one hears, for example, in the repeated warnings by Yale deans Thomas Appelquist and Richard Brodhead that graduate students who withhold grades will find that such "actions . . . must be expected to carry consequences."

Meanwhile, elite arrogance can be deployed in one final form that simultaneously reconfirms Yale's prestige and discredits complaining graduate students. There continues to be little interest at our most distinguished institutions in the underlying cause of doctoral student unrest—the nearly hopeless job market. Departments at Harvard and Yale often have no faculty job counselor, despite the fact that the Ivy League schools have no more success at placing new Ph.D.s in tenure-track jobs than do, say, Midwestern schools like my own. Yet when told their students aren't getting jobs Yale faculty first look puzzled and then adopt what I shall call the "Yale Tableau." It's not an argument, mind you, rather more of a gestural embodiment of astonished wisdom. Hands spread, they simply say "No, no. They have the Yale degree." The Tableau's caption varies, but the intent is always the same, to correct what is obviously a cultural misunderstanding. Yale's students are set for life. End of conversation.

Particularly adept at one version of the Yale Tableau is Thomas Appelquist, dean of the Graduate School of Arts and Sciences. "Graduate Students," he wrote in the *New Haven Register* of 3 January 1996, "enter as students but leave as colleagues of the faculty." This is a traditional formulation of the eucharistic effect of bestowing the Ph.D. You are thereafter members of the eternal priesthood, among the elect of your discipline. You are entitled to profess your discipline wherever on earth you may be, however you may be otherwise employed. Of course in the real world it is a faculty job that gives you the time and social context in which to profess, and most Yale Ph.D.s will not get tenure-track faculty jobs. Appelquist offers an abstract fraternity and hopes readers will think it just as satisfying as the material one. But union members well know the difference; they have long been offered "pie in the sky / when they die" in place of any earthly benefits.

To the extent the public believes this little charade as well, sympathy for graduate student "workers" will be a rare commodity. Here, of course, the burden for changing perceptions falls on student employees themselves, something GESO has sought to alter by building alliances with other area unions. But alliances with union leaders are easier to create and sustain than alliances with the rank-and-file membership.

Yet are academics in any real sense *workers?* Are they paid for their labor? Can English graduate students put their shoulders to the wheel of a Keats poem? Is it demeaning for people paid for intellectual labor to focus on their material working conditions? Can academics build substantive alliances with electricians, secretaries, and cafeteria workers once they rethink the nature of their own labor and the power relations in the university workplace? It is questions like these that churn not far beneath the surface of the Yale struggle. As graduate students and progressive faculty try to answer them they begin to learn something of the limits of intellection in academia. For it is not sweet reason alone that rules all these debates. Fear and ideology, the twin engines driving faculty consensus at Yale, block discussion not only of the union but of all these other pertinent questions as well. Sometimes, GESO's leaders have learned, it is not so much reasoned argument as dogged persistence that finally wins a hearing. The fiftieth conversation on the same topic may suddenly break through inbred resistance. Few on the faculty are eager to admit the existence of such a dynamic. What is clear is that if we do not begin to have such conversations tenured faculty will eventually be as rare as passenger pigeons.

Yet in some ways, to be fair, it is not surprising that tenured faculty across the country are in widespread and deep denial. At the 1995 MLA convention, the University of Pennsylvania's Wendy Steiner was trotted out to update a set speech Sandra Gilbert had given a few months earlier. It is the last stand for the madmen and madwomen in the ivory tower, so their compensatory rhetoric is predictably ever more inflated. Steiner reiterated that we are training adepts in a spiritual discipline, not job candidates. Yet few wish to confront the fact that the material instantiation of disciplinarity in Ph.D. programs, faculty positions, curriculum requirements, budget allocations, course offerings, and departmental autonomy has a largely economic basis. If there are no jobs, why are we training Ph.D.s? Blather about spiritual quests is unlikely to sway anyone making budget allocations either within the university or outside it. What's worse, from the vantage point of those in denial, is that the whole infrastructure supporting and sustaining disciplinary boundaries and prerogatives is economically grounded. In other words, the existing disciplines survive in their present size and configuration because of their economic justification. If there is no useful function a history Ph.D. can serve, why train one? And why, under these conditions, separate history from English or philosophy? Climbing up on ever higher horses will not sustain our present dispensation, yet that is all the leadership we have seen so far from Yale's administrators or the officers of the MLA.

The strangely intertwined destinies of Yale and the Modern Language Association underwent yet one more phase in 1996. In anticipation of the MLA membership's vote on the resolution condemning Yale that was approved by the Delegate Assembly in December, anti-union Yale faculty wrote several letters of protest to MLA headquarters. In what seems to me the most unabashedly partisan act by the staff and officers during the thirty years in which I have followed the association, MLA decided to send these letters to all members without giving its pro-union or pro-resolution constituency an opportunity to respond. Instead of sending a balanced mailing, then, MLA designed an expensively produced brochure—almost like a keepsake from a vanity press—composed exclusively of anti-union and anti-resolution letters and mailed it to the entire association. The message could not have been more clear: here is how the MLA office wants you to vote.

Margaret Homans in her letter argues, in effect, that graduate teaching assistants do not need a union and thus should not be permitted to have one. It is hard to send a wake-up call to someone so drowsy with power and privilege, but the point here is that it is up to employees themselves, not their employers or supervisors, to decide whether and how they should be represented. Like other employees, teaching assistants have a right to determine for themselves whether they want to enter into collective bargaining. Annabel Patterson too misses the basic nature of U.S. labor law—that it is facilitative, designed to enable workers to make their own decisions about such matters—but the low point of the brochure's discussion of general issues may well have been Patterson's false and contemptuous claim that Yale might have negotiated with GESO—*if* the union had not decided to affiliate with maintenance and cafeteria workers![6] As the number of tenured faculty members continues to decline nationwide and as universities increasingly opt for part-time employees in all job categories, we may well recall Patterson's disgust at the thought of making alliances with the working people in her campus community, her disgust indeed at any notion of community beyond idealization with no material consequences. So much for the virtues of enlightenment thought she advocates in her scholarship. In any case the class contempt self-righteously paraded before MLA's membership in this mailing may well have backfired; the membership ratified the resolution in the summer of 1996. Yale's denial of community and mutual responsibility has once again shown us how not to face the future.

If the categorical contempt for the working class may have offended many of the MLA members who read this mailing, little did they know how appalling some of these letters actually are. Hidden behind rhetoric of professional outrage is the most astonishing and unprincipled departmental attack on a graduate student I have ever encountered. I refer to Homans's and Patterson's defense of Richard Brodhead's now notorious letter of recommendation and their decision to mount a public attack on the (unnamed) student involved. As I pointed out in chapter 9, the 1994 letter sent to a donor from the GESO office was signed by four students. Here is how Patterson describes it: "The alleged 'reprisal' involving faculty recommendations concerns a letter written months before the grade strike, a letter that takes pains to make clear that it refers not to unionizing activities but to far-fetched and questionable personal behavior" (6). Of course the whole campaign about "Daily Themes" was precisely a union activity, a standard union effort to represent employees' complaints about unfair compensation. A March 22 headline in the *Yale Daily News* reads "GESO upset with changes in Daily Themes." As to whether the behavior—cosigning a letter to donor Perry Bass—was far-fetched, questionable, or even substantively personal, readers may judge for themselves.[7] In her own letter Margaret Homans writes "I would see it as a violation of my own academic freedom to be prevented from alluding to the judgment and ethics exhibited by a student while engaged in university activities if I thought they were predictive of a student's future behavior as a colleague. . . . Nor do the AAUP's guidelines exist to shelter unprofessional and dishonest behavior of the kind that some students have engaged in in the name of unionization. One student who complained publicly of a letter in her file has engaged in campus activities that are unethical and that violate university policies, activities that have nothing to do with unionization or even the grade strike" (10). About Yale, all I can say is that its highly rated English department may no longer be altogether fit to run a graduate program; perhaps it should be under independent control to assure that faculty misconduct is restrained. Certainly a debate about whether the department belongs in receivership would be instructive. As to Sandra Gilbert and Phyllis Franklin, respectively MLA president and executive director, the best I can say is that it appears they unwittingly aided and abetted a smear campaign.

Some time early in the next millennium, the remaining tenured faculty may find themselves herded together in attenuated humanities and social science departments, with scientists and engineers confined to doing product research for Dow Chemical. If there is an alternative to such a future, faculty denial will not help bring it to pass. Nor will blindly destroying the careers of our present doctoral candidates. Two generations of unemployed students are hardly the constituency best positioned to help us create a future worth entering. On the other hand, perhaps those unemployed can send faculty and administrators a wake-up call.

One could imagine a world in which administrators realized that making graduate student teachers full partners in defining viable programs with fair compensation might improve higher education, not threaten it. Certainly it could make any given campus more attractive to prospective students. On the other hand, perhaps some administrators realize that employees with no future do not count, that they are literally and irredeemably expendable. The depressed job market, in other words, leads administrators to what I might call the *Blade Runner* strategy. In the 1982 film based on a Philip K. Dick novel, incredibly realistic androids called "replicants" are for all practical purposes indistinguishable from real humans. Realizing they are potentially dangerous to their masters and wanting to make them disappear when their usefulness is at an end, the corporation guarantees that each one is irreversibly programmed to die at an early age. Why should academia's graduate student replicants be made part of the governing process? Why can't they just die when their time has come? Perhaps the formal conferring of the Ph.D. could activate the mortality chip. In the low-budget academic version of this film I foresee a former MLA president in the Tyrell role, head of the corporation that makes and markets replicants. Just before Tyrell is murdered by one of his products, they meet face-to-face; the replicant has come to plead for a modification so his life can be extended. In one of the many features that make the scenario so well adapted to academia,

Tyrell does not just refuse; like the Yale faculty, he declares the change in status a categorical impossibility:

> *Tyrell:* You were made as well as we could make you.
> *Replicant:* But not to last.
> *Tyrell:* The light that burns twice as bright burns half as long. And you have burned so very brightly, Roy. Look at you. You're the prodigal son—you're quite a prize.

The perfect faculty member, with his parchment skin and formal manner, Tyrell makes his remarks in self-justifying commercial ecstasy, in spiritual communion with his ideology. How many faculty members at Yale, how many MLA officials, have done screen tests for this role? The blessed of the earth, we may recall, was Peter Brooks's phrase for dedicated graduate students with no futures; they burn very brightly indeed. More recently, Sandra Gilbert, having won little praise for her contention that jobless Ph.D.s were ungrateful wretches, has decided that they may after all be among the wretched of the earth, at least if they accept their status without blaming tenured faculty. Blessed wretches, then, so long as they know their place.

One could imagine, alternatively, a professoriate whose academic organizations were devoted to testing and coordinating efforts to deal with higher education's multiple crises. One could imagine the MLA, the AHA, the APA, encouraging their member departments to design alternative degree programs directed toward careers outside academia. M.A. programs would clearly be most adaptable, and they have the advantage of avoiding the psychological damage done by research-oriented doctoral programs that come to nothing. Some of those M.A. programs might cross disciplinary boundaries. Meanwhile, considerable pressure must be applied to avoid further reductions in the number of full-time tenured and tenure-track faculty, lest the unique and important cultural and intellectual work they do be curtailed. Since large-scale access to undergraduate education remains desirable and since it is structurally dependent on cheap graduate student instructional labor, closing down graduate programs entirely would have serious social consequences. Yet retaining a system now based on exploitation and inertia, defended by dishonorable posturing, will prove increasingly unacceptable, especially if graduate students continue to organize and act collectively. Dialogue and debate about such matters might absorb much of our organizations' resources. Unfortunately, that presently seems little more likely than that Yale will publicly take pride in its GESO activists.

Meanwhile, both at Yale and in the hiring process across the country, part of the problem is clearly with the unfettered, unreflective sense of privilege and noblesse oblige departments feel entitled to flaunt. One might like to imagine the National Labor Relations Board hauling a couple of Yale faculty members off to jail for illegal retaliation against union organizers, but that is unlikely. In the meantime, one weapon against the abuses of the job wars is frank testimony in print. That is what I have offered here and elsewhere. Yet in response to the first in my series of "Lessons from the Job Wars" essays, one reader complained that it was inappropriate to protect institutions by not revealing their names. So I shall now name some names, something that seems especially appropriate when the schools have successfully promoted a more exalted image of themselves.

In the mid-nineties a friend of mine, Ph.D. in hand from an Ivy League school, was undergoing interviews at the annual MLA meeting. A session with the University of Chicago went particularly well. Yet weeks after the convention he'd still heard nothing from them. When things began to develop at other schools, he called Chicago to let them know his prospects and give them a chance to respond. Ah, one search committee member replied, we never had any intention of hiring in your area. But we admired your work and granted you an interview as a mark of our respect. That was a *courtesy* interview.[8] Apparently they thought he should be grateful to receive such an honor. Needless to say, he felt neither courteously treated nor honored. He'd paid for his plane fare and hotel room because he wanted a job. Chicago, one can well imagine, no doubt felt itself a magnanimous department, generously bestowing its attention even when self-interest was not at issue.

In one of those fantasy worlds in which justice always triumphs, the interview would never have been completed. Instead, two MLA guards with truncheons kick in the door of the Chicago suite and demand to know if a courtesy interview is in progress. They proceed to teach Chicago a lesson in humility. Ah well, even fantasy requires *some* self-restraint. Let's say they levy an on-the-spot fine instead.

In fact some of these courtesy interviews can be just a bit discourteous. Perhaps it was a courtesy interview that I had, in another life, with the University of Massachusetts at the 1969 Denver MLA. I was ushered into the room by two young gentlemen of Amherst, and the conversation opened when they recalled with pleasure a Paris restaurant each had visited on different trips in recent years. Had I been there, they asked? Actually, I replied, I've never even been to Paris. Unfazed, they continued to compare meals in France. Have you ever been to *La Coupole?* No, I said again, since I haven't been to Paris, you can assume I've never been to any Paris restaurants. Well, the interview, if that's what it was, never broke its culinary frame. Was it a test? Was I supposed to begin describing my dissertation unasked? Had they already decided whom to hire? I'll never know. Even at the time I was as much amused and incredulous as annoyed. I had other interviews and, as it happened, got a job, though the job came from the school where the interview—or so it seemed to me—went least well.

But then people being interviewed are often not well positioned to judge how the interview went. So too with this last group of stories, which I offer in part as testimony about the very difficulty inherent in the policing function I want professional organizations to undertake. The Chicago story I have told exactly as it was told to me—in this case by an exceptionally talented and confident young scholar. He too had other interviews and had little reason to worry. Meanwhile, other more politic members of the Chicago search committee would no doubt characterize the interview differently. And some might have a completely different understanding of how the search was conducted. But the point here is not Chicago's culpability; the point, which the story dramatizes, is that such practices, wherever they occur, should be curtailed. That there are fake or nonserious interviews taking place I have no doubt. In fact such practices have gone on for years. In 1976, for example, Williams College went ahead and interviewed people for a job that had been canceled because they thought it would be interesting to meet them!

Part of what we need as a profession is a relativistic, context-specific ethic of hiring. It's a case where recent theory can help us to clarify our present dilemma. In a market replete with jobs a courtesy interview would do no harm; it might even give a candidate valuable practice and feedback. But what if it represents a candidate's *only* interview and he or she spends $1,000 on airfare and hotel to get there? Obviously departments need to take special care *in the current economic context* to interview only people they are serious about considering for employment.

To take on the responsibility of identifying victims and naming departments guilty of professional misconduct, however, is necessarily to enter a zone of hallucination, misrepresentation, and multiple interpretation. Yet if standards of professional conduct are to be followed, there will need to be some potential for a price to be paid when they are not. The deterrence value of a few well-publicized cases would be considerable. Yet even when the events are completely clear, when no one disagrees about what happened, it may be that no one would want them pursued.

In the 1980s, for example, the English department at the State University of New York at Buffalo was interviewing a woman for one of those senior positions that might or might not materialize. "According to one of my colleagues, we've been hiring so many women lately," one of the interviewers remarked, "that the department feels like it's wall-to-wall pu**y." It was hardly a characteristic comment from a SUNY-Buffalo faculty member, but there it was nonetheless. The woman being interviewed took it as a studied provocation, a test to see if she was the sort of feminist who had a sense of humor and replied in kind. She had nothing to gain from pursuing the matter. Nevertheless, the matter seems unresolved. Where *are* those truncheons?

Having told a series of stories where misconduct is uncertain or punishment irrelevant, however, I would be remiss in closing without a story of a different sort. It is a story that takes us back to the introduction to *Manifesto,* where I talked about the vicissitudes of publishing, for this is a story about how a publisher may have destroyed a job candidate's chances and perhaps terminated his career as well. I believe it is a story with victims, villains, and spineless bystanders alike. It is a story too, I suppose, about how much moral fibre some respected members of the profession have.

In 1993, one of my former students, a 1991 Ph.D., submitted his revised dissertation in American literature to a well-known book series published by Cambridge University Press. In the fall of 1993 he received a strongly positive reader's report and encouragement from the series editor, a faculty member at a distinguished university, that the book would be taken if he did the requested revisions. That he did, and some months later returned the manuscript. The series editor called to express his satisfaction with the revisions and to reassure the author that he expected everything to go well when the book went before the Cambridge board. The timing looked perfect. The MLA job list was due out just about the time the final word was due from Cambridge. It was the fall of 1994. Three years after finishing his degree, my former student was beginning his fourth search. I felt he needed a book to have a chance at getting interviewed. Now it certainly seemed he did.

A day or two before the Cambridge board was to meet, a staff member at the New York office tried to call my former student at home. He was not available, because his wife had had a miscarriage, and he was at the hospital with her. She e-mailed him instead, telling him Cambridge's marketing department had decided the book might not sell enough copies and thus refused to let the book go to the board. So sorry. So much for that year's job search. Two years later, another publisher has accepted the book, but Cambridge had torpedoed him at the key moment. He does not expect to have a career.

I have no objection to a market evaluation of a book, though both I and others think Cambridge's evaluation was ill-informed, but market evaluations should be done either when a manuscript is first turned in or immediately after the first reader's report is received. To tell an author to do all the revisions and *then* many months later reject the book on the basis of a market report is unconscionable. As for the academic editor, he should have threatened to resign if the book was not accepted and promptly resigned if it was not.

Both the departments interviewing at the MLA and those in power at Yale and Cambridge imagine that negative consequences flow only one way in academia—toward those most vulnerable, those least able to advocate for themselves. Richard Brodhead, dean of Yale College, has reiterated his chosen theme of "consequences" at every stage of Yale's labor conflicts. Each threatened punishment, every reprisal for collective action, is figured as a naturally or institutionally ordained "consequence" of student action. Those who think they can act without consequences, he repeatedly intones, are deceiving themselves. Yet faculty who sabotage student letters of recommendation, or seek to expel union leaders, or lure students into job-training programs when there are no jobs imagine themselves above criticism or penalty. There is more than one group of exploited labor in academia that must act to correct that imbalance. My own recommendation is this, and I direct it especially to those who know they have nothing left to lose: when the princes of Yale or the MLA sit down to decide your future—bright pennants waving over their vitas—let them know that you are there.

NOTES

NOTES TO THE INTRODUCTION

1. As Michael Bérubé points out in *Public Access,* the title of Roger Kimball's *Tenured Radicals* gets some of its force from the fact that "tenure is also thought by both left and right to be antithetical to political progressivism" (22).

2. The emerging crisis in scholarly publishing has several causes, but certainly one of them is faculty members failing to work hard enough to protect library budgets. Indeed, most faculty ignore such matters. Other causes include the meteoric rise in the price of scientific journals, a pattern initiated when the late Robert Maxwell decided libraries were a captive audience for such publica-

tions and started a number of new journals (with salaried editors) that had prices ten or more times what had been traditional; Maxwell was looking for high profits and succeeded in getting them. Organized resistance from scholars and librarians at the outset might have stopped that practice. More recently, paper costs have increased much more rapidly than the rate of inflation.

Can anything be done? Decreasing library sales produce increased book prices, which in turn decrease library sales still further. The only solution is increased funding for libraries. The robber baron profits available to publishers of scientific journals need still stronger organized resistance. And finally, publication subventions may need to be far more common in the future. But many scholarly projects without significant audiences are doomed.

The solution of computerized publication is quite promising for journals but unattractive for books, since reading whole books on computer is highly unappealing and piles of printed-out pages less than convenient. Evaluating computerized publications for tenure and promotion also presents real problems, since standards of evaluation in prepublication reviews are unlikely to survive cost-free publication.

3. Arguments that tenure protects free speech are often dismissed by tenure's opponents. Indeed, even those who support tenure could cite faculty experience during the height of McCarthyism in the 1950s to prove that tenure's free speech guarantees may be worth little in times of national repression. At a less dramatic level, however, tenure does offer significant free speech protection. I offer this book and my professional activities promoting the positions I advocate here as evidence to support that claim. The arguments I make here are not all popular with faculty members or administrators, as responses to them have shown. I name names and make strong statements about professional practices and beliefs. In support of graduate student unionization efforts in Urbana I have published essays, written public letters, and filed a notarized affidavit. None of this makes the upper administration at Illinois happy, but the campus administration supports faculty free speech and I am reasonably well protected by tenure in any case. If I were an unprotected adjunct or part-time faculty member at many other schools, however, I could easily lose my job for these actions. The official reason might well be some other minor infraction, like turning in grades late, but the real reason would be to silence someone taking controversial positions. A recent *Lingua Franca* article by Emily Eakin describes me as a professor "known for his radical views." That, and my public statements, would be all, say, a conservative religious or community college administrator would need to send me on my way. Even at my own university, moreover, I can think of departments where I would not advise an assistant professor to file an affidavit criticizing the administration unless he or she had an exceptionally strong case for tenure.

NOTES TO CHAPTER 1

1. See, for example, Baker et al., eds., *Black British Cultural Studies.*
2. At talks in the 1980s Bate was fond of opening with a salvo against deconstruction. "I don't call it *deconstruction,*" he would announce, simultaneously whipping a handkerchief out of his pocket and waving it before the audience, "I call it *decongestion* and blow it out of my nose."
3. See Martha Nussbaum's *Poetic Justice* for the most recent suggestive effort to read literature as the locus of values like empathy.

NOTES TO CHAPTER 2

1. The most successful multicultural anthology of American literature is clearly *The Heath Anthology* of American Literature, under the general editorship of Paul Lauter.
2. A few years ago one of my graduate students was trying to persuade a faculty member teaching a course on the short story to include some texts by women on his all-male reading list. After some discussion of the general issues involved and suggestions of particular stories of possible interest, the faculty member asked, with a trace of irritation, where he could *find* the stories the student had suggested. The answer was straightforward but startling: "In the anthology you assign for your course." Of course we have long known that including works by women and minorities in anthologies is no guarantee faculty members will assign them; some faculty members cling to the skeleton of an older anthology that remains within the body of a new one. But this anecdote extends the uncertainty about how anthologies will be used to a new level—uncertainty about whether teachers will even *read* the new texts made available to them.
3. The best review of the issue of evaluation is Barbara Herrnstein Smith's *Contingencies of Value.* For an application of this problem to a specific historical context see my *Repression and Recovery.* Although this is not the place for a full discussion of the issue, I should at least confirm that I believe value is not intrinsic to literary works but rather culturally constructed and variable. Editing broadly multicultural works requires recognizing that literature can serve different cultural functions and thus at least maintaining multiple standards of evaluation simultaneously. Editing multicultural anthologies thus requires subjecting supposedly permanent notions of value to the contingencies of history. On the question of quality versus history see Paul Lauter's letter to the editor of the *New Criterion.*
4. Langston Hughes, "White Shadows."
5. Stuart Hall, "The Problem of Ideology—Marxism without Guarantees."

NOTES TO CHAPTER 3

1. For that reading see Walter Benn Michaels, "The New Modernism."
2. See Hayden White's *Tropics of Discourse, Metahistory,* and *The Content of the Form.*

219

3. A number of reviews of *Repression and Recovery* have taken up the bait I set down and paid some attention to H. H. Lewis. My favorite passage is in a 1991 review by David Perkins: "When I read [H. H. Lewis's 'Thinking of Russia'] I remember Pisarev's remark that potatoes are better than Shakespeare. Of course they are if you lack potatoes, and such a stanza may also have its utilitarian value. Since H. H. Lewis wrote this in verse, I'm willing to call it a poem. It is part of our literary and cultural past, and I am interested in it, the more so since, perhaps, it stirred many people. But to claim, as Nelson does, that it has literary merit, is incredible . . ." (p. 158).

NOTES TO CHAPTER 4

1. For other programmatic statements on cultural studies see Lawrence Grossberg, "The Formation(s) of Cultural Studies: An American in Birmingham" and "The Circulation of Cultural Studies"; Stuart Hall, "Cultural Studies: Two Paradigms" and "Cultural Studies and the Center: Some Problematics and Problems"; Richard Hoggart, "Contemporary Cultural Studies: An Approach to the Study of Literature and Society"; Richard Johnson, "What Is Cultural Studies Anyway?"; Meaghan Morris, "Banality in Cultural Studies"; Meaghan Morris and John Frow, "Introduction"; and Raymond Williams, "The Analysis of Culture." Several of these essays, along with others attempting definitions of cultural studies, are reprinted in John Storey, ed., *What Is Cultural Studies?* Also see Cary Nelson and Dilip Parameshwar Gaonkar, eds., *Disciplinarity and Dissent in Cultural Studies,* for a detailed review and critique of cultural studies' engagements with traditional disciplines.

   For bibliographies of the work of two key figures, Raymond Williams and Stuart Hall, see "A Raymond Williams Bibliography," in Alan O'Connor, *Raymond Williams: Writing, Culture, Politics,* pp. 128–75, and David Morley and Kuan-Hsing Chen, eds., *Stuart Hall: Critical Dialogues in Cultural Studies.*

2. One such reader was apparently Diane Elam, in a 1992 paper "Doing Justice to Feminism":

   > There is a certain tendency in the American academy to police what is and is not allowed to be called cultural studies. I can think of no better example of this than Cary Nelson's essay 'Always Already Cultural Studies.' On the one hand, Nelson stresses that cultural studies is not supposed to have a fixed methodology, although it does have no less than fourteen [now sixteen] different points to which it ideally adheres. On the other hand, despite his claims for the variety of shapes cultural studies can take, Nelson seems to have a very firm (and fixed) idea of just what does and does not constitute cultural studies. Thus, he takes to task a number of people for believing that they are doing cultural studies when they are not following the tradition that Nelson has in mind. . . . Indeed, there is

a curious colonial allegiance in Nelson's stringent—even strident—defense of a strictly British heritage for cultural studies. . . . I think Nelson's assumption that not all studies of culture are cultural studies sets up an unnecessary boundary. That both Nelson and Allan Bloom would claim to be studying culture—with dramatically different results—would seem to me to indicate what is *at stake* in the study of culture. If I have more sympathy in the long run with Cary Nelson than with Allan Bloom, it's because the former leaves the question of culture more open than Bloom does, although Nelson's weakness is at times to want to slip into being a left-wing Allan Bloom. (5–6)

Obviously, I am not eager to be seen as *policing* cultural studies, an activity that is quite impossible in any case. With so many competing versions of cultural studies evident in print, the field has passed the point where it could be uniformly policed. Of course individual reviewers and groups of reviewers will police their own venues, but that is always the case. My aim is to help sustain a continuing debate about what cultural studies is, a debate that I see as a necessary part of its self-definition and social effectivity. I persist in thinking that, if people actually read and think about the individual points in my manifesto, as opposed to reacting viscerally to the manifesto form, they will find it open to a wide range of different kinds of writing. Of course my insistence on some familiarity with the British cultural studies tradition may seem more restrictive, but many of the points in the manifesto make rather different sorts of demands of the field. As to the demand that people familiarize themselves with the British cultural studies tradition and conceptualize its relationship with their own work, I am not certain why any responsible intellectual would feel colonized or coerced by an injunction to read and think.

NOTES TO CHAPTER 5
1. Balch and Warren, "A Troubling Defense of Group Preferences," A44.
2. For an extended analysis of white poets taking up the issue of race, see Aldon Lynn Nielsen, *Reading Race: White American Poets and the Racial Discourse in the Twentieth Century*. Two important anthologies to consult are Langston Hughes and Arna Bontemps, eds., *The Poetry of the Negro*, which includes a section of "tributary poems by non-negroes," and Maureen Honey, ed., *Shadowed Dreams: Women's Poetry of the Harlem Renaissance*.

I have also taught a unit on race in modern American poetry in which I assign a group of poems by black and white poets without identifying the race of the poet until after we complete part of the discussion. My list of poems for that assignment was: Maxwell Bodenheim, "Negroes," Kay Boyle, "A Communication to Nancy Cunard," Sterling Brown, "Scotty Has His Say," "Slim in Hell," Witter Bynner, "Defeat," Hart Crane, "Black Tambourine,"

Countee Cullen, "Incident," "For a Lady I Know," e. e. cummings, "Theys SO Alive," Charles Henri Ford, "Plaint," Sol Funaroff, "Goin Mah Own Road," Angelina Weld Grimké, "The Black Finger," "Tenebris," "[fragment]," Langston Hughes, "Ku Klux," "The Negro Speaks of Rivers," "White Shadows," "Lynching Song," V. J. Jerome, "A Negro Mother to Her Child," Stanley Kimmel, "Niggers," Aqua Lalula, "Lullaby," Vachel Lindsay, "The Congo," A. B. Magil, "They Are Ours," Dorothea Matthews, "The Lynching," Claude McKay, "Mulatto," "The White City," "The Lynching," "To the White Fiends," Kenneth Patchen, "Nice Day for a Lynching," Carl Sandburg, "Jazz Fantasia," "Nigger," Lew Sarett, "Scalp-Dance," Anne Spencer, "White Things," Genevieve Taggard, "To the Negro People," Lucia Trent, "Black Men," John Wheelwright, "Plantation Drouth," and Richard Wright, "Obsession."

NOTES TO CHAPTER 6

1. People wishing to purchase (for educational use) a copy of the videotape of "The Politics of Race and Sex on Campus" as broadcast on C-Span may order it (tape no. 03781) from:

     Public Affairs Video Archives
     School of Liberal Arts
     Purdue University
     West Lafayette, Indiana 47907

   Throughout this paper, transcriptions are my own.

2. See, for example, Paul Lauter's " 'Political Correctness' and the Attack on American Colleges."

3. See Michael Bérubé, "Public Image Limited: Political Correctness and the Media's Big Lie," *Village Voice.*

4. A transcript of this firing line debate may be ordered from:

     Firing Line Debate
     P.O. Box 5966
     Columbia, South Carolina 29250

5. One passage from Silber's remarks is worth quoting because it suggests some of the reasons why conservatives find recent skepticism in theory so disturbing. In Silber's case it also helps explain why, as president of Boston University, he feels free to terminate faculty members who express such views:

> What bothers me is how one maintains any function for the university when we reduce the pursuit of truth and the claim of the capacity to transcend the individual and to know other minds, that people come up with the thesis that our knowledge is dependent on our perspective as either a male or a female, as a member of one race or another race, as a member of one class or another class, or as a person living in a period of history as opposed to another. The

denial of transcendence that is implicit in all these statements is inimicable to the very life of the mind and to the very function of the university.

NOTES TO CHAPTER 7

1. For a report of early efforts to draft campus speech codes that includes sample rhetoric from several regulations see Felicity Barringer, "Free Speech and Insults on Campus," *New York Times,* April 25, 1989, pp. 1, 11. For comments on the text of the code adopted at Stanford in 1990 see Nat Hentoff, "Are People of Color Entitled to Extra Freedom of Speech?" *Village Voice,* September 18, 1990, pp. 26–27. Also see Hentoff's series of 1992 *Village Voice* articles on municipal and campus speech codes: "This is the Hour of Danger for the First Amendment" (January 28), "Trading in the First Amendment for 'Hate Speech' Laws" (February 4), "The Bitter Politics of the First Amendment" (February 11), and "Mari Matsuda: Star of the Speech Police" (February 18), as well as his book *Free Speech for Me But Not for Thee: How the American Left and Right Relentlessly Censor Each Other.*
2. See Michele Collison, "Hate-Speech Code at U. of Wisconsin Voided by Court." There was a subsequent effort at Wisconsin to rewrite the hate speech code more narrowly.
3. Leon Botstein, president of Bard College, spoke at a special Firing Line debate titled "Resolved: Freedom of Thought Is in Danger on American Campuses." The debate was broadcast on educational television on 6 September 1991.
4. Brown University's decision to expel Douglas Hann was widely reported. See, for example, the 25 February 1991 issue of *U.S. News and World Report.* It was also widely debated, despite the probability that the whole story was never fully revealed. For quotations from a variety of media responses and for the Brown University president's defense of his actions see the May 1991 issue of *Brown Alumni Monthly.* Also see Nan Hunter, "A Response on Hate Speech," paper presented at a Brooklyn College of Law conference on hate speech on 10 April 1991.
5. For a commentary on the antipornography movement that places it in the broader context of differing feminist positions on sexuality see Ann Ferguson et al., "Forum: The Feminist Sexuality Debates." This forum includes citations to contemporary reactions to the antipornography legislation proposed in Minneapolis. Also see the chapter "The Popularity of Pornography," in Andrew Ross, *No Respect: Intellectuals and Popular Culture.*
6. R.A.V. v. City of St. Paul, 112 S. Ct. 2538 (1992).

NOTES TO CHAPTER 8

1. The most useful overviews of the Left in America are the massive two-volume *Socialism and American Life,* ed. Donald Drew Egbert and Stow Persons and

the *Encyclopedia of the American Left,* ed. Mari Jo Buhle, Paul Buhle, and Dan Georgakas.

2. See Hester L. Furey, "Poetry and Rhetoric of Dissent in Turn-of-the-Century Chicago."

3. See Mark Van Wienen, "Women's Ways in War: The Poetry and Politics of the Woman's Peace Party, 1915–1917."

4. Edwin Rolfe, *Collected Poems.* All quotations by Rolfe are taken from this edition and are cited parenthetically by page number.

NOTES TO CHAPTER 9

1. The final paragraph of Brodhead's letter has been distributed to members of the press, some of whom, including Emily Eakin, have referred to it and quoted phrases from it in their stories. Yale faculty member Michael Denning warned the student about the letter (and described it at a public rally) after reading her dossier when it was sent to his department (American Studies). At that point she wisely had the letter removed. Yale's English department, incredibly enough, had supposedly reviewed the dossier and approved it for distribution with Brodhead's letter included. The student knew that Brodhead disapproved of her union activity and thus had reason to be anxious about his letter, but she had no idea it would be so negative. I had a photocopy of the full letter, along with copies of all other letters referred to here, available to me while I was writing this chapter. Let me say, finally, that the first two paragraphs of Brodhead's letter, though positive, follow a standard form for lazy writers of recommendations who are not members of a student's doctoral committee; he praises the seminar papers she wrote years ago but makes no effort to familiarize himself with her dissertation.

2. Yale's "Daily Themes" course was in fact the subject of a number of GESO letters, beginning with letters sent to Yale administrators. The course was also the subject of numerous letters and columns in campus newspapers, so the controversy surrounding its funding was no secret. The GESO letter to Perry Bass, a donor who helped fund the course, may be read in its entirety in note 7 to chapter 12 of *Manifesto.*

   What had happened was that graduate students in 1993 had urged Yale to recognize that tutors were spending ten hours a week on the course, not the five hours for which they were being paid. The administration agreed and raised the pay scale. Then the English department decided the extra $20,000 a year was too expensive and decided to raise the number of students being tutored by each instructor, thereby of course throwing the hours off again and making graduate assistants once again work beyond the hours for which they were being paid. It was at that point, in February 1994, that the whole issue broke into public debate.

The graduate student in question had actually signed two letters about the course on behalf of GESO—the February 24 letter to Perry Bass to which Brodhead refers and a letter to a group of course alumni, which she wrote herself and sent out from GESO as part of the group effort; she wrote the second letter (in March) individually because she was a Yale graduate and GESO felt having one of its members who was a Yale graduate express concern was a good strategy. That letter lays out the recent history of the course and urges alumni to express support for its adequate funding.

Why anyone would get exercised about either of these letters is hard to guess. They are certainly not rabble-rousing; they seem a responsible effort to get donors and alumni involved in supporting full funding for "Daily Themes," nothing more. They make no threats and ask no threats of their addressees. Unlike conservative efforts to involve alumni, they do not suggest involvement in course content or recommend withdrawing gifts.

3. For a chronology of the grade strike see Cynthia Young, "On Strike at Yale." Also see the essays published in Cary Nelson, ed., "A Yale Strike Dossier," *Social Text* (Fall 1996).

NOTES TO CHAPTER 10

1. See Ernst Benjamin, "A Faculty Response to the Fiscal Crisis: From Defense to Offense."

2. About fifty of these courses—remedial composition courses that require extensive one-on-one tutorial work—count as two courses each.

3. Faculty members at Illinois, for example, have their health insurance paid for them, whereas graduate students do not. The main benefit graduate students receive is free tuition, a benefit only economically meaningful if there are jobs available for new Ph.D.s. One of the notable effects of the salary differential is that most graduate students find it impossible to get through the summer without taking an extra job. Faculty members, on the other hand, can usually spend the summer reading and writing. Given that the teaching responsibilities are comparable (except for those faculty who take on extra tasks, like directing theses), this one economic inequity seems particularly galling.

4. Making this calculation for the campus as a whole would be more difficult. In my department, where most courses are limited to twelve to thirty-six students, graduate students go through a training program and then, for the most part, teach their own independent courses. Depending on the level of the course, there are some constraints on the course syllabus, but other than that the responsibility is the graduate student's alone. Thus the graduate student meets all classes, gives all lectures, and grades all assignments. To assign faculty members to teach the courses would require a straightforward one-for-one replacement. The situation is more complicated for those departments that offer very large lecture courses where the graduate students meet discus-

sion sections and grade exams. That might require changing the nature of the courses taught. The costs there too would be considerable. A calculation for the university as a whole would also have to take into account the sometimes wide disciplinary differences in faculty salaries. A very rough estimate is that replacing graduate assistants with faculty members would cost the campus at least $80 million. My thanks to Rene Wahlfeldt for providing me with the raw data on which my calculations are based; she is not, of course, responsible for any of my conclusions.

5. The ideology of professionalism not only turns graduate student rage inward; it also discourages them from unionizing and *using* the potential economic power they have.

6. See the list of recommendations for graduate programs in the introduction to Michael Bérubé and Cary Nelson, eds., *Higher Education under Fire: Politics, Economics, and the Crisis of the Humanities.*

NOTES TO CHAPTER 11

1. On the unpredictable and unreadable character of the market see Terry Caesar's "Getting Hired."

2. See Steven Watt, "The Human Costs of Graduate Education" (1995).

3. See Michael Bérubé and Cary Nelson, eds., *Higher Education under Fire: Politics, Economics, and the Crisis of the Humanities.*

4. In their 1996 review essay "Public Access," Neilsen and Meyerson also make the ill-informed and rather paranoid argument that those who argue for closing marginal programs stand to gain professionally and financially! How that is supposed to happen I cannot imagine. They thus attack the introduction I wrote with Michael Bérubé to *Higher Education under Fire:* "Although we don't mean to impugn their motives, it's worth noting that this proposal requires no sacrifice of Bérubé and Nelson. In fact, it works to their advantage, there being little chance that the graduate program at the University of Illinois would be closed. In addition, their status (both in professional reputation and financial reward) is likely to be enhanced" (272).

Well, the program at Illinois is indeed unlikely to be closed, but it has been radically downsized. In the fall of 1970, when I arrived on campus, there were 268 graduate students in residence in my department. In the fall of 1995 the number had fallen to 117. In the fall of 1970 we admitted 33 new students, in the fall of 1995 we admitted 19. These numbers have been deliberately reduced in a gradual fashion over twenty-five years.

The only personal benefit I could receive from closing other programs would be increased chances for my Ph.D. students to get jobs, but we cannot close enough programs to make this increased chance statistically relevant. Closing graduate programs in fact makes *me* less mobile; it reduces the job market for senior research faculty and thus reduces the only real opportunity I would have for measurable financial gain. Now if we could close the English

Ph.D. programs at Berkeley, Chicago, Duke, Harvard, Hopkins, UC-Irvine, Princeton, UCLA, and Yale, *then* Illinois would shoot up in the rankings and my department and I as a member of the graduate faculty would gain in prestige, but I did say close *marginal* programs, which rumor has it these are not. Neilson and Meyerson would be well advised to test their fantasies against the material world.

By the way, it is worth noting that in 1970 my department had another 40 Ph.D. candidates no longer in residence; they had caught the job wave of the 1960s boom years and landed tenure-track jobs before finishing their Ph.D.s.

5. See "Association Seeks Way to Improve the Image of the Professoriate," *Chronicle of Higher Education,* June 23, 1995, A16.

NOTES TO CHAPTER 12

1. For a debate about job application requirements, see the letters by Cary Nelson, Eric Sundquist, and Steven Watt in, respectively, the Summer 1995, Fall 1995, and Spring 1996 issues of the *MLA Newsletter.*

2. It is notable that the AAUP's resolution was adopted despite the objection of a number of faculty members in Yale's AAUP chapter. Eager to build membership in the Yale chapter, the national organization preferred to avoid a confrontation. Meanwhile, the rest of Connecticut's higher education community, heavily unionized and no great admirers of Yale, were ready to censure Yale's AAUP chapter if they had taken a formal stand against graduate assistant collective bargaining rights. It is significant that the AAUP's national office stood by its principles and issued the statement I reprint here.

3. I was obviously not present at this meeting. My sources are several tenured faculty members whom I interviewed by phone. I felt it important to limit my conversations to tenured faculty in the light of Yale's keen interest in finding targets for reprisals. Elsewhere in the essay I draw on insights and observations gained from conversations with numerous GESO members over a period of two years. I have decided it would be best not to name any of these people.

4. See the letter Peterson coauthored with Ruth Bernard Yeazell in the February 1996 MLA mailing about the resolution censuring Yale. There they write "The university's decision not to reappoint those who have refused to fulfill their responsibilities as teachers seems to us altogether just and appropriate" (p. 12).

5. One reason administrators make this argument at a large research university has nothing to do with its truth or falsehood. They are actually protecting constituencies worried about the financial cost of unionization. Thus scientists may worry about the number of hours assistants actually work in their labs, or about the cost of increased benefits. Anything that increases the size of their grant requests may make them less competitive than campuses that

do not monitor research assistant working hours or conditions closely or that offer fewer benefits. Since administrators cannot mount an argument against fairness by saying it's too expensive, they claim instead that students are not employees.

6. The passage in Patterson's letter reads: "The university administration, whose leaders are all Yale faculty, has consistently refused to recognize them [GESO] as a union, not only because it does not believe this to be an appropriate relationship between students and faculty in a non-profit organization, but also because GESO has always been a wing of Locals 34 and 35 of the Hotel Employees and Restaurant Employees International Union, who draw their membership from the dining workers in the colleges and other support staff. Yale is not prepared to negotiate academic policy, such as the structure of the teaching program or class size, with the Hotel Employees and Restaurant Employees International Union. Yale administrators have made it perfectly clear that they have no objection to working with an elected graduate student organization other than GESO, one that is not tied to the non-academic unions on campus" (6).

7. Here, in its entirety, is the 24 February 1994 GESO letter to Texas donor Perry Bass, cosigned by four union members, that produced the collective anger of Brodhead, Homans, and Patterson:

> Dear Mr. Bass,
>
> We write to inform you of a recent and disturbing change in one of Yale's most successful courses. "Daily Themes," the tutorial writing class underwritten by the bass Writing Program at Yale, has been "down-sized," and as former tutors for the course we feel bound to speak up in its defense. The number of tutors for Daily Themes has been cut from twenty to ten, student enrollment has been cut from one hundred to 75, and tutors now teach seven students for the same pay that last year's Graduate School Dean (current Yale President Richard Levin) recommended for teaching *four* students. All this to save approximately $20,000 per year.
>
> Last Spring, Yale's Graduate School discovered how much work it takes for a tutor to give four students the kind of serious attention that our undergraduates expect from Daily Themes. Concerned that the excellence of the course was in danger, Levin made sure that last year, at least, tutors would be paid for the *actual* amount of work they did. But this year the English Department decided that it could not afford the additional $20,000 per year that it would cost to keep doing this.
>
> So the Department restructured Daily Themes. Tutors are now instructed to read each theme *only once,* without comments in the margins and without reviewing earlier work. According to the new

guidelines for the course, tutors need not even read the themes in advance: they simply look quickly at the week's five essays before meeting with the student to ask the questions that come to mind. That's it. Further, recent guidelines direct tutors to simplify their evaluations of students' progress in the course by "discarding as dross over 90% of daily efforts."

In the past, the long wait-list for Daily Themes has been largely unneeded. Not this year. Even though the course began with 25 fewer slots, the Department has had to use the *entire* wait-list and even offer admission to students below the wait-list. And enrollment is still dropping. Word travels fast among Yale undergraduates, and the word on Daily Themes is, *It's not what it used to be.*

As former Daily Themes tutors, we ask you to help rescue this unique and important pedagogical tradition. We know that President Richard Levin and the rest of Yale's leaders hold your opinion in the highest regard, and we urge you to remind them that Daily Themes is too successful and too important to become just another casualty in the budget-cutting war. Please feel free to contact us with any questions.

8. My Chicago anecdote reports events as the interviewee related them to me. Thus in some (though not all) of the anecdotes in this chapter, I have had to rely on testimony from other people. In other cases, including the SUNY-Buffalo story, I had first-hand knowledge. I am not, needless to say, a committee empowered to investigate departmental practices, so there is certainly potential for not representing all points of view in the way I have operated here. Of course I believe professional organizations should have such committees; if these stories lead people to evaluate their own practices and to discuss the possibility of professional ethics committees, then they will have served their function.

BIBLIOGRAPHY

Allison, Alexander, ed. *The Norton Anthology of Poetry*. New York: Norton, 1990.

Baker, Houston, Manthia Diawara, and Ruth H. Lindeborg, eds. *Black British Cultural Studies*. Chicago: University of Chicago Press, 1996.

Balch, Stephen H., and Peter N. Warren. "A Troubling Defense of Group Preferences." *Chronicle of Higher Education,* June 21, 1996, A44.

Baldick, Chris. *The Social Mission of English Criticism: 1848–1932*. Oxford: Oxford University Press, 1983.

Barringer, Felicity. "Free Speech and Insults on Campus." *New York Times,* April 25, 1989, 1, 11.

Batsleer, Janet, Tony Davies, Rebecca O'Rourke, and Chris Weedon. *Rewriting English: Cultural Politics of Gender and Class*. New York: Methuen, 1985.

Benjamin, Ernst. "A Faculty Response to the Fiscal Crisis: From Defense to Offense." In *Higher Education under Fire,* ed. Michael Bérubé and Cary Nelson.

Bérubé, Michael. *Marginal Forces/Cultural Centers: Tolson, Pynchon, and the Politics of the Canon.* Ithaca: Cornell University Press, 1992.

———. *Public Access: Literary Theory and American Cultural Politics.* New York: Verso, 1994.

———. "Public Image Limited: Political Correctness and the Media's Big Lie." *Village Voice,* June 18, 1991, 31–37.

Bérubé, Michael, and Cary Nelson, eds. *Higher Education under Fire: Politics, Economics, and the Crisis of the Humanities.* New York: Routledge, 1994.

Bowen, William G., and Neil Rudenstine. *In Pursuit of the Ph.D.* Princeton: Princeton University Press, 1992.

Bowen, William G., and Julie Ann Sosa. *Prospects for Faculty in the Arts and Sciences: A Study of Factors Affecting Demand and Supply, 1987 to 2012.* Princeton: Princeton University Press, 1989.

Brooks, Cleanth. *Modern Poetry and the Tradition.* 1939. Rpt. New York: Oxford University Press, 1965.

Buhle, Mari Jo, Paul Buhle, and Dan Georgakas, eds. *Encyclopedia of the American Left.* New York: Garland, 1990.

Caesar, Terry. *Conspiring with Forms: Life in Academic Texts.* Athens: University of Georgia Press, 1992.

———. "Getting Hired." *minnesota review* 45–46 (1996): 225–45.

Cheney, Lynne V. *Telling the Truth: Why Our Culture and Our Country Have Stopped Making Sense—and What We Can Do About It.* New York: Simon & Schuster, 1995.

Collison, Michele. "Hate-Speech Code at U. of Wisconsin Voided by Court." *Chronicle of Higher Education,* October 23, 1991, A1, 2.

Crosby, Harry. "Pharmacie du Soleil." In *Chariot of the Sun.* Paris: Black Sun Press, 1931.

Cullen, Countee. "Incident." In *Caroling Dusk: An Anthology of Verse by Negro Poets,* ed. Countee Cullen. New York: Harper & Row, 1927.

cummings, e. e. "Theys SO Alive." In *Complete Poems, 1913–1962.* New York: Harcourt, 1972.

D'Souza, Dinesh. *Illiberal Education: The Politics of Race and Sex on Campus.* New York: Free Press, 1991.

———. *The End of Racism.* New York: Free Press, 1995.

Eagleton, Terry. *The Function of Criticism: From the Spectator to Post-Structuralism.* London: Verso, 1984.

Eakin, Emily. "Walking the Line." *Lingua Franca* (March/April 1996): 52–60.

Egbert, Donald Drew, and Stow Persons, eds. *Socialism and American Life.* Princeton: Princeton University Press, 1952.

Elam, Diane. "Doing Justice to Feminism." Paper presented at the conference Rethinking Culture, University of Montreal, April 3–5, 1992.

Ellmann, Richard, and Robert O'Clair, eds. *The Norton Anthology of Modern Poetry.* New York: Norton, 1973.

Fearing, Kenneth. "Dirge." In *Poems.* New York: Dynamo, 1935.

Ferguson, Ann et al. "Forum: The Feminist Sexuality Debates." *Signs* 10 (1984).

Fish, Stanley. "Consequences." In *Against Theory: Literary Studies and the New Pragmatism,* ed. W. J. T. Mitchell. Chicago: University of Chicago Press, 1985, 106–31.

———. "There's No Such Thing as Free Speech and It's a Good Thing, Too." In *Debating P.C.: The Controversy over Political Correctness on College Campuses,* ed. Paul Berman. New York: Dell, 1992.

———. *Professional Correctness: Literary Studies and Political Change.* New York: Oxford, 1995.

Ford, Charles Henri. "Plaint." In *The Garden of Disorder.* London: Europa, 1938.

Funaroff, Sol. "What the Thunder Said: A Fire Sermon." In *The Spider and the Clock.* New York: International, 1938.

———. "Goin Mah Own Road." In *Exile from a Future Time.* New York: Dynamo, 1943.

Furey, Hester L. "Poetry and Rhetoric of Dissent in Turn-of-the-Century Chicago." *Modern Fiction Studies* 38 (autumn 1992): 671–86.

Gilbert, Sandra. "Business Week." *MLA Newsletter* (summer 1996): 3–5.

Gilman, Sander L. "The Job Market and Survival." *GSC Newsletter* (winter/spring 1995): 2.

———. "*Habent Sua Fata Libelli;* or, Books, Jobs, and the MLA," (Presidential Address). *PMLA* (May 1996): 390–94.

Graff, Gerald. "The University and the Prevention of Culture." In *Criticism in the University,* ed. Gerald Graff and Reginald Gibbons. Evanston: Northwestern University Press, 1985, 62–82.

———. *Professing Literature: An Institutional History.* Chicago: University of Chicago Press, 1989.

Graff, Gerald, and Michael Warner, eds. *The Origins of Literary Studies in the United States: A Documentary Anthology.* New York: Routledge, 1988.

Grossberg, Lawrence. "The Circulation of Cultural Studies." *Critical Studies in Mass Communication* 6 (1989): 413–21.

———. "The Formation(s) of Cultural Studies: An American in Birmingham." *Strategies* 2 (1989): 114–49.

Grossberg, Lawrence, Cary Nelson, and Paula A. Treichler, eds. *Cultural Studies.* New York: Routledge, 1992.

Guillory, John. *Cultural Capital: The Problem of Literary Canon Formation.* Chicago: University of Chicago Press, 1993.

Hall, Stuart. "Cultural Studies and the Center: Some Problematics and Problems."

In *Culture, Media, Language: Working Papers in Cultural Studies,* ed. Stuart Hall et al. London: Hutchinson, 1980.

———. "Cultural Studies: Two Paradigms." *Media, Culture, and Society* 2 (1980): 57–72.

———. "The Problem of Ideology—Marxism without Guarantees." *Journal of Communication Inquiry* 10, no. 2 (1986): 28–44.

———. *The Hard Road to Renewal: Thatcherism and the Crisis of the Left.* New York: Verso, 1988.

Hentoff, Nat. "Are People of Color Entitled to Extra Freedom of Speech?" *Village Voice,* September 18, 1990, 26–27.

———. *Free Speech for Me But Not for Thee: How the American Left and Right Relentlessly Censor Each Other.* New York: HarperCollins, 1992.

Hoggart, Richard. "Contemporary Cultural Studies: An Approach to the Study of Literature and Society." C.C.C.S. Occasional Paper, 1969.

Honey, Maureen, ed. *Shadowed Dreams: Women's Poetry of the Harlem Renaissance.* New Brunswick: Rutgers University Press, 1989.

Horwitz, Tony. "Class Struggle: Young Professors Find Life in Academia Isn't What It Used to Be." *Wall Street Journal,* February 15, 1994, A1, A8.

Hughes, Langston. "The Negro Speaks of Rivers." In *The Weary Blues.* New York: Knopf, 1926.

———. "Union." In *A New Song.* New York: International Workers Order, 1938. The poem was first published in *New Masses* in 1931.

———. "The Bitter River." In *Jim Crow's Last Stand.* Atlanta: Negro Publication Society of America, 1943.

———. "White Shadows." In *Good Morning Revolution: Uncollected Writings of Social Protest,* ed. Faith Berry. Westport, Conn.: Lawrence Hill, 1973. The poem was first published in *Contempo* in 1931.

Hughes, Langston, and Arna Bontemps, eds. *The Poetry of the Negro: 1746–1949.* Garden City, N.Y.: Doubleday, 1949.

Jameson, Fredric. *The Political Unconscious: Narrative as a Socially Symbolic Act.* Ithaca: Cornell University Press, 1981.

Jerome, V. J. "A Negro Mother to Her Child." In *The Rebel Poet* 15 (August 1932): 1.

Johnson, Richard. "What Is Cultural Studies Anyway?" *Social Text* 6, no. 1 (1987): 38–80.

Jolas, Eugene. "Mountain Words." In *I Have Seen Monsters and Angels.* Paris: Transition, 1938.

Kimball, Roger. *Tenured Radicals: How Politics Has Corrupted Our Higher Education.* New York: Harper & Row, 1990.

Laclau, Ernesto, and Chantal Mouffe. *Hegemony and Socialist Strategy.* London: Verso, 1985.

———. "Post-Marxism without Guarantees." *New Left Review* 166 (1987): 27–41.

Laluah, Aqua. "Lullaby." In *Shadowed Dreams: Women's Poetry of the Harlem Renais-*

sance, ed. Maureen Honey. New Brunswick: Rutgers University Press, 1989. The poem was first published in the *Crisis* in 1929.

Lauter, Paul. "Letter to the Editor." *New Criterion* (December 1990): 87.

———. " 'Political Correctness' and the Attack on American Colleges." In *Higher Education under Fire,* ed. Michael Bérubé and Cary Nelson.

———, ed. *The Heath Anthology of American Literature.* 2d ed. 2 vols. Lexington, Mass.: D.C. Heath, 1994.

McKay, Claude. "The Lynching." "To the White Fiends." In *Selected Poems of Claude McKay.* New York: Bookman Associates, 1953.

Michaels, Walter Benn. "The New Modernism." *ELH* 59 (1992): 257–76.

Morley, David, and Kuan-Hsing Chen, eds. *Stuart Hall: Critical Dialogues in Cultural Studies.* New York: Routledge, 1996.

Morris, Meaghan. "Banality in Cultural Studies." *Discourse* 10, no. 2 (1988): 3–29.

Morris, Meaghan, and John Frow. Introduction to *Australian Cultural Studies: A Reader,* ed. Meaghan Morris and John Frow. Urbana: University of Illinois Press, 1993.

Nelson, Cary. *Repression and Recovery: Modern American Poetry and the Politics of Cultural Memory, 1910–1945.* Madison: University of Wisconsin Press, 1989.

Nelson, Cary, and Michael Bérubé. "Introduction: A Report from the Front." In *Higher Education under Fire,* ed. Michael Bérubé and Cary Nelson.

Nelson, Cary, and Dilip Parameshwar Gaonkar, eds. *Disciplinarity and Dissent in Cultural Studies.* New York: Routledge, 1996.

Nelson, Cary, and Lawrence Grossberg, eds. *Marxism and the Interpretation of Culture.* Urbana: University of Illinois Press, 1988.

Nielsen, Aldon Lynn. *Reading Race: White American Poets and the Racial Discourse in the Twentieth Century.* Athens: University of Georgia Press, 1988.

Neilson, Jim, and Gregory Meyerson. "Public Access Limited." *minnesota review* 45–46 (1996): 263–73.

Nussbaum, Martha C. *Poetic Justice: The Literary Imagination and Public Life.* Boston: Beacon Press, 1995.

O'Connor, Alan. *Raymond Williams: Writing, Culture, Politics.* New York: Blackwell, 1989.

Ohmann, Richard. *English in America: A Radical View of the Profession.* New York: Oxford University Press, 1976.

Olsen, Tillie. "I Want You Women Up North to Know." *Partisan* 1, no. 4 (1934): 4.

Patchen, Kenneth. "Nice Day for a Lynching." In *First Will and Testament.* New York: Padell, 1948.

Paull, Irene. "Ballad of a Lumberjack." In *We're the People.* Duluth: Midwest Labor, c. 1941.

Perkins, David. Review of *Repression and Recovery, Style* (Spring 1991).

———. "The Future of Keats Studies." Keats Bicentenary Conference, Clark Library, University of California at Los Angeles, April 1995.

235

Perry, Richard, and Patricia Williams. "Freedom of Hate Speech." *Debating P.C.: The Controversy over Political Correctness on College Campuses.* New York: Laurel, 1992.

Pratt, Linda Ray. "Going Public: Political Discourse and the Faculty Voice." In *Higher Education under Fire,* ed. Michael Bérubé and Cary Nelson.

Quin, Mike. "The Glorious Fourth." In *More Dangerous Thoughts.* San Francisco: People's World, 1940.

Rolfe, Edwin. *Collected Poems,* ed. Cary Nelson and Jefferson Hendricks. Urbana: University of Illinois Press, 1993.

Ross, Andrew. *No Respect: Intellectuals and Popular Culture.* New York: Routledge, 1989.

Sandburg, Carl. "Jazz Fantasia." "Mammy." "Nigger." In *The Complete Poems of Carl Sandburg.* New York: Harcourt, 1970.

Simpson, David. "Raymond Williams: Feeling for Structures, Voicing 'History.' " In *Cultural Materialism: On Raymond Williams,* ed. Christopher Prendergast. Minneapolis: University of Minnesota Press, 1995.

Smith, Barbara Herrnstein. *Contingencies of Value: Alternative Perspectives for Critical Theory.* Cambridge: Harvard University Press, 1989.

Sosnoski, James J. *Token Professionals and Master Critics: A Critique of Orthodoxy in Literary Studies.* Albany: State University of New York Press, 1994.

Spacks, Patricia Meyer. "Voices of the Membership." *MLA Newsletter* (fall 1994): 3.

Spencer, Anne. "White Things." In *Shadowed Dreams: Women's Poetry of the Harlem Renaissance.* New Brunswick: Rutgers University Press, 1989. The poem was first published in the *Crisis* in 1923.

Storey, John, ed. *What Is Cultural Studies? A Reader.* London: Arnold, 1996.

Taggard, Genevieve. "Ode in Time of Crisis." "To the Negro People." In *Long View.* New York: Harper & Row, 1941.

Tichenor, Henry. "Onward, Christian Soldiers." In *Rhymes of the Revolution.* St. Louis: National Ripsaw, 1914.

Trent, Lucia. "Parade the Narrow Turrets." "A White Woman Speaks." In *Children of Fire and Shadow.* Chicago: Robert Packard, 1929.

Van Wienen, Mark. "Women's Ways in War: The Poetry and Politics of the Woman's Peace Party, 1915–1917." *Modern Fiction Studies* 38 (autumn 1992): 687–714.

Warren, Kenneth W. "The Problem of Anthologies." Paper presented at the annual meeting of the Midwest Modern Language Association, November 6, 1992.

Watkins, Evan. *Work Time: English Departments and the Circulation of Cultural Value.* Stanford: Stanford University Press, 1989.

Watt, Steven. "The Human Costs of Graduate Education; Or, The Need to Get Practical." *Academe* (November–December 1995): 30–35.

White, Hayden. *Metahistory: The Historical Imagination in 19th Century Europe.* Baltimore: Johns Hopkins University Press, 1973.

———. *Tropics of Discourse: Essays in Cultural Criticism.* Baltimore: Johns Hopkins University Press, 1978.

———. *The Content of the Form: Narrative Discourse and Historical Representations.* Baltimore: Johns Hopkins University Press, 1987.

Williams, Raymond. "The Analysis of Culture." In *The Long Revolution.* New York: Columbia University Press, 1961.

Wilson, John K. *The Myth of Political Correctness: The Conservative Attack on Higher Education.* Durham: Duke University Press, 1995.

Young, Cynthia. "On Strike at Yale." *minnesota review* 45–46 (spring 1996): 179–96.

Young Bear, Ray. "Grandmother." "In Viewpoint: Poem for 14 Catfish and the Town of Tama, Iowa." "It Is the Fish-Faced Boy Who Struggles." In *Winter of the Salamander.* San Francisco: Harper & Row, 1980.

———. "The Personification of a Name." "The Significance of a Water Animal." In *The Invisible Musician.* Duluth, Minn.: Holy Cow! Press, 1990.

INDEX

Batsleer, Janet, 20, 26
Benjamin, Ernst, 178, 225n. 1
Bennett, William, 24, 97, 98, 99, 101–2, 105–8, 109, 121, 146, 149–50
Berlin, James, 54
Bérubé, Michael, 109, 166, 178, 222n. 3, 226n. 4; *Higher Education under Fire: Politics, Economics, and the Crisis of the Humanities* (1994), 226nn. 3, 4; *Marginal Forces/Cultural Centers* (1992), 14; *Public Access: Literary Theory and American Cultural Politics* (1994), 217n. 1
Bessie, Alvah, 132
Black studies, 25
Bodenheim, Maxwell, 221n. 2
Bontemps, Arna, 33, 221n. 2
Boston University, 222n. 5
Botstein, Leon, 110, 118, 223n. 3
Bowen, William, 155
Boyle, Kay, 221n. 2
Brodhead, Richard, 142–43, 207, 210, 216, 224nn. 1, 2, 228n. 7
Bromwich, David, 141
Brooks, Cleanth, 15
Brooks, Peter, 196–99, 212
Brown, Sterling, 94, 221n. 2
Brown University, 118, 223n. 4
Buchanan, Patrick, 111
Buckley, William F., 110, 121
Buhle, Mari Jo, 224n. 1 (ch.8)
Buhle, Paul, 224n. 1 (ch.8)
Burgan, Mary, 193
Burroughs, William, 147
Bynner, Witter, 221n. 2

Caesar, Terry, 20
California Board of Regents, 108
California-Santa Cruz, University of, 195
Cambridge University Press, 215
Canon revision, 97–114
Carby, Hazel, 199
Centre for Contemporary Cultural Studies at the University of Birmingham, 53
Chavez, Cesar, 140
Chen, Kuan-Hsing, 220n. 1
Cheney, Lynne, 35, 97, 98, 102, 104, 105–8, 109, 111, 140, 149–50
Chicago, University of, 213
Collison, Michelle, 223n. 2 (ch.7)
Cott, Nancy, 143–44, 197–98
Crane, Hart, 221n. 2
Crosby, Harry, 92–93

Cullen, Countee, 94, 115, 118, 222n. 2 (ch.5)
Culler, Jonathan, 53, 57
Cultural studies, 24, 52–74, 98, 127; and Marxim, 46
cummings, e. e., 94, 222n. 2 (ch.5)

Dade County Community College, 138
Dartmouth Review, 97, 111–12
Davies, Tony, 20
Davis, David Brion, 143–44, 199
Davis, Robert Con, 52, 53
Debs, Eugene, 129
Deconstruction, 18–19, 51, 73, 98, 99, 100, 101, 219n. 2 (ch.1)
de Man, Paul, 18, 51, 100
Denning, Michael, 199, 224n. 1
Derrida, Jacques, 18–19, 46, 51, 86, 100
Dick, Philip K., 211–12
Dissent, 144
D'Souza, Dinesh, 80, 97, 99, 102–3, 105–8, 109, 110, 111
Dunbar, Paul Lawrence, 14

Eagleton, Terry, 20
Eakin, Emily, 181, 218, 224n. 1
Egbert, Donald Drew, 223n. 1 (ch.8)
Elam, Diane, 220n. 2
Eliot, T. S., 44
Essentialism. *See* Anti-essentialism

Fearing, Kenneth, 87, 88
Feminism, 20, 22, 41, 48, 55, 58, 65, 87
Ferguson, Ann, 223n. 5
First Amendment, 123–25
Fish, Stanley, 20–21, 110, 123–24
Ford, Charles Henri, 94, 222n. 2 (ch.5)
Foucault, Michel, 86
Franklin, Phyllis, 211
Freud, Sigmund, 123
Frow, John, 220n. 1
Fry, Paul 142
Fry, Northrup, 158
Funaroff, Sol, 93, 94, 222n. 2 (ch.5)
Furey, Hester L., 130, 224n. 2 (ch.8)

Gaonkar, Dilip Parameshwar, 220n. 1
Georgakas, Dan, 224n. 1 (ch.8)
Georgetown University, 113
Gilbert, Sandra, 154, 176, 177, 179, 209, 211, 212
Gilman, Sander, 176, 201–4
Gingrich, Newt, 140

INDEX

241

ABOUT THE AUTHOR

CARY NELSON is Jubilee Professor of Liberal Arts and Sciences at the University of Illinois at Urbana-Champaign. He is the author of *The Incarnate Word: Literature as Verbal Space* (1973), *Our Last First Poets: Vision and History in Contemporary American Poetry* (1981), *Repression and Recovery: Modern American Poetry and the Politics of Cultural Memory, 1910–1945* (1989), and *Shouts from the Wall: Posters and Photographs Brought Home from the Spanish Civil War by American Volunteers* (1996). His edited and coedited books include *Theory in the Classroom* (1986), *Marxism and the Interpretation of Culture* (1988), *Cultural Studies* (1992), Edwin Rolfe's *Collected Poems* (1993), *Higher Education under Fire: Politics, Economics, and the Crisis of the Humanities* (1994), *Madrid 1937: Letters of the Abraham Lincoln Brigade from the Spanish Civil War* (1996), *Disciplinarity and Dissent in Cultural Studies* (1996), and *Will Teach for Food: Academic Labor in Crisis* (1997).